NAIS

Journal of the NATIVE AMERICAN *and* INDIGENOUS STUDIES ASSOCIATION

VOLUME 3.2

2016

NAIS (ISSN 2332-1261) is published two times a year by the University of Minnesota Press, 111 Third Avenue South, Suite 290, Minneapolis, MN 55401-2520. http://www.upress.umn.edu

Postmaster: Send address changes to *NAIS*, University of Minnesota Press, 111 Third Avenue South, Suite 290, Minneapolis, MN 55401-2520.

Information about manuscript submissions can be found at naisa.org, or inquiries can be sent to journal@naisa.org.

Books and other material for review should be addressed to *NAIS*, Department of American Studies, University of Kansas, Bailey Hall, Room 213, 1440 Jayhawk Boulevard, Lawrence, KS 66045-7594.

Address subscription orders, changes of address, and business correspondence (including requests for permission and advertising orders) to *NAIS*, University of Minnesota Press, 111 Third Avenue South, Suite 290, Minneapolis, MN 55401-2520.

SUBSCRIPTIONS
- **Individual subscriptions to *NAIS*** are a benefit of membership in the Native American and Indigenous Studies Association. NAISA membership is $50 annually. To become a member, visit http://naisa.org/.
- **Institutional subscriptions to *NAIS*** are $100 inside the U.S.A., $105 outside the U.S. Checks should be made payable to the University of Minnesota Press and sent to *NAIS*, University of Minnesota Press, 111 Third Avenue South, Suite 290, Minneapolis, MN 55401-2520.
- **Back issues of *NAIS*** are $25 for individuals (plus $6 shipping for the first copy, $1.25 for each additional copy inside the U.S.A.; $9.50 shipping for the first copy, $6 for each additional copy, outside the U.S.A.).
- **Digital subscriptions to *NAIS* for institutions** are available online through the JSTOR Current Scholarship Program at http://www.jstor.org/r/umnpress.

Journal of the NATIVE AMERICAN *and*
INDIGENOUS STUDIES ASSOCIATION

CONTENTS

VOLUME 3 ● ISSUE 2

2016

Articles

KEVIN BRUYNEEL

1 Race, Colonialism, and the Politics of Indian Sports Names and Mascots:
The Washington Football Team Case

KATHRYN WALKIEWICZ

25 Affirmative Exclusions: The Indigenous Exception in Oklahoma's Official
English

DEVON MIHESUAH

45 Indigenous Health Initiatives, Frybread, and the Marketing of Nontraditional "Traditional" American Indian Foods

KASEY KEELER

70 Putting People Where They Belong: American Indian Housing Policy in
the Mid-Twentieth Century

DREW LOPENZINA

105 Letter from Barnstable Jail: William Apess and the "Memorial of the
Mashpee Indians"

Reviews

ALYSSA MT. PLEASANT

128 *Laura Cornelius Kellogg: Our Democracy and the American Indian and Other Works* edited by Kristina Ackley and Christina Stanciu

JARED EBERLE

130 *First Nations, Museums, Narrations: Stories of the 1929 Franklin Motor Expedition to the Canadian Prairies* by Alison Brown

RICHARD MACE

132 *Transformable Race: Surprising Metamorphoses in the Literature of Early America* by Katy Chiles

MELANIE KENDALL TOTH

134 *The Civil War and Reconstruction in Indian Territory* edited by Bradley R. Clampitt

THEODORE (TED) JOJOLA

136 *Thatched Roofs and Open Sides: The Architecture of Chickees and Their Changing Role in Seminole Society* by Carol Dilley

HAYLEY G. BRAZIER

138 *Cattle Colonialism: An Environmental History of the Conquest of California and Hawai'i* by John Ryan Fischer

JESSICA LESLIE ARNETT

140 *Attu Boy: A Young Alaskan's WWII Memoir* by Nick Golodoff

KRISTOFER RAY

142 *Cherokee Medicine, Colonial Germs: An Indigenous Nation's Fight against Smallpox, 1518–1824* by Paul Kelton

SHAUN A. STEVENSON

144 *The Land We Are: Artists and Writers Unsettle the Politics of Reconciliation* edited by Gabrielle L'Hirondelle Hill and Sophie McCall

KYLE T. MAYS

146 *MTV Rebel Music: Native America*

MICHELLE STOKELY

148 *The Darkest Period: The Kanza Indians and Their Last Homelands, 1846–1873* by Ronald D. Parks

CHARLOTTE COTÉ

150 *The Seas Is My Country: The Maritime World of the Makahs, an Indigenous Borderlands People* by Joshua Reid

CURTIS FOXLEY

152 *The Settlers' Empire: Colonialism and State Formation in America's Old Northwest* by Bethel Saler

CHRISTOPHER J. ANDERSON

154 *Capture These Indians for the Lord: Indians, Methodists, and Oklahomans, 1844–1939* by Tash Smith

Contributors

KEVIN BRUYNEEL

Race, Colonialism, and the Politics of Indian Sports Names and Mascots: The Washington Football Team Case

Introduction

IN JULY 2014 the Center for American Progress released a study titled *Missing the Point: The Real Impact of Mascots and Team Names on American Indian and Alaska Native Youth*. Written by Erik Stegman and Victoria Phillips, this study further substantiated that the use of Indian team names and mascots has a clear negative social and psychological impact on Indigenous people, especially young people (Stegman and Phillips 2014; Fryberg et al. 2008). To introduce and publicize the report, the Center invited guest speakers and a panel to address the topic. The keynote speaker was Congresswoman Betty McCollum (D-Minn.), who in discussing the controversy over the Washington, D.C., football team's name noted that if a derogatory word for people who are Jewish, African American, or Chinese was proposed as a sports team name, it "wouldn't be allowed, no one would stand or it, but for some reason, the term 'Redskin' gets a free pass" (Center for American Progress 2014). Rep. McCollum is firmly on the side of those seeking to end the use of these names and mascots for sports teams at the high school, college, and professional levels in the United States. At the same time, her "for some reason" statement reveals an underlying confusion about why this is even an issue at all, and why there has not been comprehensive indignation and swift action to end this practice. McCollum is not alone in her confusion, as it is articulated often by those who oppose such names and mascots. The source of this confusion is the inability to grasp the manner in which settler-colonialism is both ubiquitous and, for most people, relatively invisible in U.S. political and cultural life. The history and present of settler-colonial violence toward and dispossession and appropriation of Indigenous people's bodies, territory, and identity is ever present in the sports names and mascots issue. However, what most political actors and observers see and discuss in this debate is not settler-colonialism but rather race and racism. To deem as racist names such as the "Redskins" is not so much wrong as it is analytically incomplete and thus politically off the mark for grasping why these names and mascots get a "free pass"—why they were created in the first place, persist, and are so vehemently defended today by those who seek to maintain the status quo.

The present debate and politics regarding Indian sports names and mascots, such as with the case of the Washington football team's name, provides an excellent opportunity to politicize and center settler-colonialism as a historical and contemporary structuring force of the United States. The sports names and mascot issue is a persistent and public practice of U.S. settler-colonial rule. It is a mnemonic device that disavows the dispossession of Indigenous territory and the violent and aggressive assimilatory practices against Indigenous peoples. Paying attention to the political functioning of memory matters here because understanding and intervening in this and other issues requires more than just getting the historical facts straight. Facts matter, but an awareness of facts will not do enough politically to generate change, and this is where we need to see and directly engage with collective memory, specifically settler memory. Settler memory refers to the mnemonics—that is, the functions, practices, and products of memory—of colonialist dispossession, violence, appropriation, and settlement that shape settler subjectivity and governmentality in liberal colonial contexts such as the United States. Settler mnemonics include not only places and teams named after Indigenous peoples, but also calendric commemorations such as Columbus Day and Thanksgiving, military nomenclature such as the Apache helicopter, and many other examples. These mnemonics are so ubiquitous that they are, at once, present and absent in American collective memory. That is, in settler memory Indigenous people are both there and not there at the same time, before our eyes across American culture but also disavowed of active political meaning in and by the settler imaginary—ubiquity and invisibility as two sides of the same settler-colonial coin. This disavowal is not a forgetting of colonialism and settlement. The problem with American settler society's relationship with its past resides in the manner in which the nation and its component parts remembers and reproduces its past, as facts and myths, and the important role of this remembering in the re-legitimation of contemporary violence, dispossession, and appropriation. This cycle replays and reproduces settlement on a mnemonic loop. Indian team names and mascots are a public example of this contemporary loop in the American settler memory and imaginary, whereby Indigenous people are both everywhere in symbolic appropriative form but relatively invisible as active, contemporary political subjects.

In this article I turn first to the history of the issue, seeing the emergence and development of these names and mascots as coterminous with and reflective of U.S. Indian policy and settler-colonial practices of the late nineteenth century and first half of the twentieth century. On this basis, I then examine the role of race in the contemporary debate over this issue, revealing the prevalence of this discourse and its popularity in mainstream American political culture, especially to the degree that it relies on and reproduces the presumptions of racial liberalism. The predominance of the discourse of race makes invisible the practices of colonialism and leaves Indigenous people to be seen, if they are seen, as another minority group within the United States, rather than as Indigenous nations that have a history of nation-to-nation treaty-based relationships with the U.S. federal government. The point of this critique is not to marginalize race for the sake of colonialism, but rather to approach our analyses with an appreciation of their distinctive dynamics and co-constitutive relationship. In that regard, what I see at work here in perpetuating the Indian sports name and mascot phenomenon are the dynamics of colonial racism, which racially categorizes and generates hierarchies in the name of preserving settler-colonial relations and white supremacy. After setting out a corrective that centers settler-colonialism, I analyze and critique two popular claims made in defense of these team names and mascots: that it is a tradition of the team and an honoring of Indigenous people. While I focus on the example of the Washington team name, I see the dynamics at work in that case to be representative of the wider politics and discourse around this issue.

The Historical and Political Context: The Allotment Era

The history of the Washington football team's name points to how this naming practice is deeply tied to settler-colonial governance. In 1933 George Preston Marshall renamed his Boston-based National Football League (NFL) team the "Redskins"; the name had been the "Braves" in 1932, the team's inaugural season. As to the name itself, while the etymology of the term "Redskins" can be traced back to the late eighteenth and early nineteenth centuries when, according to one historian, it was not derogatory or negative, by the late nineteenth century one could no longer make such a case (Goddard 2005, 1). For example, in the wake of the U.S.—Dakota War of 1862 an ad in the September 24, 1863, edition of the *Winona Daily Republican* in Minnesota offered the following: "The State reward for dead Indians has been increased to $200 for every red-skin sent to Purgatory. This sum is more than the dead bodies of all the Indians east of the Red River are worth" (see also Routel 2013). The genocidal tone and aims for which "red-skin" is utilized in this public forum shows that the word fit comfortably as part of settler-colonial discourse and practices of the time. This colonialist racialization dehumanizes Indigenous bodies as objects of commodification through genocidal violence. This is colonial racism. Putting the team name in historical and political context also reveals that the naming of the Washington team in 1933 marked the end, or close to the end, of a defining era in U.S. Indian policy.

In his comprehensive study of the history of the topic of Indian team names and mascots, J. Gordon Hylton discovered that "the practice of identifying professional teams by Indian names most likely began in 1886" (2010, 895). Prior to that there were no such names for professional teams, but soon after they begin to proliferate; most of the team names with which we are now familiar emerged between 1886 and 1933. The baseball Boston Braves (eventually relocated to Milwaukee and then to Atlanta) got their name in 1912, the Cleveland Indians in 1915, the Chicago Blackhawks in 1926, and then the Washington football team in 1933. After 1933, one still sees intermittent cases of such naming—the Kansas City Chiefs in 1960, for example—but there is a clear decline, and there have been no new names of this sort since 1963. Hylton's study, however, does not point out the relevance of this time period that starts with 1886 and ends, for the most part, in 1933. Infamously, 1887 marks the passage of the General Allotment (Dawes) Act, commencing the massive dispossession of Indigenous people's territory through the allotment of collectively owned tribal property into individual parcels to adult male tribal members who were expected to earn U.S. citizenship over time and assimilate by becoming private property holders in a liberal capitalist polity. The surplus of land beyond that distributed to Indigenous adult males was then made available for sale as private property on the free market. This process reduced Indigenous territorial holdings from 138 million acres in 1887 to 48 million acres in 1934 (Hoxie, ed., 1996, 154; Hirschfelder and Kreipe de Montano, eds., 1993, 20–22). Also, 1890 marks the low point in terms of the recorded population of Indigenous people in the U.S. context, at 248,000 people (Thornton 1987). These are just two features of a time period that saw massive land dispossession and appropriation by and into liberal capitalism, which went hand in hand with the genocidal practices and policies that involved not only direct killing of Indigenous people but also the effort to remove Indigenous people from their nations and assimilate them into the American population. In this regard, consider President Theodore Roosevelt's words, from 1901: "In my judgment the time has arrived when we should definitely make up our minds to recognize the Indian as an individual and not as a member of a tribe. The General Allotment Act is a mighty pulverizing engine to break up the tribal mass." Along with General Allotment Act, other settler-colonial measures taken to "pulverize" tribes and forcibly assimilate Indigenous people included the 1924 Indian Citizenship Act, which unilaterally made Indigenous people U.S. citizens, regardless of whether they consented (Bruyneel 2004). Also, as Jennifer Guiliano (2010,

2015) demonstrates in her studies of the gendered discourse of Indigenous sports naming and mascotry, the growth of college and professional sports during this historical period provided an important vehicle for the expression and production of the racial and gendered superiority of white middle-class masculinity in the United States by means of white male participation in and support of an emergent, popular sports culture. In all, the U.S. Indian policies and related political developments from the 1880s through the 1930s shaped the context for the emergence and flourishing of the naming of professional sports teams after Indigenous people. The timing of these two developments is not a coincidence, as they mark the compatible relationship between the ubiquity and invisibility of settler-colonial governance and of Indigenous people in the American settler imaginary.

Policies such as the General Allotment Act and the Indian Citizenship Act were components of a public, active, comprehensive effort to make Indigenous people disappear, either through death or forced assimilation, and to destroy tribal communities and landholdings. The increasing invisibility of Indigenous people as distinctly Indigenous in their territorialized, collective existence, both as a reality in some sense as a consequence of said policies and more actively as a component of the American settler vision of Indigenous people as a disappearing people, opened the space for and was also fostered by the active symbolic appropriation of Indigenous identity for the sake of the reproduction of American settler identity and belonging. As American state actors and American settlers forced Indigenous people more to the margins through policies and practices of displacement, violence, and assimilation, symbolic Indigeneity moved increasingly and necessarily to the center of the settler imaginary. This mutually constitutive dynamic reflects the relationship among the three pillars of settler-colonialism, focusing on territory, people, and identity. The appropriation of territory and the violence toward and forced assimilation of Indigenous people are two key pillars of settler-colonialism, and the third pillar is the appropriation of Indigenous identity and culture. The naming and mascot phenomenon is just such an appropriative settler practice, which requires the first two pillars to clear the way for and are also facilitated by the third. I refer to this as a settler practice because it helps to constitute and acculturate a sense of settler belonging on this land through the production of a settler tradition that both acknowledges the presence of Indigenous people as historical beings while disavowing their presence as contemporaneous beings. Thus, to the settler imaginary, Indigenous people and settler-colonialism itself are both everywhere and nowhere, ubiquitous and invisible, a vibrant, generative, if tragic part of America's past rendered absent in the American present. It is this dynamic that shapes and constrains the politics over team names and mascots to this day.

To conclude this section, I return to the history of the Washington football team. George Preston Marshall's motivation for giving the team this name derived from his "longtime fascination with Native Americans" and in honor of the identity of his coach, William "Lone Star" Dietz, who was "believed to be a Native American," from the Sioux Nation, although in all likelihood he was not (Hylton 2010, 888; Waggoner 2013, 1). Dietz's previous positions included coaching at the Haskell Indian School, and he recruited six Indigenous men, a number from Haskell, to play for the 1933 Boston team (Hylton 2010, 888–89). As well as introducing the new name, that year Marshall also required Coach Dietz to "walk the sidelines wearing a Sioux headdress" and he had the players, white and Indigenous, "wear war paint when they took the field" (902). In this way, the white settler owner imposed not only the name but an entire performance of stereotypical Indigeneity, one reflective not of actual Indigenous practices but of the owner's settler imaginary. This settler imaginary is also deeply shaped by anti-blackness, as Marshall's actions showed after he moved the team to Washington, D.C., in 1938.

By 1961 the Washington football team stood as the only the NFL team to have never had a black player on its roster. Under the new John F. Kennedy presidential administration and with the advent of an increasingly powerful civil rights movement, Kennedy's secretary of the interior, Stewart Udall, pressured Marshall to sign a black player so that the team residing in the nation's capital would no longer be, in Udall's words, "lily-white," or the "paleskins" as he called them. Marshall resisted, cementing his reputation as a notorious, open white supremacist, stating at one point, "We'll start signing Negroes when the Harlem Globetrotters start signing whites." Marshall had supporters in his effort to resist the Kennedy administration's pressure to integrate the team. Notably, the American Nazi Party marched in support, and one photo shows two distinct signs carried by the uniformed Nazis. The first is a banner stating "America Awake," with a swastika positioned between these two words. Next in line is a marcher holding a sign that says "Mr. Marshall: Keep Redskins White!" (Park 2013).

Udall eventually compelled Marshall to cede on this issue and integrate his team because the secretary had important leverage over the owner. Marshall had recently signed a thirty-year lease on the stadium in which his team would play, and that stadium—at the time called D.C. Stadium, later RFK Memorial Stadium—resided on federal lands. As such, Marshall's landlord was the Department of Interior, and Udall threatened to deny use of these lands if the team persisted in its discriminatory practices (Smith 2011). Here settler-colonial invisibility and its modern functionality and material presence came in to play. These lands are part of the traditional territory of the Piscataway people, a composite of Algonquin-speaking nations. British colonizers and settlers seized this land in the late seventeenth and early eighteenth century. In the late eighteenth century, ten square miles of the land was turned over to the federal government in order to locate and build the nation's new capital in Washington, D.C. We can see in the history of Marshall's ownership of the team the mutually constitutive relationship between settler-colonialism and white supremacy, which also foreshadow the contemporary debate over the team's name.

To start, take note of the American Nazi wish to "Keep Redskins White," which echoed Marshall's effort to keep black players off his team. Here, the preservation of whiteness is maintained through direct anti-blackness, the core of U.S. white supremacy. It also premised on a foundation of settler-colonialism in which an overt claim to an identification with and appropriation of Indigeneity in the early 1930s does not upset the desire for racial purity, because in settler memory Indigenous people have disappeared either through assimilation into the American social body or through death. Either way, Indigeneity is made functionally absent, a safe part of the past. This is the work of a white settler tradition that deploys settler-colonial practices of appropriation and dispossession to generate settler belonging and also the work of white supremacist practices of anti-blackness that affirm white racial superiority. This particular story ends with the Kennedy administration succeeding with regard to ending Marshall's practice of a particular form of anti-blackness, that being the exclusion of black people from the marketplace—in this case that of professional athletics—due to racial discrimination. Marshall was violating a tenet of racial liberalism, in the nation's capital no less. The settler government's claim over this land proved to be the leverage needed for Marshall to eventually and very reluctantly allow for the inclusion of Black players on his team. This was a victory for racial liberalism won through the deployment of settler-colonial governing power over land dispossessed from Indigenous people. The difficult relationship of settler-colonialism to white supremacy and also Indigeneity to race that we can discern from this historical moment resonates in the contemporary debate, revealing both potential problems but also possibilities in how to understand, reframe, and intervene in the public discussion occurring over this issue.

The Contemporary Debate: The Anti-naming Claim of Racism

Just as in the early 1960s when the Washington football team stood at the center of a storm over a violation of racial liberalism and the owner's anti-blackness, in the contemporary era this same franchise in the most profitable professional sports league in the United States is under intense scrutiny over the team's name. A wide range of Indigenous and non-Indigenous political actors have voiced their opposition to the name, demanding that present team owner Dan Snyder change it. They include Suzan Shawn Harjo, the Cheyenne and Muscogee writer and activist who legally challenged the trademark status of the team name; the Oneida Nation under the leadership of Ray Halbritter; the National Congress of American Indians; the Leadership Council on Civil and Human Rights (a coalition that includes the National Association for the Advancement of Colored People, the American Civil Liberties Union, Human Rights Campaign, the National Council of La Raza, and the American—Arab Anti-Discrimination Committee), and President Barack Obama, who stated that if he was the owner of a team with a name "that was offending a sizeable group of people, I'd think about changing it" (Vargas and Shin 2013). Halbritter, while leading the Oneida Nation's public campaign against the name, also wrote a 2014 editorial critiquing what he saw to be hypocrisy in the NFL pondering a plan to penalize players for saying the word "nigger" on the field while the Redskins remained the name of one of its franchises. Comparing the N-word and the R-word, Halbritter (2014) argued that the latter is like the former in that it is a well-recognized racial slur. And in the wake of the National Basketball Association banning Los Angeles Clippers' owner Donald Sterling in April 2014 for making racist statements in what he assumed was a private setting, a number of public figures have used this moment as an opportunity to demand the NFL take action on the Washington team name, seeing the two situations as analogous. Football player Richard Sherman, when asked if he thought the NFL would have taken the same stance on racist statements as did the NBA, stated, "No, I don't. Because we have an NFL team called the Redskins." Senator Majority Leader Harry Reid (D-Nev.) implored the NFL to follow the NBA's lead, mocking those who defend the Washington team name as a matter of tradition, stating, "What tradition? A tradition of racism." Representative Henry Waxman (D-Calif.) has called for a congressional hearing on the team's name, stating that the Committee on Energy and Commerce "could play a constructive role in challenging racism" by calling Goodell and Snyder to testify and defend the name. And on May 21, 2014, fifty U.S. senators, all Democrats, signed on to a letter to Commissioner Goodell calling for a change to the Washington team's name. The letter also builds on the NBA example and includes the following claims and statements:

> . . . that racism and bigotry have no place in professional sports;
>
> What message does it send to punish slurs against African Americans while endorsing slurs against Native Americans?
>
> This is a matter of tribal sovereignty—and Indian Country has spoken clearly on this issue.
>
> At the heart of sovereignty for tribes is their identity. Tribes have worked

for generations to preserve the right to speak their languages and perform their sacred ceremonies. . . . Yet every Sunday during football season, the Washington, D.C., football team mocks their culture.

The NFL can no longer ignore this and perpetuate the use of this name as anything but what it is: a racial slur. (U.S. Senators 2014)

This issue may be getting close to a so-called tipping point, as an increasing number and range of individuals and organizations feel comfortable taking a clear public stance against the Washington football team's name. This emerging movement against the team name is a positive development in that it may mean the name will be changed in the not-too-distant future. On the other hand, one 2013 poll found that 79 percent of Americans think the Washington team should not have to change its name (Steinberg 2013). Thus, while the issue has gained momentum to the degree that mainstream political and public figures are comfortable speaking out against the name, a significant portion of the public does not see it as a serious problem. To make sense of these twinned dynamics, we need to take a close look at the politics and discourse of race deployed here.

The predominant claim made by those opposing the Washington team name is that the name is racist, a slur on Indigenous people. One can find this claim throughout the public realm, and especially across social media as people call out and protest the use of the identities and imagery of Indigenous people for team names and mascots. The claim that this practice is racist, or a racist slur, is clearly defensible in that the Washington football team is a dictionary-defined slur and a dehumanization of Indigenous people. The problem here is not the charge of racism itself, but that it has become hegemonic in the debate. In so doing, this discourse marginalizes to the point of making invisible the idea and claim that these team names and mascots are persistent practices of settler-colonalism that exist in a constitutive relationship with white supremacy. The relative invisibility of settler-colonialism in this debate is as much a product of a disavowal of distinct Indigenous status and claims as it is a consequence of a lack of knowledge or a mere byproduct of the predominant focus on race. For example, the letter from the U.S. senators asserts that the issue is a matter of tribal sovereignty, which thus conveys their knowledge of that fact Indigenous nations stand in a distinct relationship to the United States. This assertion might have opened a path to defining this naming practice as a settler-colonial one—one of appropriation built on genocidal and dispossessive practices against peoples who assert their status as sovereign nations. But the senators' letter closes with the presumptive assertion that the team's name is "what it is: a racial slur." This is unsurprising, as U.S. senators—specifically Democratic ones—can comfortably stand against racism in this particular form while also standing, if implicitly, for the maintanance and reproduction of American settler-colonialism in the form of liberal colonialism. By liberal colonialism I mean polities comprising institutions, norms, and practices that reflect a compatible encounter between liberal democracy and colonialism in the political development and contemporary formation of nations such as the United States. Within a liberal colonial context there is no tension between an open opposition to practices that explicitly violate racial liberal principles and the simultaneous disavowal and reproduction of settler-colonialism. They go hand in hand.

To be more precise on racial liberalism, the liberal discourse about race is one that marks out for attention and potential amendment those evident exclusions and discriminations that could forestall some form of standing as equal or with the potential to be equal in the U.S. polity, as defined by civil rights—era norms of inclusion to an ideal of a racially egalitarian, even post-racial, American republic. With the Washington football team of the early 1960s we saw government intervention to stop then team owner Marshall from excluding black players from eligibility to be employed by his team. In the early twenty-first century, mainstream politicians, public actors, and activists are seeking to get present owner Snyder to change the Washington team name based on the claim that it is a form of racial discrimination that excludes Indigenous people from realizing the norm of equal treatment under racial liberalism. This emerging popular and mainstream movement against the Washington team name is built on a very narrowly tailored sense of what counts as racism. To refer to the issue of the Washington team name as a matter of racial discriminaton frames the problem and the solution within the assimilatory logic of racial liberalism, which does not allow room to mention productively, let alone debate and challenge, the role of historical and contemporary settler-colonialism. Rather, as with the conflict over the Washington team's exclusion of black players in the 1960s, the existence of settler-colonial governance is presumed, both invisible and ubiquitous.

The political theorist Robert Nichols sheds light on the tensions that emerge when antiracist politics and critiques that focus on closing the gap between the ideals of a racially egalitarian society and the reality of a racially unjust society presume the persistence of settler-colonialism and the settler state. He notes, "Antiracist critique may inadvertently reproduce the official state narrative of the settler colony, in which the (colonial) state is the best approximation of the ideal social construct and indigeneity is understood as a derivation or deviation from this ideal, in need of additional normative justification. . . . In fact, it is often through the removal of so-called race-based barriers to integration and subsequent enclosure and incorporation of previously self-governing Indigenous polities that settler colonialism has operated" (2014, 103). As a consequence, "Insofar as this form of antiracist critique enables settler colonial sovereignty to structure the terms of its own contestation, it is classically hegemonic" (113). It is this hegemony that is in play in the race-based critique of team names and mascots, one in which race-based discriminations and barriers become the primary focal point of the discourse such that not only is settler-colonialism rendered invisible, but the resolution to this racial violation follows the logic of inclusion within and thus affirmation of settler-colonial governance. The resolution to the exclusion of black players from the Washington football team in the early 1960s came by means of settler state actors using as leverage against a white supremacist team owner the fact that said team owner sought to profit from long-term access to lands dispossessed from Indigenous peoples. Racial inclusion was achieved and settler-colonial governance was the means to achieving this aim, which thereby reaffirmed the settler state's status and authority over territory dispossessed from Indigenous people. When settler-colonial governance shapes the "terms of its own contestation" in this way, the deeper historical and political sources and meanings of the appropriation of Indigenous identity and imagery for team names and mascots get subsumed and disavowed. As a consequence, so does the distinction between various group experiences in relation to American liberal colonialism.

With this critical perspective in mind, I see in the example of the letter from the fifty U.S. senators as well as other forms of opposition to the Washington team name and similar sports names a form of liberal colonial discourse at work. This discursive work can be seen in the popular rhetorical trope referenced by Representative McCollum, by which one posits a hypothetical in which there is an analogous appropriation of the identities and imagery of non-Indigenous racial and ethnic others to the white Christian norm. A visual example of this device can be seen in the image widely shared across social media that shows three baseball caps side by side, that of the New York Jews, the San Francisco Chinamen, and the Cleveland Indians, each with its own derogatory caricature of an individual from these respective groups.

FIGURE 1. Poster by the National Congress of American Indians, 2013.

This particular image is from a poster and social media campaign produced and disseminated by the National Congress of American Indians. The image includes the following tagline: "No race, creed or religion should endure the ridicule faced by the Native Americans today. Please help us put an end to this mockery and racism by visiting www.ncai.org" (Graham 2013). The point being made here is that if one finds unacceptable the hypothetical New York and San Francisco teams names and mascots, then one should by racial liberal analogy find the third, that being the actually existing Cleveland Indians and their grotesque logo/mascot Chief Wahoo, also unacceptable. As short-term political maneuvering it may make sense for activists to utilize this form of race-based discourse to generate public attention to the issue. However, this is likely less a calculated political move than an example of the hegemonic power of the discourse of race, and racial liberalism in particular. It is fair to question at a practical level whether this race-based approach does indeed work best in the short term in the effort to address and overcome the arguments made to defend such names/mascots and, connectedly, what this approach means in the long-term effort to maintain and further generate an anticolonial politics. The potential problems with a discursive move such as the example of the three baseball caps are that, first, it is premised on the idea that the experiences and resolutions to the injustices perpetuated on these groups are analogous; and second, in so doing it also undermines the effort to grasp why Indigenous sports names and mascots persist. The baseball cap analogy does not answer the question of why Indian team names and mascots get the "free pass," but instead unintentionally serves to further inscribe this pass. The question that the hypothetical poses—how can we tolerate the Cleveland Indians when we would not tolerate the New York Jews or San Francisco Chinamen?—means to expose the hypocrisy or inconsistency in the application of racial liberalism, but it masks the deeper, disavowed problem: that colonial relations define the production and persistence of names like the Redskins and mascots such as Chief Wahoo, which exist in a constitutive relationship to race but cannot be collapsed as a matter of race, and race alone.

The creation and the persistence of these naming and mascot practices are deeply tied to the Allotment-era appropriations of land and the violence and assimilative practices toward Indigenous peoples that remain structuring forces of U.S. liberal colonialism. Thus, the point of deconstructing the baseball cap analogy for the settler dynamics at work here is not to reveal that in contemporary life most people would not tolerate the New York Jews or San Francisco Chinamen as team names and mascots. Instead, this approach sheds light on the fact that in U.S. history the creation of such professional sports team names and mascots would not have made sense in the first place. This is the critical historical and political point that is missed when settler-colonialism is not placed at the center of this debate. Compared to settler appropriations of Indigenous identity, settler memory finds much less identificatory fuel in anti-Semitic or racist anti-Asian representations. This is not to say that Jewish and Asian people did and do not experience structural discrimination productive of American political identity and development, but rather that there is a more distinct, constitutive role for Indigenous identity and settler-colonialism in relation to American settler identity and political development. Without such a shift of registers from racial liberalism to settler-colonialism and its corollary colonial racism, the issue as presently and predominantly debated is more likely to reproduce than challenge and disrupt settler-colonialism. I turn now to address a couple of the main arguments made in defense of Indian team names and mascots to reveal the theoretical and political benefit of directly upsetting the productivity of settler memory in the contemporary debate.

Two Defenses of Naming/Mascots, and Anticolonial Responses

There are two prevalent contemporary arguments made to defend the practice of Indian team names and mascots: (1) for the team and its fans, the name or mascot is an important tradition worthy of respect and preservation, and (2) these names and mascots are meant to honor Indigenous people, culture, and traditions, and in that spirit they are utilized to reflect and enhance team pride. These two arguments are often articulated in the defense of the Washington football team's name, and they are important to analyze because of their constitutive relationship to white settler memory and identity. In particular, the argument that these names are meant as an honor to Indigenous people reveals settler practices that are tightly tied to white supremacist presumptions.

IT'S A TRADITION
In an October 9, 2013, letter to the season ticket holders of the Washington football team, team owner Dan Snyder addressed the controversy over the team's name. While stating that "he respects the feelings of those who are offended by the team name," over the course of the letter Snyder invokes a number of common defenses of the name, in particular that of it being a tradition and an honoring. I start with the way he concludes the letter:

> So when I consider the Washington Redskins name, I think of what it stands for. I think of the Washington Redskins traditions and pride I want to share with my three children, just as my father shared with me—and just as you have shared with your family and friends.

I respect the opinions of those who disagree. I want them to know that I do hear them, and I will continue to listen and learn. But we cannot ignore our 81-year history, or the strong feelings of most of our fans as well as Native Americans throughout the country. After 81 years, the team name "Redskins" continues to hold the memories and meaning of where we came from, who we are, and who we want to be in the years to come.

We are Redskins Nation and we owe it to our fans and coaches and players, past and present, to preserve that heritage. (Snyder 2013)

Dan Snyder's assertion that the team's name is a tradition that is meaningful to him and to the fans should be taken as a sincere, legitimate claim. He is right, it is a tradition: a settler-colonial tradition. In no small part, a settler-colonial tradition is one that supplants and replaces Indigenous people's history and presence with a settler history that seeks to establish a sense of settler belonging in the territory. Historian and Indigenous studies scholar Jean O'Brien refers to this as a "replacement narrative" that effects a "stark break from the past, with non-Indians replacing Indians on the landscape" (2010, xxii–xxiii). O'Brien's focus is on the production of the replacement narrative in nineteenth-century New England, and she finds "five locations" in which it can be read: "the erection of monuments to Indians and non-Indians, the celebration of historical commemorations of various sorts, the enterprise of excavating Indians sites, the selective retention of Indian place-names, and claims Non-Indians made to Indian homelands" (57). I see Indian sports names and mascots as forms of a monument and historical commemoration that serve a similar purpose of establishing settler belonging at the expense of Indigenous presence, and Snyder's words explicitly concede the production of such a narrative.

In response to protests, Snyder counters with a claim premised on the weight and meaning of the over eighty-year history of the Washington team's name. It is his team's history, what he refers to as a "Nation," that he positions as under threat from those who seek to change the name. For Snyder, this eighty-year historical span has generated a collective identification and belonging, explicitly avowed in his assertion that the name "continues to hold the memories and meaning of where we came from, who we are, and who we want to be in the years to come." These are settler memories built on the appropriation, representation, and replacement of Indigenous identity and presence by an emergent settler tradition and identity. Snyder constructs a "we" comprising non-Indigenous people, settlers, who find in the Washington team a mnemonic bond that links together fans and players of the "past and present." Snyder's construction of the "we" is demonstrated by the fact that he starts his mnemonic tale with the meaning the name has for his own family, extends that feeling out to "your family and friends," and finally to "most of our fans as well as Native Americans." The latter is a telling construction in that it splits off a settler fan base from Indigenous people. And even if Snyder included settlers and Indigenous people in his "we" of the "Redskins Nation," the tradition he is defending is a settler tradition in its creation, development, and purposes. This a tradition built on locating active Indigenous identity in the past that settlers then *honor* via appropriation in the present day. In this way, the Washington team name and the team name / mascot phenomenon in general are active components of a contemporary replacement narrative that constitutes and with each articulation reconstitutes the story of settler belonging as a tradition unto itself.

To take at face value the claim to tradition and then deconstruct and consider the meaning of such a claim is to engage in an anticolonial critique by marking it as an appropriative practice that serves in the constitution of settler identity. This goes further politically and critically than the claim that the name is racist. This approach refuses to allow settler-colonial governance to set the terms of this debate. It does so by putting the team name's into historical and mnemonic perspective as part of a persistent, deeply rooted settler-colonial logic and set of practices traceable from the past to the present and thereby tying it to, rather than cleaving if off from, the history and present of settler-colonial governance. Thus, when Dan Snyder makes the claim that names and mascots matter because they convey memories about "where we came from, who we are, and who we want to be in the years to come," opponents of such names and mascots can concur with him and then take him up on the very historical arc invoked here, one that goes right back to the Allotment era and all that it has wrought. As well, this critical approach places settler-colonialism at the center of this debate such that it can facilitate the articulation of a racial critique that goes beyond the parameters of racial liberalism. I draw this relationship out in the next section, regarding the claim that these names and mascots honor Indigenous people.

IT'S AN HONOR

The claim that this naming practice is not a slur but is, to the contrary, an honoring of Indigenous peoples is closely bound up with the view that Indian team names and mascots are a tradition. Both the claim to tradition and to honoring articulate an implicit concern with defending settler identity, meaning, and memory. Below are three examples of its deployment in reference to the Washington team name. First, the following is an excerpt from NFL Commissioner Roger Goodell's June 2013 letter to two congressional representatives: "Neither in intent nor use was the name ever meant to denigrate Native Americans or offend any group. The Washington Redskins name has thus from its origin represented a positive meaning distinct from any disparagement that could be viewed in some other context. For the team's millions of fans and customers, who represent one of America's most ethnically and geographically diverse fan bases, the name is a unifying force that stands for strength, courage, pride and respect." Second, in an August 2014 interview with the television sports network ESPN, Dan Snyder offered the following in response to the question, what is a Redskin? "A Redskin is a football player. A Redskin is our fans. The Washington Redskin fan base represents honor, represents respect, represents pride. Hopefully winning. And it's a positive" (Steinberg 2014). Finally, the website RedskinsFacts.com, a team alumni website funded by Dan Snyder with the listed support of such former players as Joe Theismann, Billy Kilmer, Mark Moseley, and Clinton Portis, makes the following claim: *We believe the Redskins name deserves to stay. It epitomizes all the noble qualities we admire about Native Americans—the same intangibles we expect from Washington's gridiron heroes on game day. Honor. Loyalty. Unity. Respect. Courage. And more."

Just as original team owner Marshall saw the name as an honorific that would stand as a positive symbol for his team in 1933, the parties supporting the name in the early twenty-first century are likely being sincere when they say that the name speaks to the "noble qualities" they admire about Indigenous people. In the conclusion to his book *Playing Indian*, the historian and Indigenous studies scholar Philip Deloria spoke to the function that "playing Indian" serves for Americans in the production and meaning of their national identity: "The self-defining pairing of American truth with American freedom rests on the ability to wield power against Indians—social, military, economic, and political—while simultaneously drawing power from them. Indianness may have existed primarily as a cultural artifact in American society, but it has helped *create* these other forms of power, which have then been turned back on native people" (1998, 191). The key word here is power. The comments of Goodell, Snyder, and the team alumni website authors articulate a vital, constitutive relationship between the honor that the name purports to convey to and about Indigenous people and the power that the team and its fans get from the name, as a "unifying force," signifying "intangibles" they "expect from Washington's gridiron heroes on game day. Honor. Loyalty. Unity. Respect. Courage." The components and purpose of honoring as defined here by significant figures of the NFL and the Washington team expressly invokes a process of drawing power from Indigeneity as a cultural artifact for the sake of enhancing the power of the collective identity of the team and its fans. The purpose here is to constitute settler identity, as the claim to honoring shows itself to be an appropriative practice for which the Washington team name is a metonym for the wider dynamic constitutive of American self-identity. This appropriative practice of honoring is also a form of replacement narrative, in which settler-collective identity—the American nation, the "Redskins Nation"—draws power from Indigeneity conceived as cultural artifact that in its noblest form is ubiquitous in the past and invisible in the present. The replacement narrative here implicitly asserts that noble Indigenous people have tragically disappeared and we, the settlers, honor them by taking up their name as our own in contemporary settler form.

In referring to honoring as a practice of appropriating Indigenous identity, I mean this as both building on and occurring alongside the appropriations/ dispossession of Indigenous territory and the effort to eliminate and undermine Indigenous people as a distinct people. Regarding this latter point, in their study of the psychological impact of American Indian mascots, the psychologist Stephanie Fryberg and colleagues discovered that there are indeed negative effects to such names and mascots, especially for Indigenous youth, and these "effects are not due to negative associations with mascots" (Fryberg et al. 2008, 216). They found that even when Indigenous youth have, in Dan Snyder's terms, a positive association with an Indian team name or mascot there was still a negative impact on the self-esteem of these young Indigenous people. These researchers conclude:

> Although pro-mascot advocates suggest that American Indian mascots are complimentary and honorific and should enhance well-being, the research presented runs contrary to this position. American Indian mascots do not have negative consequences because their content or meaning is inherently negative. Rather, American Indian mascots have negative consequences because, in the contexts in which they appear, there are relatively few alternate characterizations of American Indians. The current American Indian mascot representations function as inordinately powerful communicators, to natives and nonnatives alike, of how American Indians should look and behave. American Indian mascots thus remind American Indians of the limited ways in which others see them. (Fryberg et al. 2008, 216)

In sum, the appropriation here diminishes and confines the ways in which many young Indigenous people understand and enact their sense of identity. This is a deeply colonialist practice premised on the enforced invisibility of Indigenous people as contemporary agents, and the ubiquity of limited representations of Indigenous people through such cultural forms as sports team names and mascots. And as a colonial practice it concomitantly serves to embolden settler identity, as supported by Fryberg and colleagues, who reference two studies which "revealed that after exposure to various American Indian representations, European Americans reported higher self-esteem compared to the control condition and to a nonnative mascot, namely, the University of Notre Dame Fighting Irish" (Fryberg et al. 2008, 216). As such, just as the colonialist appropriation of Indigenous territory reduces and limits the territory of Indigenous people in the process of enhancing the territorial claims of the settler population, so does the appropriation of Indigenous identity through team names and mascots undermine the self-esteem and sense of identity of many young Indigenous people while enhancing the self-esteem of settlers—that is, of European Americans.

The relationship between appropriation of territory and of identity is indicative of the wider colonialist dynamics at work here. What I marked out as a mutually constitutive relationship during the Allotment era continues to this day. As with the response to the tradition defense, an anticolonial response to the honoring defense does not need to challenge the idea of it being a positive representation, an honor, or a sign of admiration. Whether an image is meant to honor or to disparage is not the fundamental point, as the psychological studies themselves show. Rather, the point to be made is that these names and mascots are created by the colonizer to represent the identity and existence of the colonized, drawing power to the former from the latter at a symbolic and cultural level that is tightly tied to the appropriations and violence which occur in the material and political sense. This anticolonial response to the honoring defense refuses to allow this debate to be reduced to race alone and also provides the opportunity to reveal the constitutive relationship between colonialism and white supremacy that is at work here.

While in the history of U.S.—Indian policy the period from the 1880s to the 1930s is known infamously as the Allotment era, in the history of formalized white supremacy this time period also represents a portion of the Jim Crow era that did not formally end until the mid-1960s. In a nation built on the cheap labor garnered through the violent enslavement of Africans and their descendants and the cheap territory gained through violent dispossession of territory from Indigenous people, during the Allotment / Jim Crow eras, sports teams turned to Indigenous identity to draw power in order to generate their honorable, noble, and courageous team identities. However, they did not turn to African American identity for this same purpose. The production of white American settler identity did involve the appropriation and drawing of power from African American identity, but in different form and with distinct meaning. As Eric Lott (1993) shows in his book *Love and Theft*, since well before the U.S. Civil War the wearing of "blackface" by white Americans was a product of their feelings of both admiration of and repulsion for African Americans, and these minstrel performances served in the production of, in particular, white American male working-class identity that was negotiating and defining the parameters of racial designations, meanings, and hierarchies. There are two important differences between these appropriations of Indigenous and African American identity that speak to why a debate over team names and mascots reduced to the terms of racial liberalism also misses out on the more fundamental and persistent role of anti-blackness at work here. First, blackface minstrelsy presumed and continues to presume the presence of African Americans in an abject state at the bottom of the racial hierarchy of U.S. white supremacy, whereas Indian team names and mascots presumes the disappearance of the noble Indigenous people who are honored as a cultural artifact. Second, in the post—civil rights era, blackface minstrelsy has become culturally and politically taboo, almost universally accepted as offensive and inappropriate, whereas the presence of Indian team names and mascots remains acceptable to many. In white American settler memory, the abjected, everpresent black American at the bottom of the hierarchy of U.S. white supremacy and the noble Indigenous person made tragically invisible by U.S. settler-colonial practices signify two distinct and compatible, constitutive imaginaries. In the white settler imaginary, the abjected presence of blackness stabilizes white superiority in the U.S. racial hierarchy and noble, disappearing Indigeneity stabilizes the settler replacement narrative and claim of settler belonging. When looked at in this way one can safely posit that to white settlers in the early twentieth century the idea of looking to draw power from black American identity so as to create an honorable team name was, quite literally, unimaginable, whereas utilizing Indigenous identity was readily imaginable, ubiquitously so. In this regard, original Washington team owner Marshall's views exemplify the manner in which anti-blackness and the claim to honoring while replacing Indigeneity go hand in hand.

While present-day fans of the team would certainly disavow previous owner Marshall's open white supremacy, as well as the wish of the American Nazi Party to "Keep Redskins White," the team's very public history on this account is not a mere exception to the rule of settler memory and tradition, but rather speaks to a collaborative relationship between settler-colonialism and white supremacy in the U.S. context. This collaborative dynamic matters a great deal when attending politically to the likes of Goodell, Snyder, and so many others who do not view the use of the N-word and the R-word as being analogous, because while they concede the N-word is a slur they insist that the R-word is an honor. That the likes of Goodell and others do not see the two words to be analogous was only further proven in 2014 when, as noted above, the NFL seriously considered instituting a new on-field penalty for the use of the N-word by one player toward another, a situation that occurred primarily among African American players (Burke 2014). To those opposed to the Washington team name, this further demonstrated that the R-word was a getting a free pass (Moya-Smith 2014). While this response has its merits, these two situations are seemlessly analogous only if one sees them through the framework of racial liberalism. An anticolonial perspective, however, reads the banning of the N-word and the maintenance of the R-word as evidence of the view of black Americans as abjected presence, as the un-honorable who need white American protection from further dishonor so as not to violate the tenets of racial liberalism and upset the white American myth that we now exist in a post-racial society. One can see colonial racism at work here in the manner in which a profound anti-blackness is subtly woven into the honoring defense, especially in light of the potential N-word ban. In the context of the NFL proposed policy regarding the N-word, the claim that the Washington team name honors Indigenous people implies that one particular group, Indigenous people, is worth the honor of white settler admiration while another group, African Americans, is worthy of only white liberal paternalism from further symbolic denigrations that openly reference abjected presence. To draw on Andrea Smith's formulation, these moves in relation to the R-word and the N-word mutually reinscribe the binaries of Indigenous—settler and black—white. The former binary presumes the disappearance/invisibility of Indigenous people. The latter binary presumes the presence and abjection/exploitability of black Americans (Smith 2012). This pairing of the honoring/invisibility of Indigenous people and abjection/presence of black people forms the core of colonial racism. However, this tightly tied historical and political relationship is not a significant part of the debate over team names and mascots in the twenty-first century, and this absence undermines the effort to generate more radical political arguments, interrogations, and alliances in the effort to oppose settler-colonialism and white supremacy.

An anticolonial approach in this debate would make clear that the disappearing, noble, and honorable Indian that Dan Snyder and his supporters posit relies historically and logically on the co-constitutive dishonorability, exploitability, and ever presence of African Americans. In so doing, this more radical approach maintains the focus on settler-colonialism and white supremacy as deeply interrelated structures. It does so by taking the honoring defense at face value and reposing it as one that relies on both Indigenous invisibility/honorability and black American abjection/exploitability. This approach does not appeal to the inclusive, assimilatory framework of racial liberalism, but instead sees the team name as a component of a larger dispossessive, appropriative, exploitative, and violent set of colonial racist practices. In response to the honoring defense, an anticolonialist argument does not say we would never tolerate a derogatory name like the New York "Negroes" so we should not have the Washington "Redskins," but instead asks why would the former have never entered the white settler imaginary in the first place whereas the latter was ubiquitous in its formative period and persists to this day—and what is the relationship between these two dynamics today? This more radical political question speaks to the history and present of settler-colonialism and white supremacy so as to push the way toward a more profound and disruptive response to the honoring defense. Such a response begins with not reducing the issue to a solely racial discourse in which colonialism is rendered invisible, but instead traces and interrogates the role of colonialism and colonial racism in the politics of Indians team names and mascots.

Conclusion

The free pass enjoyed by the Washington football team persists to the degree that settler-colonialism remains invisible in this political debate. In making this case, the purpose of this article is not to discredit the efforts of those seeking to do the important work of bringing an end to these names and mascots, but rather to consider the implications of the arguments that are deployed and to suggest alternative, historically attentive and politically radical ways to intervene in the debate and politics of this issue. The political efforts to oppose names and mascots offer an opportunity to upset the mnemonic loop that reproduces settler-colonial logic. They can do so through a direct focus historically on the Allotment era in order to argue that this present practice of names and mascots is part of a connected chain of appropriations and dispossessions that continues right on up to our day. However, if these efforts to raise and engage Indigenous political issues remain within the logic and narrative of racial liberalism in a post—civil rights era paradigm that defines the mascot issue as a matter of offensiveness, exclusion, and discrimination rather than an anticolonial focus on appropriation, dispossession, and violence, they are more likely to reproduce, even if unintentionally, settler memory as a practice that sustains liberal colonialism. The present politics of Indian team names and mascots can bring the politics of settler-colonialism to the center of public debate, and this can be done not at the exclusion of questions of race but as a way to push this discussion in even more radical antiracist directions. In the least, it is imperative to engage in a politics that works to refuse the invisibility of settler-colonialism and Indigenous people. While this may complicate the argument a bit more than it is at present, the benefit would be to compel the widening of the discourse on this issue beyond the narrow parameters of racial liberalism.

KEVIN BRUYNEEL is professor of politics in the History and Society Division of Babson College in Wellesley, Massachusetts.

Note

I would like to thank the Babson College Research Fund for providing support in the researching and writing of this article. I was also greatly assisted by the comments and suggestions received from the anonymous reviewers for the journal and from discussants and audience members during the presentation of this work at the 2014 Native American and Indigenous Studies annual meeting and the 2014 inaugural workshop of the Tufts University Consortium of Studies in Race, Colonialism, and Diaspora.

Bibliography

Bruyneel, Kevin. 2004. "Challenging American Boundaries: Indigenous People and the 'Gift' of U.S. Citizenship." *Studies in American Political Development* 18, no. 1: 30–43.

Burke, Chris. 2014. "NFL Competition Committee Passes on N-Word Rule, Considers Extra Point Changes." *Sports Illustrated.* March 19. http://www.si .com/nfl/audibles/2014/03/19/nfl-competition-committee-passes-on-n -word-rule-considers-extra-point-changes.

Center for American Progress. 2014. "Missing the Point: The Real Impact of Mascots and Team Names on American Indian and Native Alaskan Youth." Event held at Center for American Progress, Washington, D.C., July 22. http://www .americanprogress.org/events/2014/07/14/93821/missing-the-point-the -real-impact-of-native-mascots-and-team-names-on-american-indian -and-alaska-native-youth/.

Deloria, Philip J. 1998. *Playing Indian.* New Haven, Conn.: Yale University Press.

Fryberg, Stephanie, Hazel Rose Markus, Daphna Oyserman, and Joseph M. Stone. 2008. "Of Warrior Chiefs and Indian Princesses: The Psychological Consequences of American Indian Mascots." *Basic and Applied Social Psychology* 30, no. 3: 208–18.

Goddard, Ives. 2005. "I Am a Red-Skin: The Adoption of a Native American Expression (1769–1826)." *Native American Studies* 19, no. 2: 1–20.

Goodell, Roger. 2013. "Letter to Congressman Cole and Congresswoman McCollum." Washington, D.C., June 5. http://indiancountrytodaymedia network.com/2013/06/11/nfl-commissioner-tells-congress-redskins -positive-name-149843.

Graham, Regina F. 2013. "Racism of Sports Logos Put into Context by American Indian Group." CBS Cleveland / AP. October 8. http://cleveland.cbslocal .com/2013/10/08/racism-of-sports-logos-put-into-context-by-american -indian-group/.

Guiliano, Jennifer. 2010. "Gendered Discourse: Higher Education, Mascots, and Race." In *The Native American Mascot Controversy: A Handbook*, ed. C. Richard King, 41–45. Lanham, Md.: Scarecrow Press.

———. 2015. *Indian Spectacle: College Mascots and the Anxiety of Modern America.* New Brunswick, N.J.: Rutgers University Press.

Hallbritter, Roy. 2014. "The 'N-Word' and the 'R-Word.'" *Huffington Post.* February 28. http://www.huffingtonpost.com/ray-halbritter/the-n-word-and-the-r-word_b_4877660.html.

Hirschfelder, Arlene, and Martha Kreipe de Montano, eds. 1993. *The Native American Almanac.* New York: Prentice Hall.

Hoxie, Frederick E., ed. 1996. *Encyclopedia of North American Indians.* Boston: Houghton Mifflin.

Hylton, J. Gordon. 2010. "Before the Redskins Were the Redskins: The Use of Native American Team Names in the Formative Era of American Sports, 1857–1933." *North Dakota Law Review* 86, no. 4: 879–903.

King, C. Richard, and Charles Fruehling Springwood. 2001. *Team Spirits: The Native American Mascots Controversy.* Lincoln: University of Nebraska Press.

Lott, Eric. 1993. *Love and Theft: Blackface Minstrelsy and the American Working Class.* New York: Oxford University Press.

Moya-Smith, Simon. 2014. "NFL May Throw Flag on N-Word, but What about the 'R-Word'?" *CNN.* February 26. http://www.cnn.com/2014/02/25/opinion/moya-smith-nfl-flag-r-word/.

Nichols, Robert. 2014. "Contract and Usurpation: Enfranchisement and Racial Governance in Settler-Colonial Contexts." In *Theorizing Native Studies,* ed. Audra Simpson and Andrea Smith, 99–121. Durham, N.C.: Duke University Press.

O'Brien, Jean M. 2010. *Firsting and Lasting: Writing Indians Out of Existence in New England.* Minneapolis: University of Minnesota Press.

Park, Alex. 2013. "That Time Nazis Marched to 'Keep Redskins White.'" *Mother Jones.* November 7.

Rifkin, Mark. 2014. "The Silence of Ely S. Parker: The Emancipation of the Sublime and the Limits of Settler Memory." *NAIS: Journal of the Native American and Indigenous Studies Association* 1, no. 2: 1–43.

Roosevelt, Theodore. 1901. "First Annual Message, 1901: The President Defends the Dawes Act." Washington D.C. Document located through *Digital History,* "Struggle for Self-Determination, Digital History ID 720." http://www.digitalhistory.uh.edu/disp_textbook.cfm?smtid=3&psid=720.

Routel, Colette. 2013. "Minnesota Bounties on Dakota Men during the U.S.–Dakota War." *William Mitchell College of Law: Legal Studies Research Papers.* No. 2013-01, October.

Smith, Andrea. 2012. "Indigeneity, Settler Colonialism, White Supremacy." In *Racial Formation in the Twenty-First Century,* ed. Daniel Martinez HoSang, Oneka LaBennett, and Laura Pulido, 66–90. Berkeley: University of California Press.

Smith, Thomas. 2011. *Showdown: JFK and the Integration of the Washington Redskins.* Boston: Beacon Press.

Snyder, Dan. 2013. "Letter from Washington Redskins Owner Dan Snynder to Fans." *Washington Post.* Octover 9. http://www.washingtonpost.com/local/letter-from-washington-redskins-owner-dan-snyder-to-fans/2013/10/09/e7670bao-30fe-11e3-8627-c5d7deoao46b_story.html.

Stegman, Erik, and Victoria Phillips. 2014. *Missing the Point: The Real Impact of Native Mascots and Team Names on American Indian and Alaska Native Youth.* Washington, D.C.: Center for American Progress.

Steinberg, Dan. 2013. "AP Finds Support for Redskins Name." *Washington Post.* May 3. http://www.washingtonpost.com/blogs/dc-sports-bog/wp /2013/05/03/ap-poll-finds-support-for-redskins-name-redskins-com -rejoices/.

———. 2014. "Daniel Snyder: 'A Redskin Is a Football Player. A Redskin Is Our Fans.'" *Washington Post.* August 5. http://www.washingtonpost.com/blogs /dc-sports-bog/wp/2014/08/05/daniel-snyder-a-redskin-is-a-football -player-a-redskin-is-our-fans/.

Thornton, Russell. 1987. *American Indian Holocaust and Survival: A Population History since 1492.* Norman: University of Oklahoma Press.

U.S. Senators. 2014. "Letter to NFL Commissioner Roger Goodell." Washington D.C., May 21.

Vargas, Theresa, and Annys Shin. 2013. "President Obama Says, 'I'd Think about Changing' Name of Washington Redskins." *Washington Post.* October 5. http://www.washingtonpost.com/local/president-obama-says-id-think -about-changing-name-of-washington-redskins/2013/10/05/e170b914 -2b70-11e3-8ade-a1f23cda135e_story.html.

Waggoner, Linda M. 2013. "On Trial: The Washington R*dskins' Wily Mascot: Coach William 'Lone Star' Dietz." *Montana: The Magazine of Western History* (Spring): 24–47.

KATHRYN WALKIEWICZ

Affirmative Exclusions:
The Indigenous Exception
in Oklahoma's Official English

THE DECADE FOLLOWING 9/11 saw a wave of state and federal legislative efforts to secure borders and identify terrorists. As evidenced perhaps most famously by the creation of the Department of Homeland Security and the passage of the Patriot Act, the "era of terror" ushered in a new relationship between national security, mobility, and surveillance that functioned in tandem with decreased regulation and transparency of national security efforts. Panic about the falling numbers of jobs and resources during the economic recession that followed the 2008 housing market crash, along with heightened militarization, catalyzed a reactionary swing to the far right that assigned significant blame for these national "crises" onto the figure of the "foreigner" as the cause of this terror. As legal scholar Leti Volpp has shown in her work on post-9/11 hate crimes and racial profiling, the terrorist and the immigrant become figures of suspicion which threaten U.S. surveillance of bodies and capital that travel within its parameters unmonitored.[1] Moreover, they become conflated—almost one and the same. In the post-9/11 United States, immigration has produced a correlative relationship between the "illegal immigrant" (often read as Spanish-speaking) and the "foreign terrorist" (often read as a Muslim extremist)—both seen as threats to the state's militarized autonomy and economy, and both aligned in racially and historically loaded ways.

In the mid-2000s, official English legislation (also known as the "English-only movement") gained short-term popularity as a way for states to assert a political stance on autonomy, foreign affairs, and multiculturalism under the valence of patriotism. Thus English became a weapon in the global war on terror, and non-English-speaking individuals became suspect, made synonymous with the figure of the threatening outsider, the immigrant other. Arizona's official English debates received the lion's share of media attention, but Idaho, Kansas, and Oklahoma followed suit by passing legislation of their own. In this essay I argue that the Oklahoma Official Language Implementation Act, authorizing an amendment to the state constitution, marked a key rhetorical shift in Indigenous—settler relations. By including an exception for Native language use in the amendment, Native nations are understood as "affirmative exclusions" (or positive exceptions) to the legislation, in contrast to the perceived foreign "other" targeted under the changes. I begin by outlining the stakes of these changes and presenting an analysis of the exception made for Indigenous languages in the amendment. I then provide historical context for current Indigenous—settler relations in Oklahoma. After situating the amendment in a longer regional history, I move into an analysis of the legislative debates and their contemporaneous press coverage, as well as a discussion of the logics of neoliberal multiculturalism that undergirded the debates. I end with considerations of the larger impact official English may have both in Oklahoma and beyond its borders.

The amendment received overwhelming support in a 2010 general vote, but while under discussion in both houses of the legislature in 2009 it garnered outspoken criticism from some key constituents. English symbolically registered national and state pride for many Oklahomans, but compulsory language use also triggered memories of the state's long colonial history. As State Representative Mike Brown (D) emphatically insisted in 2009 legislative debates, official English "reek[ed] of forced assimilation."[2] The legislation echoed language debates of a prior era in which Native peoples, particularly children, as a method of assimilation and colonial acculturation were forcibly required to stop speaking their Indigenous languages and only speak English; history threatened to repeat itself (yet again) in Oklahoma.[3] But legislators who supported the bill insisted that it was not about repeating the sins of Oklahoma's colonial past. Rather, they assured, it was about protecting current citizens from the threat of a cultural and economic terror ushered in by an imagined inundation of immigrants.

The 2010 official English amendment, now Article XXX of the state constitution, was part of a post-9/11 conservative turn in state-level politics that proposed anti-immigrant xenophobic reform and asserted a return to states' rights as necessary to protecting the nation-state.[4] The amendment was not only an anti-immigration action but also attempted to rework the logics of state inclusion and exclusion by reifying conservative values. Despite the presence of long-standing Muslim communities across Oklahoma, a post-9/11 culture of fear was deployed in making the argument that nonwhite immigrant bodies posed a terrorist threat to the status quo. Importantly, this legislation did so by simultaneously reworking Indigenous—settler relations. By "indigenizing" prior settlers, particularly white settlers who illegally moved to the region in the late nineteenth century, and by insisting that they, like Native peoples, have claims to the land that precede those of other groups, the sins of settler colonial violence became background to the foregrounded threat of nonwhite immigrant terrorizing.[5]

Combined, the terrorist/immigrant symbol functions as both an economic and a security threat. This is a tricky move, however, in a state whose identity is deeply and fundamentally tethered to a narrative of settlement by (often illegal) immigrants who terrorized Native individuals and communities, eventually usurping geopolitical control of the region and weakening the autonomy of tribal control. In his ethnographic study of post-9/11 Islamophobia, Junaid Rana describes such responses as a "racial panic" in which heightened fear legitimates racist backlash and reinforces racial hierarchies.[6] For Rana this xenophobic paranoia is manifested in the figure of the Muslim terrorist who "is racialized not only in relation to terror, but also in relation to ideas of illegality and criminality that historically have been associated with racialized populations in the U.S."[7] Furthermore, the figure of the Muslim terrorist becomes a conflation of multiple racial "others" seen to pose a variety of threats to white supremacist colonialism. The non-English-speaking immigrant figure is alluded to, time and again in the legislative discussions surrounding the official English amendment, as a conflation of the terrorist and the Spanish-speaking immigrant.

House discussions of the bill tended to gloss over the history of settlement, racial stratification, and erosion of Indigenous autonomy that shaped the land and governance for well over 150 years. Sidestepping this history demonstrated one attempt to remap Oklahoma's borders and refigure a legacy of colonial trauma and migration that indelibly mark the space. Instead, representatives framed Oklahoma as a space of what affect theorist Sara Ahmed calls "happy multiculturalism." For Ahmed, "happy multiculturalism" offers a promise of happiness through immersion into hegemonic culture on the part of the migrant or the historically disenfranchised by finding common values with the privileged, as well as a release from a sense of anger or frustration with past wrongs.[8] While the debate and the popular vote inadvertently acknowledge the relationships between Indigenous peoples and the land that is currently Oklahoma, it also attempts to inoculate Oklahoma from this same historical memory.[9] The House debates reveal a great deal about the logics that undergird U.S. colonialism's machinations. Rhetorical justifications launched back and forth between representatives palpably demonstrate the clear connections between U.S. colonialism of Indigenous people and the war on terror.

By aligning the hegemonic state and Indigenous identity, the amendment works to "indigenize" whiteness and states' rights in order to redefine the geopolitical parameters of the space. The official English amendment's investment in governmentally regulated language use functions as an attempt to determine who does and does not have access and rights to mobility, capital, and land in ways that are deeply complicated by the long history of oppression, violence, and exploitation that have defined Oklahoma statehood.

This notion of the white-dominant settler state is coded into some of the claims made by the bill's author, Representative Randy Terrill (R). During legislative discussions Terrill claimed that other, more diverse states had already passed similar legislation. However, in Terrill's final remarks on March 11, 2009, he deployed a Winston Churchill quote about the "gift of a common language" as a "priceless inheritance" to frame multiculturalism and recognition of difference as threats to U.S. hegemony. He argued:

> It is our common American language, the language of English, and that melting pot process that is supported that has made this country *this* [his emphasis] country, the most successful multiethnic nation in the history of the world. Today, however, it is that priceless inheritance that is in danger. And it's under attack by those people who stand to gain by dividing American into separate communities that do not share a common language and have little in common except the same geographic location. They use the code word "multiculturalism" when, in fact, they are teaching a doctrine of linguistic apartheid.[10]

For Terrill, multiculturalism is a divisive force, but his claim that it is a form of "linguistic apartheid" is a poor choice of words at best. By this strange logic he inverts South African colonialism and oppression, aligning racialized institutional violence enacted by settlers to the erosion of English; multiculturalism, somehow, becomes a form of segregation and exclusion. Following his critique of multiculturalism (and one could argue an implied multilingualism), he—somewhat inaccurately—offered a quote from President Theodore Roosevelt on assimilation and the English language: "We have one language here and that is the English language, and we intend to see that the assimilation crucible turns our people out as Americans, not as hyphenated Americans, but as Americans."[11] This rescaling also attempts to shrink the temporal, cultural, and political differences between white Oklahomans and Native Oklahomans. In Terrill's amendment, the only "hyphenated Americans" explicitly allowed are the state-approved exceptions: Indigenous peoples. He highlights a distinction between Native peoples and other "hyphenated" Oklahomans and aligns multilingualism with "apartheid" in a complex move that simultaneously joins the state, white Oklahomans, and Indigenous Oklahomans against the figure of the immigrant, who is a threat to all three. While official English draws on the ghosts of Oklahoma's colonial past, it also signals new rhetorical tactics to indigenize the white settler presence in the state.

Making English Official

Legislative discussions about official English began on March 11, 2009, when the Oklahoma House of Representatives discussed House Joint Resolution 1042, the constitutional amendment proposal that would make English the official language of the state. The bill's debate included one exception: the use of Native American languages in state affairs. Less than ten minutes into the discussion, Representative Paul Wesselhoft (R) asked the author of the resolution, Randy Terrill (R), the following: "Would you concede, Representative Terrill, that this has a symbolic impact on a lot of people in Oklahoma, and that symbolic impact can actually cause, uh, some injury? Would you concede that?" Representative Terrill was not only unwilling to make this concession, which he acknowledged was in reference to Native peoples in Oklahoma, he argued that "if this were to become law and be voted on by the people, Oklahoma would be the only state, the *only* state—not just in the United States, but in the world—that would provide constitutional protection not only to English but to the Native American tribal languages."[12] Terrill, therefore, proffered the exception as a positive inclusion, calling it an "affirmative exclusion" that ostensibly protects Native languages and cultures. Nonetheless, Terrill's response elided the history of linguistic violence that both colonialism and Oklahoma statehood brought to Native peoples. As other representatives would bring up in the March 11 discussion, the linguistic censorship implicit in the bill had frightening similarities to colonial tactics of the late nineteenth and early twentieth centuries that attempted to prevent Native peoples from speaking their native tongues in a sweeping effort to assimilate them and help them become proper U.S. citizens.[13]

Official English passed through the Oklahoma legislature and was put to vote in the general election on November 2, 2010, as one of eleven State Questions (SQ). It was listed as State Question 751 on the ballot.[14] One of the other eleven, State Question 755, garnered significant attention from the national press. SQ 755 proposed a ban on the use of international law generally, and Sharia (religious law employed by some Islamic countries) more specifically, in the state courts. SQ 755 received national recognition because of its clearly anti-Islamic sentiments, but also because under preexisting legal codes Sharia already carried no juridical weight in the state. Read together (which was difficult *not* to do, since they were two of only eleven questions), SQ 751 and SQ 755 collaboratively expressed an aggressively xenophobic stance, and both gained overwhelming support from voters: over 70 percent voted yes for both, demonstrating that the majority of voting Oklahomans strongly favored the measures and the sentiments they represented.[15]

Terrill's official English bill and his notion of the Indigenous language exception as one of positive inclusion rather than injurious exclusion serves as the convergence of four moves on the part of the state: (1) an attempt to indigenize (white) Oklahoma settler identity, (2) an exception for Native people and languages that seemingly aligns Native peoples and whites as both indigenous to the space, (3) while simultaneously ignoring Oklahoma's history of settler colonialism, and (4) exclusion of the figure of the outsider immigrant as one who poses a threat to the status quo of the space. By this logic, the racialized immigrant—through illegal immigration or terrorism—poses a threat to the borders and safety of the United States. Both immigration and terrorism are seen as present threats that the state must regulate. Furthermore, the specter of immigrants *as* terrorists is juxtaposed against Oklahoma settlers and Native peoples. The terror posed is that a new wave of immigrants will dispossess the white settler state of its current status quo.[16] At the same time, prior illegal immigration in the form of the "Sooner" legacy is celebrated as sacred state mythology, but only through the narrative of white pioneer migration, which I will discuss in more detail below.[17]

Although Terrill posited the exception made for Native languages as one of multicultural sensitivity, this status in fact allows the state to renegotiate its relationship with Native nations and individuals in two particularly dangerous ways. First, it perpetuates state affirmation of a settler political structure that repeatedly attempts to obfuscate and weaken Native sovereignty, allowing the state of Oklahoma to determine which languages are "official" and why. Second, the law attempts to reinforce stratifications along lines of race, class, and nation in ways that challenge anti-imperial coalition building both within and beyond the state by distinguishing Native people from immigrants and non-English speakers. As Giorgio Agamben has argued, the exception the sovereign state makes does not place the exception outside of state control or surveillance. Rather, as an "inclusive exclusion," the exception for Native languages reinforces U.S. state power to decide both what is included and what is excluded from official state language and official state business.[18] Despite its seemingly beneficent acknowledgment of Native nations and individuals, the bill's "Indigenous exception" for Native languages not only participates in and perpetuates a long history of attempts to undermine and neutralize Native nations, communities, and individuals in the space of present-day Oklahoma, but also lays the groundwork for a new era of Indigenous—U.S. relations that has, in a few short years, already proven damaging to ongoing projects of Native sovereignty and autonomy. This gesture recycles past colonial practices of U.S. surveillance and control of Native people through language by flagging Indigeneity as an exception to the norm, but simultaneously does so by undercutting another sovereign exception—that of the immigrant. The native/nativism dialectic is used to naturalize xenophobia as an inclusivity, and in so doing the amendment complicates Agamben's notion of the exception's function.[19] Native identity is made distinct from but beholden to hegemonic state power, situated as a more acceptable or less distant exception than that of the radical outsider immigrant. It also reinforces a "domestic dependent" understanding of Native nations as put forth in the 1831 *Cherokee Nation v. Georgia* Supreme Court decision in which the Marshall court argued Native nations did not function like foreign nations or like states (in this case, Georgia), but like wards to a guardian—"domestically dependent" on the U.S. federal government. Official English serves as a template for shifting relationships between settler colonial states and Indigenous peoples that refashions the "domestic dependent" exception in a post-9/11 world. History repeats itself in the bill's exception, but does so by rescaling the proximity of inclusion and exclusion to the state.

Terror in the Territories

Geographically, Oklahoma is not a borderland in the most literal sense. Nonetheless, for over 150 years it has been a space that spawns borders. It was the forty-sixth territory to gain statehood, followed only by states whose borders physically marked the division between the United States and another nation or body of water (New Mexico, Arizona, Alaska, and Hawai'i). As territory, present-day Oklahoma has been understood as a space both inside and outside the purview of the settler nation. Prior to statehood it was a contact zone that, as Kevin Bruyneel notes, "was often referred to as *the* Indian Territory, a signal that it was not legally incorporated into or formally governed by the U.S."[20] Indian Territory was interstitial ground between a number of topographically differing regions—the South, the Southwest, and the Midwest—partially due to the territory's somewhat centralized location within the contiguous forty-eight states.

Beginning in the early 1800s numerous Indigenous peoples were forcibly removed there, most famously in the removal of Southeastern peoples on the Trail of Tears, which concomitantly shrank landholdings of Indigenous peoples already living in the region. Throughout the rest of the nineteenth century numerous other Native peoples from across the continent were also removed—every time further slicing up the land allocated to each nation within Indian Territory, and further displacing those Native peoples who had inhabited the space prior to Indian Removal. The territory was imagined as a settler annex—a distant location for eastern settlers to "disappear" the Native peoples they displaced (although this was also at the expense of renegotiating land claims of Indigenous communities and nations whose relationships with the continent have existed since time immemorial). However, these displaced Native nations maintained autonomy over land and governance, and therefore "the boundaries were governed by the nations' themselves, not the U.S. government, and thus they had a unique, uncertain relationship to the American polity."[21]

Over time, however, the United States made repeated attempts to integrate

Indigenous nations into the domestic space of the nation-state, which eventually led to the allotment policy of the Dawes Commission, the subsequent land runs in which settlers could claim "empty space" as their own property, and that transformation of Indian Territory into the state of Oklahoma. All of these had devastating effects on Native peoples within the territory. The Allotment era of the 1890s and early 1900s broke up land into individual plots, or allotments, a process that eroded the autonomy of Native tribes and nations to govern and dictate their national borders and land use. As a result, the federal government justified the dissolution of tribal governance of Indian Territory in 1906, arguing that allotment and U.S. sovereign control of the region was necessary for its eventual integration into as a state. A year later, in 1907, Oklahoma officially became the forty-sixth state of the Union. Nonetheless, the region's legacy as Indian Territory was never fully erased from historical memory. In fact, numerous elements of the Oklahoma state constitution were based on a prior movement to make Indian Territory a state—to be named Sequoyah—as an effort to maintain as much Native control of the territory as possible in the face of statehood. In more recent history Oklahoma has been a place of migration and mobility, due to the construction of railroads, cattle ranching, and later Route 66, negotiating an in-betweeness or liminality that has enabled the malleability and mutability of articulations of the space. Moreover, it is a region whose histories are repeatedly bumping up against the present, as its settler colonial past and Indigenous presence haunt liberal progress narratives that flatten race and Indigeneity.

However, the charges posed against this imagined group of threatening bodies has marked similarities to the actual immigration of white settlers into Oklahoma Territory and Indian Territory at the end of the nineteenth century, settlers who, in fact, did move to the territories for self-profiteering. Starting in 1889, the U.S. government opened what it depicted as "unused" land for settlement in a series of land runs. In these runs (also called "rushes"), settlers (called Boomers—or Sooners if they staked land before the official start of the run) could claim 160-acre plots, so long as they agreed to work the land. This "open" land was the product of increased U.S. involvement in Indian Territory, often the work of the Dawes Commission, to erode Native landownership and increase a U.S. (mostly white) presence in the state. The land rushes and the opening of previously Native-owned land created a massive influx of settlement in both Oklahoma and Indian Territory, and the number of white settlers increased almost fivefold between 1890 and 1907.[22]

Ironically, in a state with such heightened fears about immigration, Oklahoma celebrated its centennial in 2007 with the commission of a public art piece that commemorated the land rushes, signaling the weight this settler narrative has on Oklahomans' understanding of identity and mythos, even though the runs occurred years before statehood. Thus, nineteenth-century immigration is framed as a positive moment for the state and imagined as part of a longer, teleological narrative of progress, while the twenty-first-century immigrant is portrayed as a threat to the ideals and culture these nineteenth-century "pioneers" brought with them to the space. The figure of the contemporary immigrant both invokes and erases the historical memory of settler migration, and becomes understood as posing a threat to the stability of the state, regardless of whether this fear of a mass influx of immigrants is actual or imagined. In these fears, the violent history of settler colonialism is regenerated in a new manifestation that this time poses a threat to the sovereign settler state rather than Native nations. The return of the dispossessed dredges up historical memories of the state's prior sins by projecting those onto the bodies of immigrants. Dangerously, this paranoia attempts to align the sovereignty of the state of Oklahoma with Indigenous sovereignty. In so doing, it aims to naturalize a white presence in Oklahoma that invokes a purposeful forgetting of the space's history through a double move: the history of allotment, colonialism, and the erasure of Native governance in the space are obfuscated, while the history of land runs and settlement (those acts that brought a massive influx of white residents to the region) are celebrated.[23]

Despite attempts to whitewash the historical record, reminders of a far more complex past and present continually haunt the narrative of the land now called Oklahoma. The state's name itself is not an English word—it's Choctaw. And it is common knowledge in Oklahoma that the word roughly translates to mean "red peoples' land," thereby emphasizing the connection between the land and Native people (not that between settler colonists and land). An Indigenous exception is needed even in the utterance of the place name.

The State of Oklahoma Exceptionalism

It took almost three years to bring official English to a popular vote in Oklahoma, and in that time there was a great deal of internal debate between tribal officials and state legislators, often played out in the front pages of newspapers and on the House and Senate floors. Discussions of such a proposal had begun in 2007, but in 2008 it seemed the bill would die in the Senate. However, Republican Representative Randy Terrill, who became the face of official English advocacy, headed a House committee to reinvigorate the proposal. In 2008 Representative Terrill took the original language of the proposal (Senate Bill 163) and added wording that would include official English as a constitutional amendment.[24] After much debate, particularly in the House, a final draft of language was approved in May 2009 and put forward for the popular vote in November 2010. Unlike earlier versions of official

English legislation in Oklahoma, the wording of the 2010 constitutional amendment addressed two major concerns: the strong presence of Native language speakers in Oklahoma and potential violation of federally enforced civil rights for non-English speakers. An addendum created to address Native language use in state activities was produced after some concern that not only did the resolution fail to acknowledge Native people in the state of Oklahoma, but also the fact that there are over twenty American Indian languages spoken there.[25]

This exception for Native languages, one of the only exceptions offered in the actual ballot wording, is coupled with a disclaimer that implementation would follow federal rules and regulations in those areas supplied with federal funds.[26] Despite the House's willingness to include these exceptions in the bill, the spirit in which it was initially drafted remained clear and was only reinforced by its overwhelming support from voters at the polls: it was a xenophobic gesture propelled by fear and meant to reinforce the authority of the state's white majority.[27] The exceptions, like Terrill's emphasis that the bill is an official English bill and not an English-only bill, attempt to frame greater surveillance of particular bodies and communities in the state as a unifying action, rather than an attempt to highlight and alienate groups who are viewed as operating in opposition to the state.[28] Terrill argued that his bill is not an "only English" or an exclusionary act, but simply one meant to serve the legislative good of the people of Oklahoma.

One of the first responses to Terrill's House presentation on March 11, 2009, came from Representative Lisa Billy (Chickasaw/Choctaw), the first woman, the first Native representative, and the first Republican from her district.[29] After greeting Representative Terrill and speaking to him in several Native languages, including Cherokee and Choctaw, Representative Billy posed the following question to Terrill in English: "What kind of problem are we trying to solve?" Representative Billy's question poked at the most problematic aspects of the bill: Why this bill at this point in time in Oklahoma? What are the practical benefits? While Representative Terrill did not offer a concrete response to Representative Billy directly, he indirectly responded to the question in remarks made later during the session, as well as in interviews and comments to the press throughout the winter and spring of 2009. Representative Terrill claimed that providing "official actions" (services or documents) in languages other than English was currently costing the state a significant amount of money. However, when pressed, Terrill was forced to admit that Spanish was currently the only other language translated, and this was done primarily in the public safety department for driver license exams. Moreover, these exam translations cost the state approximately $50,000 annually, an infinitesimal percentage of the state's operating budget at the time.[30] Nonetheless, Terrill insisted that if the state were to begin offering additional language translations, each one would cost an additional $50,000 per translation.[31]

Chad Smith, then principal chief of the Cherokee Nation, was one of the more outspoken opponents to the official English legislation. In a *Cherokee Phoenix* editorial published in April 2009 he exposed the slippage in the proposed amendment's logic: "When Randy Terrill introduced 'English Only' last time he called me about excluding Indian languages and said the bill was 'only directed toward Hispanics.'"[32] While Terrill repeatedly claimed the amendment stemmed from economic concerns, Smith clearly outlines the intended target of "English Only" as a racialized population, while also positing Native languages as exceptions to the rule.[33] Significantly, here Native identity is temporarily removed from a historically consistent status of being the targeted racialized other and instead is aligned with that of white Oklahomans in opposition to immigrants. Doing so is an attempt by the state to temper the threat of Native resistance to the resolution and also to bury the history of language oppression enacted by the state of Oklahoma on Indigenous people.

As pointed out by Representative Terrill numerous times while defending his official English proposal's acknowledgment of Indigenous language use, Oklahoma is a "*unique* [my emphasis] environment" with a "*unique* [my emphasis] political history," and because of this it sometimes demands "unique" forms of legislation.[34] Additionally, this proposed amendment emerges at a "unique" moment in Oklahoma history, an era in which Oklahoma posits itself as a space of exceptionalism—understood not only by its loyalty to the nation, but also by its difference from the nation. Oklahoma becomes an exceptionalist space that understands itself as holding the ground for "American values" in uneasy times and doing work the federal government is unwilling to do to protect a particular iteration of American identity. State Questions like SQ 751 (official English) and SQ 755 (Sharia law ban) become one way to demonstrate Oklahoma's stance on the political and cultural moment.

Read through Jasbir Puar's notion of exceptionalism, Oklahoma's current moment of exceptionalism aligns itself with the nation ideologically but not temporally. Puar's critique of heteronormativity unpacks exceptionalism's ability to embody a variety of manifestations. She observes, "Exceptionalism paradoxically signals distinction from (to be unlike, dissimilar) as well as excellence (immanence, superiority), suggesting a departure from yet mastery of linear teleologies of progress."[35] The term is both material and theoretical for Puar, as "exception refers both to particular discourses that repetitively produce the United States as an exceptional nation-state and Agamben's theorization of the sanctioned and naturalized disregard of the limits of state juridical and political power through times of state crisis, a 'state of exception' that is used to justify the extreme measures of the state."[36] The nation is understood as being in a moment of crisis, engaged in a "war on terror" and still reeling from the economic recession of 2008. Legislatively and culturally Oklahoma posits itself as the exception to the rule that can paradoxically reinvigorate the core ideological values of the nation by challenging the nation's authority to determine its state sovereignty—Oklahoma is imagined as ahead of the game, and its forward thinking offers a template for how the nation can (and should) move forward.

Rights Rhetoric and Neoliberalism

The logics of neoliberal multiculturalism and capital on which the amendment depends utilize a rights discourse that masks paranoia about the migration of less desirable bodies into Oklahoma.[37] Proponents of the official English amendment claimed that the resources needed to accommodate non-English-speaking individuals unnecessarily burdens taxpayers and chips away at their rights by dedicating more state energy and taxpayer money to translation services. In an interesting turn, the defense of the law balances a liberal emphasis on the personal rights of the more desirable citizen, the English-speaking individual compliant with the state's wishes, with the assertion that English allows for stronger unification and cohesion. Individuals' needs, be they desirable or undesirable in the eyes of the state, become privatized. Languages other than English become legally acceptable in two specific venues—the private sphere and the private sector. Doing so utilizes the privatized logic of neoliberal economics to allow the state to maintain a broader sense of multiculturalism in those areas where it is economically advantageous to do so, while simultaneously authoring a symbolic ban of those same practices in order to demonstrate displeasure with the necessity of making such accommodations. Neoliberalism becomes the logic by which some bodies can become individualized targets in order to appease a sense of multiculturalism or liberal values—isolate certain individuals in the name of alliance building across heterogeneous groups who might otherwise have competing interests. For example, Native nations, communities of color, queers, working-class communities, and reproductive justice organizations (all of which have been perceived as threats to Oklahoma at one point or another) might collectively align with the state and denounce the terrorizing immigrant in the name of "state security."

However, during March 11, 2009, discussions of the bill on the House floor, a number of representatives expressed concern that such a contradictory policy would actually harm the Oklahoma economy rather than help it, sending the message that Oklahoma was "close-minded" and uninterested in participating in a global marketplace. As noted by one representative, such a law is "bad for business" and sends a negative message to the world that "we don't want your kind."[38] Whenever posed this question, Representative Terrill emphatically responded that the amendment would have no impact on business transactions. Language use would be left to the discretion of owners. The exception made for business only further underscores the bill's status as a symbolic gesture of bigotry and ties it to a neoliberal centralization of capitalism. It is only useful as long as it does not prevent the flow of capital into and out of Oklahoma. Such attention to economic marketability potentially sheds more light on Representative Terrill's interest in making an exception for Native language use—the exploitation of Native language use is good for Oklahoma tourism and advertising.

Privatization of Native language is made clear in the specific wording of Article XXX. The rule is stated first, "English is the common and unifying language of the State of Oklahoma," and then the exception: "Nothing in this Article shall be construed to diminish or impair the use, study, development, or encouragement of any Native American language in any context or for any purpose."[39] In other words, what individual Oklahomans do in their private time is fine, so long as it does not interfere with their relationship to the state. However, as noted by Puar in her discussion of *Lawrence and Garner v. Texas* (2003), "the private is . . . offered as a gift of recognition to those invested in certain normative renditions of domesticity and as an antidote, with many strings attached."[40] While Puar is primarily interested in the privatization of sexuality and sexual practices, the same modes of surveillance function in the context of language, both as ways in which individuals are ideally able to express themselves and to interact with a larger world outside the body. The "gift" of private freedoms does not allow for a selfhood outside the surveillance of the state—quite the opposite, in fact. Privatizing Native language use and the suggestion that these languages exist outside civic life challenges the sovereignty of Indigenous nations.

The gift of exception allows the state to intervene in private affairs in addition to public affairs, particularly for people of color (and queers), as "the precious haven of the private, always a relative, tenuous, and often impossible affair for people of color and immigrants, is even further spatially and temporally contained through the notion of intimacy."[41] The exception made for Native languages urges their continued "use, study, development, and encouragement," but with the understanding that their use, like the use of other languages, will be relegated to the private sphere. When Representative Billy asked Representative Terrill how the amendment "would apply to [state] officials engaging in official action," using herself as an example, Terrill responded that he would assume when speaking on the House floor she would speak in English, but the language she chose to use when speaking to her constituents was up to her.[42] A clear hierarchy (albeit an inconsistent logic in the above example) is thus established in which English is the dominant language of power and the law. This unequal distribution of power may be one reason why the legislative bodies of the Five Tribes (the Cherokee, Mvskoke/Creek, Choctaw, Chickasaw, and Seminole Nations) all came out in opposition to the bill.

In response to a 2009 *Tulsa World* article outlining changes to the amendment's wording (necessitated by Department of Justice concerns that a previous version potentially violated the civil rights of limited and non-English speakers and jeopardized federal funds), one online reader posted the following: "About 25 or 30 years ago there were Cherokee families living in the hills in eastern Oklahoma that did not speak English. When their children came to kindergarten the first thing they had to learn was to speak English. I wonder if some of those folks are still around and how it will affect them."[43] As this reader notes, regulation of language use has been repeatedly employed throughout Oklahoma's history to disenfranchise Native communities and individuals (as well as communities of color). During debate on the floor on March 11, 2009, Representative Jerry McPeak (D) argued that rhetorical claims used to advocate for the proposed amendment eerily echoed past U.S.—Indigenous land negotiations. In his comments McPeak noted that "for years the Indians have been sold some kind of bill of goods as the Caucasians have come along and really actually needed their land or wanted to take their land and they've been told something by the government to make those people feel better about that. So we have as appeasement some constitutional protection for the tribes. Please forgive us if we're just a little skeptical."[44] In his comments, the Mvskoke/Creek Representative reminded the House of another set of immigrants, those settlers who moved into Indian Territory at the end of the nineteenth century, many of them illegally, to obtain Indian land. McPeak challenged the kind of historical amnesia which manufactures a narrative of Oklahoma that deploys Indigenous history to its own ends— even when the narrative is contradictory.

Back to the Future: The "Affirmative Exclusion" of Indigenous Sovereignty

While the official English amendment seemingly offers a politically progressive exception in its acknowledgment of the presence and value of Native languages, at what cost does it do so? And moreover, can an Indigenous exception ever become anything but an exception that affirms settler colonial rule? In Elizabeth Povinelli's discussion of Australian multiculturalism, she argues that "critiques of liberal forms of domination should not dismiss or take lightly the truth of the state, national, and legal caretaking," even though they "reinstate liberal law and desire at the end of difference and they help saturate locals with this dream."[45] However, I would argue that no matter how well-intentioned, any "liberal law" framed by the settler colonial state should always be suspect because its closest alliance will always be with the settler colonizer.

This has proven to be the case in Oklahoma, and in the new amendment to the state constitution it continues to repeat itself. The same November Oklahomans voted in official English they voted in a new governor, Mary Fallin. Under her governorship the era of anti-immigrant Indigenous exceptionalism has gathered steam. In June 2014 the U.S. Department of Health and Human Services established one of three shelters for undocumented children in Oklahoma at Fort Sill. Governor Fallin opposed the federal government's use of Fort Sill, and when the children were removed in August 2014 she said the following in a public statement: "I am relieved—as are many Oklahomans—to hear this facility will be closed by the end of this week. We can now use it as it was intended: as a military resource to house and train soldiers."[46] Unsurprisingly, Fallin failed to reference the fact that Fort Sill was built in the nineteenth century to pacify and incarcerate Indigenous peoples in the area—most famously, the Chiricahua Apache leader Geronimo in the 1890s. Fort Sill is a "military resource" that marks a long history of anti-Indian settler force in the region. While today the soldiers Fallin spoke of are trained to fight abroad in places like Afghanistan, the first wars fought from the fort were in Indian Territory. In Fallin's comment the official word of the state's highest representative linked overseas U.S. warfare to a repurposed colonial legacy of violence against Native people that rejiggers history; language is not just about the words spoken but rather the stories told, making all the more salient the use of "Geronimo" as the military's alleged code name for Osama bin Laden.

The affirmative inclusion mapped out in the official English amendment's Indigenous exception has ushered in an era in which Indigeneity is up for grabs when it benefits the reputation of the state, but is also deployed to rework and harden boundaries about who is an included Oklahoman and who is a suspected security threat. While Mvskoke/Creek poet Alex Posey once coyly wrote that Indian Territory itself was a rare exception to historical repetition, the current policy making in the state of Oklahoma is an exception that threatens to prove the rule in state-level politics across the United States—and exceptions are not the same as freedoms. Inclusion can mean the elision of historical difference and the reproduction of a state identity narrative that employs Indigenous history toward its own ends.[47]

KATHRYN WALKIEWICZ is an assistant professor of literature at the University of California, San Diego.

Notes

The author would like to thank Jodi Byrd, Trish Loughran, T. J. Tallie, Lisa Tatonetti, the University of Illinois Indigenous studies reading group, and the anonymous reviewers at *NAIS* for thoughtful feedback that helped shape this essay.

1. Leti Volpp, "The Citizen and the Terrorist," *UCLA Law Review* 49 (2000): 561—86.

2. All discussions in the Oklahoma House of Representatives cited in this article were pulled from electronic MP3 audio recordings available through the House's website. All direct quotes from these audio archives are my own transcriptions. See Oklahoma House of Representatives, "1038_HJR 1042," *Session Audio Archives*, March 11, 2009, http://204.126.144.31/AudioArchives /2009/3/11/1038_HJR1042%20-%20Terrill.MP3.

3. I use both the terms "Native" and "Indigenous" in this paper to denote American Indians living in Oklahoma. The term "Native American" is used in the state amendment and in legislative discussions, so it appears more frequently in this essay than do "Indigenous" or "Indigenous peoples" simply for consistency.

4. The amendment is also known as the Oklahoma Official Language Implementation Act.

5. Elizabeth Povinelli describes something similar occurring in Australian legislation and policy. See *The Cunning of Recognition: Indigenous Alterities and the Making of Australian Multiculturalism* (Durham, N.C.: Duke University Press, 2002).

6. Junaid Rana, *Terrifying Muslims: Race and Labor in the South Asian Diaspora* (Durham, N.C.: Duke University Press, 2011), 51—52.

7. Ibid., 53.

8. See Sara Ahmed, *The Promise of Happiness* (Durham, N.C.: Duke University Press, 2010), 121—59.

9. See Chadwick Allen's discussion of "blood/land/memory" for a more in-depth discussion of correlative. Allen, *Blood Narrative: Indigenous Identity in American Indian and Maori Literary and Activist Texts* (Durham, N.C.: Duke University Press, 2002), 160—93.

10. Oklahoma House of Representatives, "1038_HJR 1042," *Session Audio Archives*, March 11, 2009.

11. Ibid.

12. The official English legislation passed in Arizona in 2006 also included an exception for Native language use; however, its reference (at least in the actual language) was far more limited. Article 28, section 1, of Arizona's constitution refers to "using or preserving Native American languages," while the Oklahoma language advocates Native language use in seemingly more explicit terms: "Nothing in this Article shall be construed to diminish or impair the use,

study, development, or encouragement of any Native American language in any context or for any purpose." The Oklahoma language was clearly based, at least somewhat, on that Arizona language, but protests from Native nations in Oklahoma demanded more robust language than that found in Arizona's constitution. See *Arizona Constitution*, art. 28, sect. 1, http://www.azleg.gov/Constitution.asp?Article=28; *Constitution of the State of Oklahoma*, art. 30, http://www.oklegislature.gov/ok_constitution.html. For a discussion of the relationship between Arizona legislation and Oklahoma legislation, see Mariann M. Atkins, "Making It Official: A Constitutional Analysis of Oklahoma's Official English Amendment," *Tulsa Law Review* 46 (2010): 477.

13. See David Wallace Adams, *Education for Extinction: American Indians and Boarding School Experience, 1875–1928* (Lincoln: University of Nebraska Press, 1997); Margaret Archuleta, Brenda J. Child, and K. Tsianina Lomawaima, eds., *Away from Home: American Indian Boarding School Experiences* (Phoenix: Heard Museum, 2000); Holly Littlefield, *Children of the Indian Boarding Schools* (Minneapolis: Lerner Publishing, 2001); K. Tsianina Lomawaima, *They Called It Prairie Light: Chilocco Indian School* (Lincoln: University of Nebraska Press, 1994).

14. The state language question read as follows on voters' ballots:

This measure amends the State Constitution. It adds a new Article to the Constitution. That Article deals with the State's official actions. It dictates the language to be used in taking official State action. It requires that official State actions be in English. Native American languages could also be used. When Federal law requires, other languages could also be used.

These language requirements apply to the State's "official actions." The term "official actions" is not defined. The legislature could pass laws determining the application of the language requirements. The Legislature would also pass laws implementing and enforcing the language requirements.

No lawsuit based on State law could be brought on the basis of a State agency's failure to use a language other than English. Nor could such a lawsuit be brought against political subdivisions of the State.

Shall the proposal be approved?

For this ballot language and additional data about the ballot question, see SQ 751's *Ballotpedia* entry, "Oklahoma English as the Unifying Language, State Question 751 (2010)," https://ballotpedia.org/Oklahoma_English_as_the_Unifying_Language,_State_Question_751_(2010).

15. "Summary Results: General Election," *Oklahoma State Election Board*, November 2, 2010, http://www.ok.gov/elections/support/10gen.html.

16. Aileen Moreton-Robinson makes similar observations about the rhetorical deployment of "security" by Australian Prime Minster John Howard in his post-9/11 speeches. See Moreton-Robinson, "Writing Off Indigenous Sovereignty: The Discourse of Security and Patriarchal White Sovereignty," in *Sovereign Subjects*, ed. Aileen Moreton-Robinson (Crows Nest, N.S.W.: Allen and Unwin, 2007), 89–90.

17. "Sooner" was a moniker given to settlers who did not wait for the official opening of land during the land runs in Oklahoma Territory and Indian Territory. Sooners would sneak onto land in advance, in order to obtain more desirable tracts. Oklahoma is called the "Sooner State" and the University of Oklahoma's mascot is the Sooner in honor of them.

18. See Giorgio Agamben, *Homo Sacer: Sovereign Power and Bare Life*, trans. Daniel Heller-Roazen (Stanford, Calif.: Stanford University Press, 1998), 21–22.

19. For an additional discussion of Agamben's notion of the exception see Giorgio Agamben, *State of Exception*, trans. Kevin Attel (Chicago: University of Chicago Press, 2005).

20. Kevin Bruyneel, *The Third Space of Sovereignty: The Postcolonial Politics of U.S.–Indigenous Relations* (Minneapolis: University of Minnesota Press, 2007), 29.

21. Ibid.

22. Angie Debo calculates the percentage of the overall population in Indian Territory this accounted for, noting that by 1907 whites constituted approximately 79.1 percent of the overall population, while African Americans made up 11.8 percent and Native Americans 9.1 percent. See *And Still the Waters Run: The Betrayal of the Five Civilized Tribes* (Princeton, N.J.: Princeton University Press, 1940), 133.

23. The current fear about the threat of immigration and terrorism is an attempt to codify a sense of state identity racially (as white), maybe even regionally. However, the figure of the immigrant–terrorist as a racialized outsider was problematized by the 1995 bombing of the Alfred P. Murrah Federal Building in downtown Oklahoma City, the most infamous act of terrorism to occur within the state of Oklahoma.

24. To compare the various manifestations of the official English proposals see George Faught, *Committee Amendment for HB 1066*, Oklahoma House of Representatives, January 28, 2009; Senate Chamber, *Floor Amendment No. HJR 1042*, State of Oklahoma, April 22, 2009; Randy Terrill et al., *Enrolled House Joint Resolution No. 1042*, Oklahoma House of Representatives and Oklahoma Senate, May 6, 2009; Randy Terrill, *Committee Amendment for SB 1156*, Oklahoma Senate, April 3, 2009; Randy Terrill, *House Joint Resolution No. 1042*, State of Oklahoma, January 5, 2009. All available at http://www.oklegislature.gov /AdvancedSearchForm.aspx.

25. This refers only to the languages of those Native nations located in Oklahoma. This number does not account for the myriad other Indigenous languages spoken in the state.

26. Of note, this inclusion was added only after the state received a warning from the federal government for possibly breaching federal legal obligations.

27. My use of the term "state" is twofold. I am referencing the state of Oklahoma proper as a territorial jurisdiction within the larger United States, but also the state as a larger set of institutions that dictate the rules and regulations of a particular polity.

28. I see little distinction between the terms "official English" and "English only," as they both stem from the same impulse.

29. According to the *Chickasaw Times*, prior to her run in the House, Billy was a Chickasaw tribal legislator. She also helped found the legislature's first Native American caucus. See "Lisa J. Billy Nominated for *Journal Record*'s 'Woman of the Year' Honor," *Chickasaw Times*, December 2011, http://digital.turn-page.com/issue/49562/15.

30. According to Oklahoma State Senate, the budget for FY '09 was approximately $7,063,300,000 and the budget for "General Government and Transportation" was approximately $379,300,000. Assuming the money for the driver's license test came from the "General Government and Transportation" budget, a $50,000 hit was a little more than one one-thousandth of a percent. See Oklahoma State Senate, *2009 Legislative Summary and FY '10 Budget Review*, June 2009, http://www.oksenate.gov/publications/legislative_summary/2009_legislative_summary.html; Oklahoma House of Representatives, "1018_SA HJR 1042," *Session Audio Archives*, May 6, 2009.

31. Oklahoma House of Representatives. "1038_HJR 1042" *Session Audio Archives*, March 11, 2009.

32. Chad Smith, "Don't Let Oklahoma Be Bullied by 'English-Only,'" *Cherokee Phoenix*, April 24, 2009, http://www.cherokeephoenix.org/Article/Index/2592.

33. Chad Smith is critical of the official English movement, but it must also be noted that this debate occurs at the same time as one about inclusion/exclusion within the Cherokee Nation concerning the Cherokee Freedmen. While the intent of the debates are somewhat different, it is important to note that at the same time the state of Oklahoma is policing its borders—physical, linguistic, and cultural—there is also heated debate within Native communities about who should have access to Cherokee citizenship, and who gets to determine the process of this decision making.

34. Oklahoma House of Representatives, "1018_SA HJR 1042," *Session Audio Archives*, May 6, 2009.

35. Jasbir Puar, *Terrorist Assemblages: Homonationalism in Queer Times* (Durham, N.C.: Duke University Press, 2007), 3.

36. Ibid.

37. I am thinking here of neoliberal multiculturalism as described by Jodi Melamed. See *Represent and Destroy: Rationalizing Violence in the New Racial Capitalism* (Minneapolis: University of Minnesota Press, 2011), 138.

38. Oklahoma House of Representatives, "1038_HJR 1042" *Session Audio Archives*, March 11, 2009.

39. *Constitution of the State of Oklahoma*, art. 30, http://www.oklegislature.gov/ok_constitution.html.

40. See Puar, *Terrorist Assemblages*, 124.

41. Ibid., 126. While queers were not explicitly included in the language debates as other communities, anti-queer and homophobic practices and policies have followed a similar trajectory in which queers are posited as anti-Oklahoman and threats to the (hetero)norms that legislate the state's culture and political climate.

42. Oklahoma House of Representatives, "1018_SA HJR 1042," *Session Audio Archives*, May 6, 2009.

43. Jim Myers, "Oklahoma's English-Only Amendment Clears a Hurdle," *Tulsa World*, July 30, 2009, http://www.tulsaworld.com/news/.

44. Oklahoma House of Representatives, "1038_HJR 1042" *Session Audio Archives*, March 11, 2009.

45. Povinelli, *Cunning of Recognition*, 268.

46. Barbara Hoberock, "Facility Housing Illegal Immigrant Minors at Fort Sill to Close by Friday," *Tulsa World*, August 5, 2014, http://www.tulsa world.com/news/capitol_report/facility-housing-illegal-immigrant-minors -at-fort-sill-to-close/article_405d2d87-6a34-51aa-9118-97bda042eb0b.html.

47. Alexander Lawrence Posey, "Letter No. 62," in *The Fus Fixico Letters*, ed. Daniel F. Littlefield, Jr., and Carol A. Petty Hunter (Lincoln: University of Nebraska Press, 1993), 237–40.

DEVON MIHESUAH

Indigenous Health Initiatives, Frybread, and the Marketing of Nontraditional "Traditional" American Indian Foods

Frybread, the staple of our Native Culture. Yep it just wouldn't be a perfect meal without it!
        —ANONYMOUS COMMENT ON NAVAJOFRYBREAD.COM, SEPTEMBER 24, 2012

I am so glad to shout from the rooftops that "Frybread" is not "our" Indigenous food and I hate that we have allowed it a place of reverence in our communities.
        —JOELY PROUDFIT, PECHANGA BAND OF LUISEÑO INDIANS,
            PERSONAL COMMUNICATION

FRYBREAD VARIES FROM TRIBE TO TRIBE in diameter, thickness, and shape, but is most commonly a plate-sized disk of flour, shortening, and salt that is fried in grease or oil. "Indian tacos" (or, as they are called in the Southwest, "Navajo tacos" and "Hopi tacos") are frybreads topped with ground meat, beans, cheese, lettuce, and sour cream. Dessert frybreads might be crowned with butter, powdered sugar, chocolate, honey, or syrup. Frybread makes its appearance at fairs, tribal commemorative marches, festivals, powwows, and restaurants. Girls running for the titles of "Tribal Princess" prepare frybread as their talent component. T-shirts are decorated with the slogans "Frybread: Breakfast of Champions," "Powered by Frybread," and "Frybread Power." Frybread enthusiasts are not deterred by *Health* magazine ranking frybread as one of the fifty fattiest foods in the country.[1]

Many Indigenous food and health enthusiasts argue that eschewing refined wheat flour, along with other unhealthy foods, in favor of traditional tribal foods is the key to eradicating the obesity and diabetes epidemic among tribal communities. Food activism, however, is not without challenges. In 2003 I wrote for the academic journal *American Indian Quarterly* about the repercussions of losing traditional foodways knowledge and opined against the overconsumption of frybread.[2] My bumper sticker, wall clock, buttons, and T-shirt that feature the word "FRYBREAD" with a red line through it appeared for sale on the website CafePress in 2004. As a result, I was assailed by frybread fans as "anti-Indian" and "not really Indian."

A year later the director of the Morning Star Institute, Suzan Shown Harjo, reiterated my notions about frybread in the popular online publication *Indian Country Today*.[3] Frybread fans reacted angrily and the controversy spread across Indian country. Despite Harjo's incorrect reconstruction of frybread's history, her essay has been mentioned in almost every newspaper article about frybread since 2005. That same year, determined Native frybread defenders pressured the South Dakota Legislature into designating frybread the "Official State Bread."[4] Elsewhere, Kiowa elder Carol Bronaugh stated that "an Indian person always gets hungry for frybread. Cutting frybread out of an Indian meal would be like cutting out the main ingredient of the entire meal."[5] Gayle Weigle, webmaster of Frybreadlove.com, stated, "It's like giving up turkey at Thanksgiving. It is a tradition."[6] Recent frybread drama occurred when fitness advocate and star of the weight-loss reality show *The Biggest Loser* star Jillian Michaels attempted to educate Yavapai Apaches about the dangers of fried flour at a 2010 tribal gathering. She dropped a plate of fried bread in the trash and called it "poison"; in return, a tribal member called her an "idiot" and threw a pile of bread at her. Afterward, she received a poor turnout for her diabetes discussion.[7]

Spokane writer Sherman Alexie has been called a "frybread expert," and he states that "frybread is the story of our survival."[8] But whose survival? Most frybread-focused stories and "traditional Native American recipes" sites proclaim frybread the creation of desperate Diné (Navajos) at Bosque Redondo in New Mexico, also known as Hwéeldi ("Place of suffering"), where the U.S. government confined Navajos from 1864 to 1868. This entrenched legend tells us that Navajo women fried their flour rations in lard and thus supplied their people with enough calories and nutrients to survive the ordeal. However, there are no government reports of Navajos at Bosque Redondo frying flour. Testimonies of Navajos whose ancestors who survived the Long Walk and lived at Bosque Redondo make no mention of frying flour either.[9]

The late George P. Horse Capture, member of the A'aninin tribe and onetime deputy assistant director for cultural resources at the National Museum of the American Indian, stated about the relation between the Creator and food: "In exchange for all the difficulties we endure, He gave us frybread and June berries." Considering the array of flora and fauna that sustained Natives for millennia prior to contact with Europeans, Horse Capture's reference to the unhealthy frybread as a gift from the Creator to distressed Natives is curious and merits a closer look.[10]

The Frybread Legend: Bosque Redondo

By 1846 Navajos lived in modern-day Arizona and western New Mexico and successfully raised horses, sheep, mules, goats, and cattle, all brought by the Spanish in the 1500s. Navajos also hunted deer, rabbits, and antelope and cultivated beans, chilies, corn, melons, squash, cactus fruits, piñon nuts, mesquite beans, and peaches they received from Hopis (who were introduced to the trees by the Spanish). Americans had moved into the Southwest by the 1860s and Navajos effectively pillaged their settlements. To stop the raiding, government officials planned to settle tribespeople onto Bosque Redondo and transform them into complacent farmers. They charged Kit Carson with gathering the Navajos and forcing them to the reservation. After an arduous and violent effort that involved much human death and destruction of tribal property, thousands of Navajos surrendered in 1866 and were forced to walk four hundred miles from Fort Defiance to Bosque Redondo. Ultimately, about 8,500 Navajos were confined along with 500 disgruntled Mescalero Apaches. While they experienced some agricultural successes during their incarceration, there were more failures and difficulties, including drought, floods, seed failure, a plague of worms, inadequate and spoiled rations, the Mescaleros' animosity, and Comanches' raiding.[11]

At various times Navajos were presented with small portions of salt, cornmeal, mutton, beef, pork, offal, wheat flour (which they did not know how to prepare), and coffee beans (which they tried to cook as they would common beans). Chiefs occasionally received sugar.[12] Despite claims to the contrary in *Smithsonian Magazine* they received no canned goods.[13] Navajos resorted to digging through horse and mule dung for undigested corn to grind into meal, and periodically they were allowed to hunt rabbits and gophers.[14] Government buyers contended with open-market prices, and many sacks of spoiled flour contained inedible objects that increased the bags' weight and cost.[15] This was not unusual. At the same time, in South Dakota at the Yankton Indian and Crow Creek Agencies, confined Natives also suffered to the point of dying of malnourishment from flour deemed "very poor," "very coarse," "sticky," and black. Those people ate wolves that had been poisoned, or sick mules, cows, and horses, as well as hooves and entrails.[16] Tough, stringy, and spoiled meat sporadically arrived at Bosque Redondo. On one occasion Navajos received a few head of cattle and they used every part of the animal, including blood they mixed with cornmeal to make what the Indian agent optimistically called "nourishing pasta."[17] They were in a dire situation and any rendered animal fat would have been quickly consumed, not saved to fry flour.

Army records mention flour being dropped in ashes to cook, mixed with water and drunk, and eaten "raw." One officer commented that a few Navajos cooked "tortilla-like substances." There were no reports of metal pots and pans and, therefore, no frying. During the same period, Civil War soldiers and tribes in the Dakota Territory received "hard tack," an undesirable rock-hard "cracker" mix of flour, water, and salt.[18] Soldiers crushed the hard bread, moistened it with water, and dropped the wad into ashes to create a softer mouthful. This would have been a logical way for Navajos to make use of the unfamiliar flour.

All the army and Navajo reports that mention flour at Bosque Redondo are bleak, conjuring reminders of sickness and death—not of survival. Indian agents wrote that flour was "unwholesome." Navajos became ill from "eating too heartedly of half-cooked bread, made of our flour, to which they were not accustomed."[19] Several Navajos testified in 1975 that their ancestors told them that many died from consuming flour.[20] It is possible that they perished from dysentery after ingesting Pecos River water that they mixed with un-cooked flour and coffee beans.[21] Their symptoms of intestinal distress are similar to those of gluten sensitivity, but there is no way of knowing for sure. No nineteenth-century Indian agent report of celiac disease exists because the connection between a body's inability to digest gluten and the ingestion of wheat was not recognized until 1952.

In 1868, Navajos signed a treaty allowing them to return to their Four Corners homeland, and eventually the reservation expanded to over twenty-seven thousand square miles. Trading posts increased on Navajo lands after 1870 and reached their peak of business between 1900 and 1930. Posts stocked their shelves with household goods, coffee, sugar, flour, baking powder, ginger snaps, oysters, deviled ham, candy, tobacco, popcorn, and canned fruit, tomatoes, and milk. Their animal herds grew exponentially, but in the 1880s Navajos in New Mexico suffered crop failures; one man stated that "we lived on [goat] milk."[22] In the late 1890s they suffered another failure, and some resorted to eating their animals and cheap flour acquired from trading posts.[23] Robb Redsteer, founder of Naataanii Alliance for Peace, says that was his great-grandparents' time and that frybread was "very rarely made."[24] Photographs of the 1913 and 1914 Shiprock Fair ("the Oldest and Most Traditional of the Navajo Fairs" that have featured frybread competitions for decades)[25] reveal impressive mounds of produce, rugs, and livestock, but no frybread. At the 1920 fair, Navajos competed in baking contests, presenting to judges loaves of wheat bread, layer cakes, biscuits, and doughnuts, and still no frybread.[26] Navajos again faced economic hardships in the 1940s. The tribe's animal herds decreased markedly and the people subsisted on "bread and coffee."[27] A 1940 photograph of a Navajo woman and a basket of frybread appears in the Sharlot Hall Museum, perhaps indicating that frybread had become a Navajo food item.[28] By mid-century the tribe economically recovered and consumed mutton, corn, beef, pork, beans, pumpkins, melons, and store-bought goods. They also made baked bread and fried "tortillas" but were not in starvation mode.[29] Throughout the 1950s Navajos ate less garden produce and more canned goods, candy, and coffee. According to Redsteer, in the 1960s frybread was more of a luxury food item. Navajos moved residences with the seasons on account of their livestock, and the heavy containers of lard and bags of flour were too cumbersome to haul.[30]

The Americanized trading post diet had consequences. By 1968 many Navajos were deficient in iron, protein, and vitamin C, and by 1981 nutritional support programs had been established to address the growing cases of deficiencies. A decade later, widespread consumption of pizza, cheeseburgers, bacon and mutton fat, sausage, canned meats, mutton sandwiches, sodas, desserts, and fried flour resulted in an obesity explosion.[31] The greasy and delicious frybread had become an everyday food. Somewhere on the vast reservation the Bosque Redondo frybread legend was created—and then spread across the country—to rationalize its mass consumption. The desire for junk food and frybread has not abated. There are only ten grocery stores on the Navajo reservation for three hundred thousand Navajos, in addition to a few gas stations and trading posts, which means residents must plan ahead and buy groceries that will last for weeks. The Diné Community Advocacy Alliance states that 80 percent of those foods are "junk." As a result, one in three Navajos is prediabetic or diabetic.[32]

There are a few deviations from the Bosque Redondo story. Some writers assert that Spanish women taught Navajo women how to make frybread in the square shape of sopaipillas and that Navajo women instead made their bread round to fit their frying pans.[33] Because the Spanish and Navajos were not friendly and the latter rigorously resisted Spanish attempts to acculturate them, it is doubtful that the few Spanish women in the Southwest and Navajo women cooked together. Moreover, one could fry square bread in a round pan. More likely is that Pueblos who lived in the vicinity of Albuquerque observed Spanish cooks making sopaipillas from flour and grease and eventually shared that knowledge with other tribes. Most Pueblos, however, baked bread in adobe ovens, and the thin Hopi blue corn piki bread is baked on hot stones.[34]

Some tribes might have learned how to use flour from French traders. By 1789 the Northwest Company traders occasionally used flour to make what they called galettes (French for flat crusty cakes or pancakes, although galettes are usually made with buckwheat) or to thicken stews. In the 1840s Frenchman Tixier traveled with Osages on the southern plains and he mentions meals that included beef fat-fried cornmeal that traders referred to as "fritters" and "beigne." French beignets, however, are square-shaped, deep-fried pastries sometimes topped with powered sugar or filled with fruit.[35] In the Northwest and Canada frybread is sometimes referred to as "bannock." Traditional bannock is dense bread made of oatmeal, barley, or other grain cooked on a griddle (or, in early days, a heated stone) and has been made in Ireland, northern England, and Scotland for centuries. Bannock can be made less dense with baking soda, and this form of bread is sometimes made by Natives, but fried bannock takes the form of a modern "Indian taco." Eighteenth-century traders and tribes rendered fat to make pemmican and normally baked breads in ovens or on hot stones, although traders sometimes mixed small amounts of flour with water and fried it in buffalo grease. Their tribal trading partners probably noted that "bannocks" were easy to prepare.[36]

Which Tribes Made Frybread?

Most tribes have always coped with poor government food commodities, including white flour. There are, however, few mentions of tribes frying flour in nineteenth-century government reports. In 1891 the physician at the Cheyenne River Agency in South Dakota wrote about the dire health issues of the tribespeople, reporting that "their bread is hardly worth the name."[37] At the Ponca Agency in 1893, the agent observed Poncas suffering from stomach ailments because of the way they prepared their bread: "Flour, water and baking powder, mixing it all together into a stiff dough; they roll it out and fry it in hot lard, making it all a very indigestible mass."[38] Another agent observed "fried bread" at a "Siwash" (probably Chinook) potlatch at Puget Sound; however, the tribespeople did not appear to be starving because they also gave away at their potlatch clams, salmon, venison, potatoes, huckleberries, and apples.[39] One agent wrote in 1892 of "several large fried cakes, made from wheat flour" among Cheyennes and Arapahos north of the South Canadian River.[40] In 1898 the Sac and Fox agent wrote that "nearly everything they eat is cooked in lard." They preferred hot fried cakes, pork, coffee, chicken, turkey, dog, and "relish skunk as a negro does opossum."[41] Francis E. Leupp, commissioner of Indian Affairs from 1904 to 1909, recounted in 1911 that Comanche Quanah Parker told him that Quahadis did not like flour because, "in our effort to get enough to extract some tastes from it, we filled our mouths, we nearly choked, and then found our teeth and tongues gummed up with a thick paste." So they dumped out the flour and used the bags for leggings.[42]

Some tribespeople did not use wheat flour at all. According to Anishinaabe Ojibway Martin Reinhardt, director of the Decolonizing Diet Project, Ojibways carried "cakes" made of rice, berries, corn, pumpkin, acorns, or meat that were cooked on heated stones.[43] Similarly, after the removal from the Southeast to Indian Territory in the 1830s, the Five Tribes (Cherokees, Chickasaws, Choctaws, Muscogees, and Seminoles) found eastern Indian Territory (now Oklahoma) crossed with waterways, rolling hills lush with nut trees and wild fruits, and populated by turkeys, deer, squirrels, waterfowl, and fish. Much of the soil was conducive to successful large-scale farming and family gardens. Tribespeople used corn, peanuts, chestnuts, acorns, and bamboo vines to make what English speakers call "breads," but these unleavened grains, nuts, and tuberous rhizomes were boiled or baked. Before long the steady stream of exploitative intruders into Indian Territory caused environmental damage and created an economic class system, resulting in many tribespeople unable to purchase food or to grow enough to sustain their families. While many members of the Five Tribes could afford to buy food, economic disparities caused some poor tribal members to suffer from a variety of ailments brought on from unsanitary conditions and lack of medical care, in addition to depression and frustration. Impoverished tribespeople received little assistance from the government and relied on cornmeal, not wheat flour, and the corn mono-diet caused malnutrition. Prior to their removal in the early 1830s, acculturated Cherokees used wheat flour to make pancakes, biscuits, gravy, piecrusts, and cookies, but not frybread.[44]

The *Indian and Pioneer Histories* consist of eighty thousand interviews of residents of Oklahoma conducted by Works Progress Administration workers in the 1930s. Many of the elderly Native and non-Native interviewees grew up in Indian Territory during the mid-nineteenth century. Only four entries mention "frybread" or "fried bread." Two are about placing biscuits in hot coals; in another, a white man observed Sac and Fox women wrapping "frybread" around raw meat and chewing until blood oozed out of their mouths;[45] and the other noticed that in Cheyenne, Arapaho, and Kiowa camps there was more "fried bread" than any other food.[46] None of the Native interviewees mentioned frying flour or bread, although some did tell of mixing purchased wheat flour with beans. Choctaws stated they did not like wheat flour and preferred cornmeal. If they did use wheat flour they did not fry it, and some used flour only to make Sunday biscuits.[47] The Cherokee Female Seminary, established in 1852 in Park Hill and rebuilt in Tahlequah after the destructive fire in 1889, served dishes with wheat flour to students every day. Cooks did not prepare frybread; however, there is plenty of documentation of physical distress from the girls' diet of excess flour, fat, sugar, and salt. Like Navajos at Bosque Redondo who had not previously consumed flour and coffee, for the Cherokee children who normally consumed garden produce and wild game at home the heavy Seminary diet of biscuits, gravy, pancakes, cakes, milk, butter, cream, and sugar resulted in a variety of digestive disorders such as "piles," "sour stomach," indigestion, "wind on the stomach," and diarrhea.

Lactose intolerance, as well as the aforementioned gluten sensitivity, were not recognized maladies. An indication of the cooks' favorite ingredient was the order placed in 1893: sixteen thousand pounds of white wheat flour for less than three hundred students.[48] Their health issues continued unabated.

Who Wants "Traditional" Food?

In the 2011 documentary *Good Meat*, Oglala Lakota Beau LaBeau is thwarted in his quest to lose weight with a traditional diet because his family prefers beef over bison, as well as processed foods procured from Wal-Mart. Whereas it was once common practice to consume squirrels, venison, and offal, now some tribal elders refuse to eat even the muscle portions of traditional meats such as elk, deer, moose, and antelope. After I spoke at Illinois State University several years ago, a Muscogee told me that his "traditional meal delivery" for elders project was not successful because his fellow tribespeople associate such fauna with being impoverished and "second class." They prefer fast foods because these are the favored fare of mainstream America.[49] Every time I teach the courses "Foodways of Latin America" and "Foodways of Native North America," Native students remark about their dislike of traditional foods such as squash, beans, bison, salmon, and venison. At Indigenous studies potlatches when I have brought elk stew, those dishes go half eaten while cheesy casseroles and desserts are immediately consumed. The answer to why processed foods are more desirable to some Natives is more complicated than frybread tasting better than pokeweed.

The topics of traditionalism, cultural change, and "food sovereignty" are beyond the scope of this article, but a cursory overview can help explain why some Natives eschew traditional foods in favor of less healthy fare. There is no monolithic "American Indian" or "Native American" culture. Tribes differed in their religions, languages, gender roles, physiologies, housing, clothing, and subsistence strategies depending on environment and their reactions to colonists. One commonalty is that tribes verbally passed sociocultural information from one generation to the next. Youngsters had the responsibility of listening to their elders and retaining the cosmological and cultural stories that instruct how to behave as a tribal member, how to interact with the natural world, and how to survive. Stories and cultural histories also situate individuals' identities within their cultural group and the larger world. This time-tested tribal knowledge, garnered through trial and error, is inexorably tied to tribal lands where ceremonies are performed, where the dead are interred, and where many tribes believed they emerged.[50] Deborah Lupton's statement that "food is instrumental in marking differences between cultures, serving to strengthen group identity," is appropriate in this context because medicinal and edible flora and fauna were, with some exceptions, particular to the tribes' homelands.[51]

Tribal foods possessed myriad symbolic connotations, including prosperity, status, wealth, luck, fertility, evil, and poverty. Tribespeople recognized the connection between sustenance and cosmological deities, often female, who presented the people with specific foods. For example, not all tribes grew maize, but among those who did, from the Aztecs in Mexica to the Choctaws and Cherokees in the Southeast to Iroquois tribes in the Northeast, corn was seen as a symbol of sustenance and fertility. Tribes followed calendars based on weather or harvests. The northern Anishinaabe divided their year into thirteen moons that match the number of sections on a turtle's shell. Their July is *Miin giizis* (berry moon). Tlingits of the northwest coast started their thirteen-month calendar in July, *Xaat disi* (salmon month), when the salmon returned. Choctaws also had a thirteen-month cycle, in which July and early August is *Hvsh luak mosholi* (month of the fires all out), and Muscogees (Creeks) referred to July as *Hiyucee* (little harvest). The same period is known among Navajos as *Bii'int'aachili*. Ceremony accompanied the stages of food acquisition. Late summer for many tribes signified that corn had reached its roasting stage and many danced (and still do) the Green Corn Dance, a thanksgiving festival that might last several weeks. Senecas, among others, recognized the importance of certain foods, evidenced, for example, by the Strawberry and Blackberry Dances. Navajos performed the Seeds Blessing and Rain Ceremonies as well as corn songs and numerous hunting rituals.[52]

Today, the definition of the tricky and debatable term "traditional" varies from person to person. How people define "traditional" depends on the extent of connection to their tribe, and how that tribe and their family confronted colonialism and its myriad socioeconomic forces such as forced education, relocations, Christian influences, economic pressures, and intermarriage with non-Indians. All tribes have been forced to change, and tribal traditions are continually invented in order to satisfy the needs of the current generation.[53] In the process of creating Navajo cultural stability after their Bosque Redondo experience, the Navajo meaning of "traditional" changed every few years to incorporate accouterments and philosophies of non-Navajo societies. They adopted more Euro-American animals and foods, learned silver and blanket making from Pueblos, embraced the peyote religion (i.e., the Native American Church) from Mexican tribes, integrated powwow regalia, drumming, and singing from Plains cultures, learned to carve and sell Hopi Kachinas, and some participate in the northern Plains tribes' Sundance. This is not unusual; most tribes adopted cultural mores from other tribes and other societies. Natives of all tribes use cell phones, wear jeans, live in homes like other non-Indians, eat fast food, and watch television; however, because they speak their language, practice religious ceremonies, appear phenotypically "Indian," and perhaps live on a reservation, they might refer to themselves as "traditional." For some Natives, "tradition" means familiarity. For example, David Fazzino conducted a study of Tohono O'odham foodways in 2003. He discovered that some tribal members considered a food "traditional" because they recalled eating it as a child. Others defined "traditional food" as their grandparents' food. Still others defined it as a food that is personally important to them. Reflecting all three criteria, young adults referred to frybread as "traditional" 37 percent more often than the middle-aged.[54] By asserting that frybread is part of their cultural heritage and therefore "traditional," some Natives simultaneously reaffirm their "Indian identity" and feel justified eating the dish.

Some Natives retain cultural knowledge while others have little or no connection to their tribal culture. More Natives live off reservations than on, and many only occasionally participate in tribal activities (such as food sovereignty initiatives) or not at all. Indigenous peoples' dietary choices, therefore, are influenced by multiple and complex factors: finances, availability, politics, religion, educational background, residence, condition of the product (polluted, GMO, farmed vs. wild), physiology of the eater (allergies, diseases, weight issues), ease of acquisition and preparation of the food, historical connection, taste preferences, advertising influences, smell, appearance, and familial and cultural pressures and expectations. Attention is paid to the way food is procured (who buys, grows, hunts, or prepares it), how it is served (who eats first, who is the server, who sits where), and what foods are labeled as taboo. Combine all these elements with how individuals view the world through the lens of their identities (gender, sexuality, cultural, religious, economic class) and it is not surprising that one Native might declare that frybread is sickening and is not a traditional food, while another cannot name a single food their tribe ate historically, and still another asserts, "I'm Navajo: frybread and mutton are my specialty."[55]

The Persistence of Fried Bread

In 2012 the Diné Policy Institute surveyed Navajo tribespeople; of 230 respondents from across the Navajo Nation, 90 percent answered yes to the question, "Would you be interested in information about traditional foods if it were available?"[56] Across Indian Country, backyard gardens of heirloom corn, squash, beans, and peppers have sprung up, as have Indigenous food sovereignty projects. Many Anishinaabe Ojibways in Minnesota and Wisconsin have attempted to remain true to their foodways traditions even after the government assigned them to reservations and took away their lands along with their essential *manoomin* (rice) stands. The tribe strategized to use sharing, reciprocity, and communal hunting to harvest wild rice, berries, and maple syrup and to hunt and catch fish. The historian Thomas Vennum observed about their wild rice that it "continues to symbolize old Ojibwe culture: it is part of the Indian world, distinct from the white."[57] Ojibway Martin Reinhardt makes it clear that frybread is not part of his "Indian world": "Our traditional Anishinaabe diet never included white flour, white sugar, and Crisco shortening."[58]

In contrast to the Ojibways' cultivation of *manoomin* is the irony of frybread. Despite tribes' lack of connection to frybread precontact and their dependency on American food manufacturers to provide the ingredients, many frybread advocates associate not eating frybread with not being Indian. Or, as one online commenter on the 2008 *Smithsonian Magazine* frybread article asserts, "Your not a real Native if u don't no how to make or eat frybread."[59] While some Natives eat frybread as a way of signifying cultural identity, others connect frybread to the inadequate foods given to tribes by the U.S. government and believe it a symbol of colonization. Indeed, none of the ingredients of frybread are indigenous to this hemisphere. Frybread creation requires no cultivating, harvesting, hunting, or gathering. Attention neither to the seasons nor to ceremony in procuring the ingredients is required. There is no oral tradition lesson to be taught about frybread, not even about it as a survival food. One can make frybread during any season with goods purchased from Dollar General. For some frybread advocates it could be that the making, selling, and consuming of frybread under the auspices of it as a "cultural food" is an act of defiance, acknowledging that the ingredients originally belonged to the Other (the colonizer), but that item made from the Others' components now belongs to them. Regardless, the lack of nutrients and the high fat and caloric content of frybread render it dangerous and undesirable except for the taste, low cost, and ease of preparation.

While some Navajos revere frybread as a symbol of their survival at Bosque Redondo, Natives a thousand miles away with their own traditional foods specific to their geographic locales consume frybread with reverence, as if the frybread story is also theirs. This is not too surprising. They want to eat it. Fat, sugar, carbohydrates, and salt can be addicting, and frybread advocates are determined to not give up such fare.[60] Historical trauma also accounts for dietary choices. Racism, stereotyping, poverty, and depression are ongoing manifestations of colonization. There is no such thing as "postcolonial" for tribespeople. The tribes' historical traumas may have taken place at different time periods and in different locales, but Natives often put all offenses against tribes into the same category. Their grief is unresolved because they feel the effects of their ancestors' sufferings. Some express their frustrations by abusing drugs, drink, or food.[61] The psychologist Billi Gordon explains that "when people are continually battered and abused, they find comfort and shelter where they can; eating satisfies the ancient brain."[62] Many Americans grew up depending on comfort food such as mashed potatoes and gravy, Cheetos, and ice cream. A lot of Natives have as well, and this includes the easily accessible frybread. Feelings of guilt and depression about having diabetes and other health problems associated with an unhealthy diet can lead people to consume the very foods that are killing them. Indigenous Arizona students in my Northern Arizona University classroom talked about "when" they develop type 2 diabetes, not "if," because every person in their family has the disease. They expect no other outcome than to become sick.

The Yavapai Apaches publish a monthly newspaper that informs tribal members about "Healthy Cooking on a Budget" courses—and, as with other tribespeople with access to wellness programs, many Yavapai Apaches choose not to take advantage of such offerings. Jillian Michaels suggests that tribal members might be apathetic, and she has a valid point. Teachers at government-run boarding schools disallowed Native children from speaking their languages, from participating in ceremonies, and from communicating with tribal elders who could teach them cultural mores, including foodway traditions. As a result they lost awareness about how to save seeds, cultivate plants, and hunt game. Every lesson ingrained in them their inferiority to whites, and this "boarding school syndrome" affected not only the children who attended the schools but also subsequent generations who learned from boarding school survivors.[63] Many Natives continue to act on their insecurities by making bad dietary and lifestyle choices. Conversely, Indigenous food activists are hopeful that a return to eating precontact foods will provide Native peoples empowering links to their tribal past. Reconnecting with their traditional Indigenous knowledges could assist them in finding historical solutions to modern health problems.

Frybread Is Here to Stay.

Game meats and organic produce are costly. Frybread ingredients are cheap. Frybread is fairly easy, albeit potentially messy, to make at home: all one needs are the ingredients, basic implements, and an electrical outlet, generator, or campfire. Cooks from Arizona to Alaska receive national attention from newspapers that feature their versions of the origin and meaning of frybread, and demonstrating one's ability to make good frybread can also bring status, as seen in various Miss (insert tribe) Princess contests, Pawhuska's annual National Indian Taco Championship, and American Indian Expositions in Anadarko (and as mocked in the wry 2010 film *More Than Frybread*). Another use of frybread is that some Natives who do not eat frybread at home will eat it among other Natives for social acceptance. "Wannabes" (non-Indians who cannot prove blood or community connection to any tribe) seeking legitimacy might eat it with Natives in an attempt to prove their connection to tribal culture, even if that identity is vague and "pan-Indian."

Frybread tastes good to most people. Because it is also popular among non-Natives there is a profit motive to sell it. Dwayne Lewis, the owner of the now-defunct Arizona Native Frybread in Mesa, Arizona, sold frybread because "everybody wants it."[64] Indian tacos are marketable to crowds looking to connect with Indian cultures, and frybread hawkers cater to Americans' tastes for greasy, salty, and fatty foods. The annual Haskell Indian Art Market in Lawrence, Kansas, for instance, offers frybread from numerous vendors, all of whom serve perpetually long lines of customers. At my university down the road from Haskell, the instructor of the Indigenous studies "Grant Writing" graduate course eschewed lessons in actual grant writing and focused on how to organize Indian taco sales. Representatives from the (not federally recognized) Houma Nation sell frybread to non-Indians at the New Orleans Jazz Fest every year, using 150 pounds of flour, 12 gallons of milk, and 12 dozen eggs per day. Cook Noreen Dardar claims that making frybread is her "tradition," but frybread was not a food among Southeastern tribes.[65] The company "Navajo Frybread" is owned by non-Indians and produces six hundred thousand twenty-five-pound bags of Blue Bird flour each year. Owner Trent Tanner states that "we wouldn't be in business without the Navajo people. It's our philosophy that it's their flour and we make it for them. Sales go up especially in the summer when kids get home from boarding school."[66] Indeed, it is not uncommon to see Native shoppers fill their carts at Flagstaff, Arizona, Safeway markets with bags of the refined flour. Some cooks rely on the mystical element to attract buyers. Although some frybread makers advise poking a hole in the dough so the edges will fry evenly, one cook clearly caters to non-Indians looking for an "authentic Native American" dish. Clark "Little Bear" Oxendine of the Lumbee Tribe cooks frybread at powwows and tells customers (and reporters) the cryptic yet unsubstantiated tribal custom that making a hole in the bread will "let the evil spirits out of it, so it'll taste good."[67]

What Is "Native American Food"?

If one searches for truly traditional Native American recipes on the web or published materials, the results are hit and miss. Marketing and selling of so-called traditional recipes takes advantage of the reality that most people know little about tribal foodways. Eric Hobsbawm and Terence Ranger define "tradition invention" as a "set of practices . . . which seek to inculcate certain values and norms of behavior by repetition, which automatically implies continuity with the past," and some of these "traditions" are "established with great rapidity."[68] Many "traditional" recipes contain more non-Indigenous ingredients than anything else; however, because Natives have been using these recipes (such as grape dumplings) for decades, producers deem them "traditional" and market them as such. The regular "Native Recipes" column in *Indian Country Today* illustrates the misrepresentation of non-Indigenous recipes as "traditional."[69]

With the popularity of chef's memoirs and foodie TV shows, the media has fervently jumped on the fryer bandwagon. Reporters romanticize frybread as an "American Indian" culinary delicacy and apply enthusiastic imagery to its preparation: "The sound of fresh dough being tossed and flattened melds with the sharp sizzle as it hits hot oil to create a pleasing culinary rhythm";[70] "Hot canola oil pangs off a stainless steel tub under the watch of a local frybread master";[71] "In this comforting Father's Day dish, homemade frybread gives the stacked entrée an indulgent foundation from which to grow";[72] and so forth. The publicity given to the stories told by frybread makers has contributed to the dish's reputation as a bona fide "Native American" food.

Natives also take advantage of the burgeoning interest in Native foods. It is obvious what is the featured item of the Frybread House in Phoenix, a restaurant owned by Tohono O'odhams who advertise their establishment as serving "Native American Food," but the other menu choices are nontraditional: fried potatoes, refried beans, beef and burro plates, along with butter, powdered sugar, and honey to adorn the frybread. The James Beard Foundation honored the Frybread House as "beloved for quality food that reflects the character of the community."[73] And that is the problem. At least half of all Tohono O'odham adults have diabetes, and it is not because they are consuming their historical diets of corn, squashes, beans, and cactus fruit.[74] The Frybread House is owned by tribal members who aim to make money. On the other hand, the opposing goals of the tribe's "Healthy O'odham People Promotion" and "Tohono O'odham Community Action" are to encourage physical activity and the consumption of traditional foods.[75]

One of the first Natives to market "Indian foods," Osage Raymond Red Corn, started HA-PAH-SHU-TSE (Red Corn) Indian Foods in Oklahoma in 1975 because, according to Raymond in 1981, "young people don't know our cooking anymore." Osages traditionally hunted, gathered, and cultivated gardens, but like every other tribe they did not traditionally use wheat, beef, or dairy products. Originally, the Red Corns served food at their establishment, including beef chuck meat pies and "Osage purple dumplings" made of flour, baking powder, shortening, butter, sugar, and Welch's grape juice.[76] Now the company is called Red Corn Native Foods and sells only frybread mix. Selling frybread has also spread to Alaska, where Indigenous peoples have never grown wheat. The Native-owned Garfield's Famous Frybread does a brisk business selling frybread to Tlingit tribal members, to the tune of 175 pounds of dough a day, along with toppings of margarine, powdered sugar, and Hershey's chocolate syrup.[77]

In 1987 WoodenKnife Co. of Interior, South Dakota, began selling a pre-made frybread mix, marketed as "the original Sioux recipe," although what the latter might be is unclear. According to government reports, tribes in the Dakotas received the same goods as did Navajos. There are no reports of them frying flour and, despite claims to the contrary on the WoodenKnife site, there are no entries in the journals of Lewis and Clark stating that tribes fried *timpsala* (prairie turnip) flour. When WoodenKnife's owners started making frybread, they added ground *timpsala* as flavoring, but they no longer do because of environmental stress to prairie plants. Today, the company markets the ordinary frybread mix in "a version of the Native American pouch bag" because "this option gives a small look into the Sioux Indian culture."[78] This is an odd keepsake; Sioux tribes did not use wheat flour while they "migrated with the buffalo"—that is, as they followed one of their main foodstuffs.

In 2010 *The Atlantic* featured the "American Indian Eatery" Tocabe. The owners of the restaurant state, "Our mission is to become the Industry Standard of American Indian cuisine," and "We need to help push it."[79] The only Indigenous ingredients offered on the Tocabe menu, however, are bison, tomatoes, beans, and possibly *wojape* (depending on how it is made; real *wojape* is fruit only, no sugar). Tocabe's menu prominently features non-Indigenous nachos and frybread with toppings of beef, chicken, cheese, sour cream, powdered sugar, as well as chips and sodas. The *Kekuli* Café in Merritt and Westbank, British Colombia, was inspired by owner's "First Nations roots." The establishment's slogan is "Don't panic . . . we have bannock!" with one "bannock taco" dish described as "piled teepee high."[80] Besides bannock, frybread, and local Saskatoon berries featured as "Indian food," the offerings are purely North Americana.

Like Tocabe, the Mitsitam Native Foods Café at the National Museum of the American Indian features an even longer list of non-Indigenous ingredients, some of which are the focal point of the pricey dishes. The restaurant claims that "each menu reflects the food and cooking techniques from the region featured." However, the Mitsitam menu features foods that were not traditionally used by tribes: crab apple, carrots, chicken, apple cider, beets, cabbage, bacon, cheese, almonds, Spanish olives, macaroons, Brussels sprouts, celery, cherries, wheat flour tortillas, sour cream, wheat rolls, leeks, saffron, cauliflower, goat, fennel, oxtail, okra, cilantro, cookies, and tarts. The adjoining Mitsitam Espresso Coffee Bar serves Tribal Grounds Coffee, a product that is grown by unidentified "Indigenous farmers."[81] Coffee plants are not indigenous to this hemisphere. The problem with Mitsitam is that it misrepresents a foundational feature of tribal cultures—food—while housed in a world-famous museum that is supposed to educate visitors about Indigenous peoples.

Cookbook authors aim their coffee table publications at those who can afford to purchase them, and those buyers usually are not tribespeople. Recipes in *Foods of the Americas* (published by Ten Speed Press in 2004) include such non-Indigenous items as flour, butter, milk, ice cream, beef, cilantro, plantain, chicken, and pork. The same can be said of *Spirit of the Harvest: North American Indian Cooking* (published by Stewart, Tabori, and Chang in 1991), which renders some "Native recipes" unrecognizable because of myriad of non-Indigenous items. *Foods of the Southwest Indian Nations* (also published by Ten Speed Press, in 2002) alternates between traditional and thoroughly non-Indigenous dishes. By including ingredients such as heavy cream, milk, butter, flour, peaches, cinnamon, chicken, and many other European-introduced items, authors miss opportunities to showcase truly traditional tribal cooking. Instead, many "Native" cookbooks present dishes made of mainly European-introduced ingredients mixed with a few native to North America.

Granted, frybread is only one cause of poor health. I know healthy and active Natives who will eat small amounts of frybread at tribal events, not out of respect to a "cultural food" but because it tastes good, as does cheesecake. The occasional indulgences in an otherwise-conscientious diet do them no harm. Some Natives, however, eat frybread and other processed foods multiple times a day, even during foodways ceremonies such as the Green Corn Dance. At the Choctaw Nation's festivals the always-crowded midway features donuts, butter-slavered corn, corn chip pie, funnel cakes, fried Twinkies, and fried bread. Next to this array of junk food stands the extensive "Healthy Living Expo" ready to assist Choctaws with their diabetes, obesity, and high blood pressure. Some festival organizers obviously can identify traditional foods such as *banaha* and *tamfula*. Still, despite my suggestion that they move *banaha* and *tamfula* to the main midway, these dishes are relegated to the "cultural demonstration" area with *ishtaboli* (stickball) games and bow and blowgun making.

Tribal Food, Tribal Health

So what is the harm of the "tradition invention" of dishes that only contain a few Indigenous items, or sometimes none at all, and marketing them as "Native American" foods? Those who profit will argue there is nothing wrong with it. For others, promoting traditional foodways is integral to becoming

aware of their tribes' history, learning their language, and becoming politically active, all of which will contribute toward building pride and shaping
their identity as Indigenous people. And while many activists urge youngsters to engage their elders, not all elder Natives are aware of their foodways.
Fazzino comments that it is not constructive to expect tribal elders to know
how to identify, cultivate, and prepare traditional foods. Many Natives have
adapted to what has been available to them. The expectations of a know-it-
all elder could be detrimental to modern food security because the assump-
tions "obliterate the processes of adaptation to and learning from one's elders and environment through rituals, experiences and just plain work under
the desert sun."[82] Indigenous food activists would agree. Besides the issue of
many Natives' inability to distinguish between traditional and nontraditional
foods, Indigenous food activists have no quarrel with the adoption of nourishing, non-Indigenous plants and animals into tribal foodways, nor with new
techniques for food sustainability, such as the Choctaw Smallwood brothers'
aquaponic farming system.[83] After all, broccoli (indigenous to the Mediterra-
nean and Asia Minor) is more nutritious than frybread. Rather, the concern
is with the overall deteriorating health of tribal peoples, their dependency on
non-tribal entities to supply their foods, and the lack of interest many have
for community-based food sovereignty and health endeavors.

Many Natives are attempting to revitalize their cultural foodways and
have altered their diets to focus on tribal foods. Navajo Robb Redsteer, for
example, says, "I personally experienced all the illnesses but overcame them
with a good diet and exercise. Frybread has to be eliminated"; now he grows
traditional plants inside the Navajo BioEnergy Dome. Martin Reinhardt
agrees: "Indian communities are in a state of emergency regarding obesity,
diabetes, heart disease, and high blood pressure. Frybread has no place as
part a healthy daily diet in Indian Country."[84]

The burgeoning "food sovereignty" movement is not the focus of this article, but it should be mentioned that tribal foodways initiatives are underway.
To name a few: Diné Inc. is a Navajo Nation community nonprofit working
to preserve Navajo cultural identity through food and to improve "the wellness" of the Navajo Nation.[85] The educational group Native Child's new site,
Navajo Recipes, posts about traditional Navajo foods.[86] The American Indian
Health and Diet Project at the University of Kansas offers tribal recipes with
only ingredients from the Western Hemisphere, as does the Facebook page
"Indigenous Eating."[87] The Decolonizing Diet Project is an ongoing study of
the relationship between people and Indigenous foods of the Great Lakes Region. In 2012, participants in the DDP embarked on the yearlong challenge
of eating only Anishinaabe foods and foods of the Great Lakes watershed.[88]
The Minnesota-based Native Harvest, a company under the White Earth Land

Recovery Project, strives "to continue, revive, and protect our native seeds, heritage crops, naturally grown fruits, animals, wild plants, traditions and knowledge of our indigenous and land-based communities," and offers *manoomin*, maple syrup, teas, and bead work items. The odd item out is frybread mix.[89] The WELRP also hosts the annual Great Lakes Indigenous Farming Conference. Native Seeds/SEARCH in Tucson is a nonprofit seed conservation organization that promotes the use of non-GMO, open pollinated seeds from the Southwest.[90] The Palouse—Clearwater Environmental Institute works with the Nez Perce tribe to restore the *qe'mes* (camas), a foundational food plant, in the Plateau region of Washington and Idaho.[91] The Cultural Conservancy is a multifaceted organization that oversees the Native Circle of Food program area and the Renewing American Indian Nutrition, Food, and Ecological Diversity (RAIN FED) projects.[92] Numerous tribes in the Northwest, such as the Makah, Nisqually, Suquamish, and Loomis, have established community food, ethnobotanical, and medicinal gardens to educate tribal peoples about their traditional ways of eating.[93] The First Nations Development Institute provides Native communities and tribes with training information, financial support, and assessment tools in their efforts to build food security and to improve health.[94] Elizabeth Hoover's project, "From Garden Warriors to Good Seeds: Indigenizing the Local Food Movement," is an exploration of an array of farming, gardening, and food sovereignty initiatives across the country.[95]

Initiatives such as the Intertribal Agricultural Council are less concerned with growing exclusively traditional foods and more with making certain that tribes can produce their own food on tribal lands. The IAC was founded "to pursue and promote the conservation, development and use of our agricultural resources for the betterment of our people." The American Indian Foods organization, under the umbrella of the IAC, is a group of tribal organizations offering Indigenous foods such as wild rice, bison, chilies, and salmon, but also non-Indigenous foods such as beef, pork, poultry, lamb, alfalfa, wheat, barley, oats, chocolate, wine, apples, cherries, pears, peaches, and asparagus. The only "Native" commonalty among the AIF groups is that Natives produce the foods.[96] Strategizing to grow enough food to sustain a tribe is not a bad thing; however, these efforts might be more effective if there is differentiation between Indigenous and non-Indigenous foods so that eaters can connect what they consume to their culture. More worrisome is that these initiatives could be compromised if the crops contain genetically modified organisms and if the animals raised are abused and treated with hormones. For example, Jim McAdory, the Mississippi State University Tribal Extension agent who advises the Mississippi Band of Choctaw farmers, supports the use of Monsanto's Roundup, Bt corn, and GMO seeds.[97]

Despite healthy lifestyle efforts, Natives will continue to eat junk food, and some will celebrate frybread as a symbol of "survival" and cultural identity. Indigenous health activists are just as determined to revitalize tribal food traditions as they are to campaign against unhealthy foods, especially frybread, the food they believe to be a representation of oppression and colonization. School and backyard garden projects are important, but they cannot provide all the food needed to nourish students and families for a significant period of time. And poor diet is only part of the escalating health problem. Children spend less time exploring and playing outdoors, and adults are increasingly isolated from the land, resulting in a diminishing interest in the natural world. Food sovereignty and healthy eating initiatives are effective only if Native peoples do not supplement their plates of garden produce with milkshakes, sugar drinks, fried chicken, gravy, and frybread. Natives must be willing to put in the effort to make healthy choices. No one else will do it for us.

DEVON MIHESUAH, the Cora Lee Beers Price Professor in the Humanities Program at the University of Kansas, is a citizen of the Choctaw Nation of Oklahoma and oversees the American Indian Health and Diet Project and the Facebook page "Indigenous Eating."

Notes

Thanks to Joely Proudfit, Robb Redsteer, Martin Reinhardt, and Elizabeth Hoover. It is preferable to refer to Indigenous people by their specific tribal names. For generalities I normally use the term "Indigenous" or "Natives," but in this article I also use the more recognizable "Indian." "Native Americans" signifies anyone born in the United States.

1. "The 50 Fattiest Foods in the States," *Health*, http://www.health.com/health/gallery/0,,20393387_42,00.html.

2. Devon Mihesuah, "Decolonizing Our Diets By Recovering Our Ancestors' Gardens," *American Indian Quarterly (AIQ)* 27, nos. 3–4 (2003): 807–39. That commentary appeared in expanded form in *Recovering Our Ancestors' Gardens: Indigenous Recipes and Guide to Diet and Fitness* (Lincoln: University of Nebraska Press, 2005).

3. Suzan Shown Harjo, "My New Year's Resolution: No More Fat 'Indian' Food," *Indian Country Today*, January 20, 2005, http://indiancountrytoday medianetwork.com/2005/01/26/my-new-years-resolution-no-more-fat-indian -food-94439.

4. See the South Dakota Legislature website at http://legis.sd.gov /statutes/DisplayStatute.aspx?Statute=1-6-16.9&Type=Statute.

5. Ron Jackson, "Fat's in the Fire: Activist Calls for Boycott of Eating Indian Frybread," *NewsOK*, August 21, 2005, http://newsok.com/fats-in-the-fire bractivist-calls-for-boycott-of-eating-indian-fry-bread/article/2908445.

6. Angie Wagner, "Cultural Icon or High-Calorie Curse?" *The Dispatch*, August 22, 2005.

7. Erin Hobday, "Live Blogging *Losing It* with Jillian Michaels: Frybread Is Making You Fat," *SELF Magazine*, July 7, 2010.

8. Jen Miller, "Frybread," *Smithsonian Magazine*, July 2008, http://www .smithsonianmag.com/arts-culture/frybread-79191/#Fog6s2ZpXwkSsMzt.99.

9. Ruth Roessel, ed., *Navajo Stories of the Long Walk Period* (Tsaile, Ariz.: Navajo Community College Press, 1973).

10. Fernando Divina et al., *Foods of the Americas* (Berkeley, Calif.: Ten Speed Press, 2004), 98–99. See also the American Indian Health and Diet Project's list of foods of this hemisphere at http://aihd.ku.edu/.

11. *Annual Report of the Commissioner for Indian Affairs* (hereafter cited as *ARCIA*) for 1864, 38th Cong., H. Ex. doc. 1, ser. 1220, p. 186; *ARCIA* for 1865, 39th Cong., H. Ex. doc. 1, ser. 1248, pp. 160–62; *ARCIA* for 1866, 39th Cong., H. Ex. doc. 1, ser. 1284, pp. 149–50.

12. Clifford Trafzer, *The Kit Carson Campaign: The Last Great Navajo War* (Norman: University of Oklahoma Press, 1982), 173–75; Gerald Thompson, *The Army and the Navajo* (Tucson: University of Arizona Press, 1976), 35, 38; Roessel, ed., *Navajo Stories of the Long Walk Period*, 113, 125.

13. Miller, "Frybread."

14. Roessel, ed., *Navajo Stories of the Long Walk Period*, 32, 191, 242.

15. Thompson, *Army and the Navajo*, 18–19, 158.

16. Joint Special Committee on Indian Affairs, *Conditions of the Indian Tribes* (Washington, D.C.: Government Printing Office, 1867), 379, 403, 405.

17. Thompson, *Army and the Navajo*, 109; Joint Special Committee, *Conditions of the Indian Tribes*, 294.

18. Joint Special Committee, *Conditions of the Indian Tribes*, 203–4, 404; Roessel, ed., *Navajo Stories of the Long Walk Period*, 214, 224, 225–26.

19. Joint Special Committee, *Conditions of the Indian Tribes*, 161, 179–80; Thompson, *Army and the Navajo*, 32.

20. Roessel, ed., *Navajo Stories of the Long Walk Period*, 82, 149, 152.

21. Ibid., 214, 233; Thompson, *Army and the Navajo*, 48.

22. Charlotte J. Frisbie and David P. McAllester, eds., *Navajo Blessingway Singer: The Autobiography of Frank Mitchell, 1881–1967* (Albuquerque: University of New Mexico Press, 1978), 32.

23. Garrick Bailey and Roberta Bailey, *A History of the Navajos: The Reservation Years* (Santa Fe, N.M.: School of American Research, 1986), 95.

24. Personal communication.

25. See the Northern Navajo Nation Fair website at http://northernnavajo nationfair.org/.

26. Peter Iverson, *Diné: A History of the Navajos* (Albuquerque: University of New Mexico Press, 2002), 126.

27. "Indians: Winter of Death?" *Time*, November 3, 1947, 23.

28. See the Sharlot Hall Museum Virtual Browsing Book online at http:// sharlot.org/img/detail_htmls/2295inn801p.html.

29. "Report with Respect to the House Resolution Authorizing the Committee

on Interior and Insular Affairs To Conduct An Investigation Of The Bureau Of Indian Affairs," pursuant to H. Res. 698, December 15, 1952, 82nd Cong., vol. 11582, H. Rpt. 2503, p. 1221.

30. Redsteer, personal communication; William Y. Adams, "Shonto: A Study of the Role of the Trader in a Modern Navaho Community," *Bureau of American Ethnology Bulletin*, January 10, 1962, H. Doc. 387, p. 81.

31. Carol Ballew et al., "Intake of Nutrients and Food Sources of Nutrients among the Navajo: Findings from the Navajo Health and Nutrition Survey," *Journal of Nutrition* 127, no. 10 (1997): 2085S—2093S.

32. Tristan Ahtone and Jolene Yazzie, "Navajo Nation's Nutrition Crisis," *Al Jazeera America*, January 14, 2015, http://projects.aljazeera.com/2015/12/navajo-malnutrition/.

33. For example, see *Canku Oka*, July 17, 2004, http://www.turtletrack.org/Issues04/Co07172004/CO_07172004_NavajoFieldTrip.htm.

34. James Hester, "Navajo Culture Change: From 1550 to 1960 and Beyond," in *Apachean Culture History and Ethnology*, ed. Keith Basso and Morris Opler (Tucson: University of Arizona Press, 1971), 51—53. For discussion about the importance of corn in Hopi society, see Dennis Wall and Virgil Masayesva, "People of the Corn: Teachings in Hopi Traditional Agriculture, Spirituality, and Sustainability," *American Indian Quarterly* 28, nos. 3—4 (2004): 435—53.

35. Gordon Charles Davidson, *The North West Company* (Berkeley: University of California Press, 1918), 267; "Bannock Awareness," available online at http://www.for.gov.bc.ca/rsi/fnb/fnb.htm; John Francis McDermott, *Tixier's Travels on the Osage Prairies* (Norman: University of Oklahoma Press, 1940), 135, 161, 196.

36. Alexander Henry, *Travels and Adventures in Canada and the Indian Territories between the years 1760 and 1776* (New York: Riley, 1809), 52; Grace Lee Nute, *The Voyageurs* (New York: D. Appleton, 1931), 52; Hartwell Bowsfield, "The Buffalo," *Manitoba Pageant* 10, no. 3 (1965): http://mhs.mb.ca/docs/pageant/10/buffalo.shtml.

37. *ARCIA* for 1891, 52nd Cong., H. Ex. doc. 1, pt. 5, ser. 2934, p. 393.

38. James H. Howard, *The Ponca Tribe* (Lincoln: University of Nebraska Press, 2010), 46.

39. *ARCIA* for 1893, 53rd Cong., H. Ex. doc. 1, vol. 2, ser. 3210, pp. 259, 398; *ARCIA* for 1895, 54th Cong., H. Doc. 5, vol. 2, ser. 3382, p. 205. The word *Siwash* is actually a derogatory term, probably meaning "no-good, drunken Indian."

40. *ARCIA* for 1892, 52nd Cong., H. Ex. doc. 1, ser. 3088, p. 669.

41. *ARCIA* for 1898, 55th Cong., H. Doc. 5, ser. 3757, p. 171.

42. *Boston Evening Transcript*, February 25, 1911.

43. Personal communication.

44. For discussion about the foodways of the Five Tribes after their removal to Indian Territory, see Devon Mihesuah, "Sustenance and Health among the Five Tribes in Indian Territory, Post-Removal to Statehood," *Ethnohistory* 62, no. 2 (2015): 263—84.

45. Byrd, *Indian and Pioneer Histories* (hereafter cited as *IPH*), 15:184—85; Baldwin, *IPH*, 4:309. The *IPH* collection is housed at the Western History Collections, University of Oklahoma, Norman, Oklahoma.

46. Forney, *IPH*, 31:193—94.

47. Edwards, *IPH*, 23:250; Cartarby, *IPH*, 19:196; Miashintubbee, *IPH*, 63:6; Culberson, *IPH*, 21:292; Ward, *IPH*, 11:191; Hampton, *IPH*, 3:343.

48. Devon Mihesuah, "Medicine for the Rosebuds," in *Cultivating the Rosebuds: The Education of Women at the Cherokee Female Seminary, 1851—1909* (Urbana: University of Illinois Press, 1993), 85—94; *Cherokee Advocate*, August 26, 1893; Frederick J. Simoons, "The Geographic Hypothesis and Lactose Malabsorption," *American Journal of Digestive Diseases* 23, no. 11 (1978): 963.

49. "Springtime in the Ancestors' Gardens: Native Health and Finding Comfort," *Spezzatino Magazine* 4 (2008), available online at http://spezzatino.com/.

50. Angela Cavender Wilson, "Grandmother to Granddaughter: Generations of Oral History in a Dakota Family," *American Indian Quarterly* 20, no. 1 (1996): 7—13; Waziyatawin Wilson, "Introduction to 'Indigenous Knowledge Recovery Is Indigenous Empowerment,'" *American Indian Quarterly* 28, nos. 3—4 (2004): 359—72; L. R. Simpson, "Traditional Ecological Knowledge: Issues, Insights, and Implications" (Ph.D. diss., University of Manitoba, 1999); Charlene Higgins, "The Role of Traditional Ecological Knowledge in Managing for Biodiversity," *Forestry Chronicle* 74, no. 3 (1998): 323—26.

51. Deborah Lupton, *Food, the Body, and the Self* (London: Sage, 1996), 25.

52. W. W. Hill, *The Agricultural and Hunting Methods of the Navaho Indians* (New Haven, Conn.: Yale University Press, 1938), 17, 52—166.

53. For discussions on culture change and identity, see Richard White, *The Roots of Dependency: Subsistence, Environment, and Social Change among the Choctaws, Pawnees, and Navajos* (Lincoln: University of Nebraska Press, 1983); Mihesuah, *Cultivating the Rosebuds*; Morris W. Foster, *Being and Becoming Comanche: A Social History of an American Indian Community* (Tucson: University of Arizona Press, 1991); Melissa Meyer, *The White Earth Tragedy: Ethnicity and Dispossession at a Minnesota Anishinaabe Reservation, 1889—1920* (Lincoln: University of Nebraska Press, 1999).

54. David V. Fazzino, "Traditional Food Security: Tohono O'odham Traditional Foods in Transition" (Ph.D. diss., University of Florida, 2007), 116—17.

55. Luci Tapahonso, *A Breeze Swept Through* (Albuquerque, N.M.: West End Press, 1987). For discussions about tribal food changes, see Harriet V. Kuhnlein and Olivier Receveur, "Dietary Change and Traditional Food Systems of Indigenous Peoples," *Annual Review of Nutrition* 16, no. 1 (1996): 417—42; Barry M. Popkin, "Nutritional Patterns and Transitions," *Population and Development Review* 19, no. 1 (1993): 138—57.

56. Diné Policy Institute, "Diné Food Sovereignty," April 2014, available online at http://www.dinecollege.edu/institutes/DPI/Docs/dpi-food-sovereignty-report.pdf.

57. Thomas Vennum, Jr., *Wild Rice and the Ojibway People* (St. Paul: Minnesota Historical Society Press, 1988), 297.

58. Personal communication.

59. Miller, "Frybread."

60. There are a variety of studies that discuss the addictive nature of such foods. See "Scripps Research Study Shows Compulsive Eating Shares Same

Addictive Biochemical Mechanism with Cocaine, Heroin Abuse," *Scripps Research Institute*, March 23, 2010, http://www.scripps.edu/news/press/2010/20100329 .html; "Burgers on the Brain," *New Scientist* 177, no. 2380 (2003): 21; Roessel, ed., *Navajo Stories of the Long Walk Period*, 214, 233.

61. See, for example, Maria Yellow Horse Brave Heart, "The Historical Trauma Response among Natives and Its Relationship with Substance Abuse: A Lakota Illustration," *Journal of Psychoactive Drugs* 35, no. 1 (2003): 7–13; Maria Yellow Horse Brave Heart et al., "Historical Trauma among Indigenous Peoples of the Americas: Concepts, Research, and Clinical Considerations," *Journal of Psychoactive Drugs* 43, no. 4 (2011): 282–90; Jessica R. Goodkind et al., "'We're Still in a Struggle': Diné Resilience, Survival, Historical Trauma, and Healing," *Qualitative Health Research* 22, no. 8 (2012): 1019–36.

62. Billi Gordon, "Symbolic Eating," *Psychology Today*, November 23, 2013.

63. Devon Mihesuah, "American Indian Identities: Comment on Issues of Individual Choices and Development," *American Indian Culture and Research Journal* 22, no. 2 (1998): 193–226; Devon Mihesuah,, "Activism and Apathy: The Price We Pay for Both," *American Indian Quarterly* 27, nos. 1–2 (2003): 325–32. For information on American Indian boarding schools, see David Wallace Adams, *Education for Extinction: American Indians and the Boarding School Experience, 1875–1928* (Lawrence: University Press of Kansas, 1995); Michael C. Coleman, *American Indian Children at School, 1850–1930* (Jackson: University of Mississippi Press, 1993); Clyde Ellis, *To Change Them Forever: Indian Education at the Rainy Mountain Boarding School, 1893–1920* (Norman: University of Oklahoma Press, 1996); K. Tsianina Lomawaima, *They Called It Prairie Light: The Story of Chilocco Indian School* (Lincoln: University of Nebraska Press, 1994); Sally J. McBeth, *Ethnic Identity and the Boarding School Experience of West-Central Oklahoma American Indians* (Lanham, Md.: University Press of America, 1983); Mihesuah, *Cultivating the Rosebuds*; Robert A. Trennert, *The Phoenix Indian School: Forced Assimilation in Arizona, 1891–1935* (Norman: University of Oklahoma Press, 1988); *American Experience: In the White Man's Image*," PBS video, 1992.

64. Miller, "Frybread."

65. Judy Walker, "Frybread Is Demonstrated at New Orleans Jazz Fest," *Times Picayune*, April 30, 2013, http://www.nola.com/jazzfest/index.ssf/2013 /04/native_americas_iconic_fry_bre.html. See also *Kenner Star*, November 2008, p. 27; and Naomi King, "New Chief to Lead American Indian Tribe," *Daily Comet*, May 14, 2010, http://www.dailycomet.com/article/20100514/ARTICLES /100519542. The picture of Thomas Dardar, Jr., that accompanies King's article gives insight into their invented traditions.

66. Carolyn Calvin, "The People's Flour," *Navajo Times*, September 30, 2010.

67. Liz F. Kay, "Frybread: Two Sides of a Powwow Staple," *Baltimore Sun*, August 23, 2006.

68. Eric Hobsbawm and Terence Ranger, eds., *The Invention of Tradition* (Cambridge, U.K.: Cambridge University Press, 1983), 1.

69. See http://indiancountrytodaymedianetwork.com/department/native -recipes.

70. Lauren Saria, "Arizona's Frybread Brings Native American Cooking into the Future," *Phoenix New Times*, November 22, 2012.

71. Jeremy Hsieh, "Frybread: An Alaska Native Treat with a Mysterious Origin," *KTOO*, June 23, 2014.

72. Melissa Elsmo, "Frybread Stacks to Honor—and Feed—Thy Father," *Evanston Review*, June 11, 2014.

73. Lee Allen, "Frybread House Honored among the Best of the Best," *Indian Country Today*, April 18, 2012, http://indiancountrytodaymedianetwork.com/2012/04/18/fry-bread-house-honored-among-best-best-108698.

74. Robert Bazell and Linda Carroll, "Indian Tribe Turns to Tradition to Fight Diabetes," *NBC News*, December 9, 2011.

75. See http://www.tocaonline.org/. See also Tohono O'odham Community Action and Tohono O'odham Community College, "Community Attitudes toward Traditional Tohono O'odham Foods," 2002, http://nptao1.arizona.edu/pdf/CommunityAttitudesTowardsTraditional5.pdf.

76. Vera Holding et al., "Indians in Industry," *Oklahoma Today*, Spring 1974), pp. 15–16; "Folks Can Feast on Indian food at Red Corn's HA-PAH-SHU-TSE," *Oklahoma Today*, Spring 1981, pp. 23–25.

77. Hsieh, "Frybread."

78. "'Necessity' Food Goes Gourmet," *Aberdeen Daily News*, October 20, 1987; WoodenKnife Co., "Campfire Talk," http://www.woodenknife.com/campfire/newsletter.asp?ID=4; "The Journals of the Lewis and Clark Expedition," http://lewisandclarkjournals.unl.edu/index.html.

79. Katie Robbins, "Frybread Nation: The Birth of a 'Native' Cuisine," *The Atlantic*, April 15, 2010, http://www.theatlantic.com/health/archive/2010/04/fry-bread-nation-the-birth-of-a-native-cuisine/38943/.

80. See the Kekuli Café website, http://www.kekulicafe.com/.

81. See the Mitsitam Native Foods Café website, http://www.mitsitamcafe.com/home/default.asp.

82. Fazzino, "Traditional Food Security," 116–17.

83. "Choctaw Brothers Pioneer Aquaponic Farming System to Tackle Food Insecurity in Indian Country," *Indian Country Today*, December 20, 2013, http://indiancountrytodaymedianetwork.com/2013/12/20/choctaw-brothers-pioneer-aquaponic-farming-system-tackle-food-insecurity-indian-country.

84. Personal communications.

85. Jackleen de la Harpe, "Back-to-the-Earth Food Movement Leads to More-Healthful Diets," *Indian Country Today*, June 8, 2011, http://indiancountrytodaymedianetwork.com/2011/06/08/back-earth-food-movement-leads-more-healthful-diets-35907.

86. See http://navajorecipes.com/.

87. See the American Indian Health and Diet Project website, http://www.aihd.ku.edu/; and the "Indigenous Eating" Facebook page, https://www.facebook.com/pages/Indigenous-Eating/478119175562387?ref=hl.

88. "2012 Week of Indigenous Eating Foods Challenge," *Anishinaabe News* 8 (Fall 2012): 11. See also the Decolonizing Diet Project blog, http://decolonizingdietproject.blogspot.com/.

89. See the Native Harvest online catalog at http://nativeharvest.com/.

90. See the Native Seeds/SEARCH website, http://shop.nativeseeds.org/.

91. Scott Driscoll, "Camas-Bulb Restoration Honors Tribal Traditions," *Horizon Air Magazine*, November 1993.

92. See the Cultural Conservancy website, http://www.nativeland.org/.

93. See http://nwicplantsandfoods.com/tribal-gardens.

94. See http://www.firstnations.org/knowledge-center/foods-health.

95. See http://gardenwarriorsgoodseeds.com/.

96. See http://www.indianaglink.com/.

97. *Choctaw Stewardship News* 1 (June 2012), available online at http://www.choctaw.org/partnerships/pdf/csnNewsVol1Issue2.pdf.

KASEY KEELER

Putting People Where They Belong: American Indian Housing Policy in the Mid-Twentieth Century

As with any group of people residing in Minnesota, the housing of the Indian population varies greatly. Some live in well-equipped, modern homes; others reside in poorly furnished, poorly constructed homes; and others exist under the most deplorable conditions. Since the number living under good housing conditions is extremely limited, no attempt will be made to consider them. These homes are generally found in the Twin City area or in towns or cities where an Indian office is located. Here, the occupants are well established economically and enjoy security.

—THE INDIAN IN MINNESOTA: A REPORT TO GOVERNOR LUTHER W. YOUNGDAHL OF MINNESOTA BY THE GOVERNOR'S INTERRACIAL COMMISSION, APRIL 1, 1947

Introduction

After four years in the United States Air Force, Jerry Flute, a tribally enrolled community member at the Sisseton-Wahpeton Reservation in South Dakota, wanted to use his earned military benefits to enroll in and attend college courses. Flute briefly drew on Operation Boot Strap, an education benefit program available to GIs, to attend college classes, but withdrew from school before he finished his degree. As an American Indian and a veteran, Jerry Flute was entitled to participate in programs and draw benefits through both the Bureau of Indian Affairs (BIA) and Veterans Affairs (VA). However, Flute, like other American Indian veterans, faced a tangled web of bureaucracy as he worked to access grants he was eligible for as a veteran and those he was entitled to as a tribally enrolled American Indian.

When Flute sought higher education assistance from the BIA, he was instead encouraged to move to an urban area for job training and placement as part of the expanded Indian Relocation Act of 1956. Determined to finish his education, Flute next contacted the VA for educational assistance. The VA would require him to pay for all his education expenses upfront and wait for reimbursement. Flute was left with few options. Feeling discouraged, he left South Dakota for Los Angeles through the BIA's Relocation Program.[1]

As a new transplant arriving in Los Angeles, the Sisseton-Wahpeton

Native and military veteran immediately knew his situation was less than ideal. Flute not only found himself trapped in a job where his wage was "below any minimum standard," he was also housed in a "slum area," both of which made subsistence "nearly impossible." After two long years in California, Flute returned to his reservation. Again he sought BIA assistance for education, again he was discouraged, and again he relocated to California. After a second, lengthier stint in California and an attempt at a new trade, auto body repair, Flute increasingly missed "home," felt discriminated against at work, and disliked the fast-paced atmosphere of Southern California. Jerry Flute traveled a well-worn path home to South Dakota.

Jerry Flute was not alone. Thousands of American Indian veterans endured similar fates in the post-WWII environment as they struggled to "reintegrate" into the dominant society and achieve the "American Dream" after military service. Across Minnesota's Twin Cities of Minneapolis and St. Paul, the geographical focal point of this article, many Indian veterans lived in slums, often raising their children in severe poverty and areas of high crime, while many proactively sought ways to move out of urban areas and into more stable and permanent housing beyond the city.[2] Though American Indians historically serve in the military at higher rates than any other racial/ethnic group, the very agency that was created to serve all veterans, the VA, rendered American Indians as incompatible with veteran status. The experience of Jerry Flute underscores the complicated issues Native veterans face when they attempt to access BIA and VA programs and benefits. The barriers Jerry Flute faced as he worked to access education benefits mirror the same obstacles American Indian veterans must navigate to access unemployment services, medical care, and housing programs they are entitled to from both the BIA and VA bureaucratic structures.

Just as Jerry Flute, numerous American Indian veterans of WWII worked to access federal programs and benefits during an unprecedented postwar suburbanization boom. The explosion in new suburban homes after WWII brings to the surface the inconsistencies in U.S. housing policies for these two seemingly incongruent groups—American Indians and veterans—at virtually the same political moment. Nearly all veterans of WWII were entitled to the programs and services of the GI Bill, including its home loan benefit. However, access to the home loan portion of the GI Bill, including a federally guaranteed loan, a low interest rate, and a small down payment, was severely curtailed for American Indians.[3] Instead, many Native veterans, faced with few options and a limited job market, had to decide between life on the reservation or participation in the BIA's Relocation Program at the war's end. While the GI Bill guaranteed federally insured home loans to construct new suburban homes for white veterans, American Indians who participated in the Relocation Program were relocated to urban areas and housed in temporary venues, including shelters and rundown apartments.[4] I juxtapose the GI Bill alongside the Indian Relocation Program to make clear the power of the federal government to create polices that essentially determine who should live where.

The careful crafting of suburbs by the federal government is clearly witnessed through the federal policies that allowed for suburban homes to be rapidly built and populated after WWII, largely to the exclusion of Indian people. The U.S. government's intervention into the housing market that began earlier in the century, namely, with the creation of the Federal Housing Authority (FHA), continued through the careful crafting and administration of the GI Bill of 1944, which largely disqualified American Indian veterans. These and subsequent interventions by the federal government into the housing sector, in particular urban renewal projects and the U.S. Housing Act of 1949, set in motion a new and dramatic wave of suburbanization that swept over the nation.[5] In Minnesota's Twin Cities, urban renewal efforts and the construction of Interstate 94, which cut directly through the heart of the cities, predominately affected communities of color, often displacing thousands of people while new (public) housing was constructed. In this article I examine the GI Bill as a continuation of federal housing policies begun earlier in the century that promoted white homeownership, increasingly in suburbs, often at the expense of people of color, including American Indian people. Furthermore, the GI Bill of 1944, as a proactive and effective housing policy that created new homeownership opportunities for many (white) veterans, thereby spurring suburban home construction, remained largely out of reach for American Indian veterans.

The GI Bill, as a federally funded housing program for veterans, stands in direct contrast to federal Indian polices of the same era, specifically relocation. I critique relocation as a policy and argue that the Relocation Program must be examined as an Indian specific *housing policy*, an aspect that is almost always ignored in lieu of a more broad focus on urbanization that includes employment, discrimination, poverty, and return migrations.[6] The intended short-term goals of Relocation were to move Indian people into temporary rental units in urban areas, while the long-term goal of Relocation was continued assimilation and reintegration of Indian people. However, I argue that the long-term goals of Relocation contradicted the short-term goals. If Relocation was intended to integrate American Indian people into mainstream, white America, then American Indian people should have been provided access to home loans while being encouraged and supported along the way to becoming suburban residents, rather than being pushed to become urban dwellers in "slum" areas in need of "revitalization" on a temporary basis.

In a process that by the 1960s was known as "white flight," more and more visibly white individuals and families moved out of the urban core and into more suburban geographies while American Indians and other people of color moved into recently vacated properties and newly constructed public housing facilities. White flight, then, largely hastened the process of redlining that sought to keep people of color (and poor whites) out of newly constructed suburban neighborhoods by making home loans in areas occupied by people of color more difficult to obtain and financially "risky" for mortgage insurers.[7] Further, we cannot fully understand the processes and extent of white flight and the housing aspects of the GI Bill without also considering the Relocation Program. Likewise, we cannot fully understand the detrimental effects of Relocation without also considering how it worked in tandem with white flight and the GI Bill. This is particularly significant because white flight has almost exclusively been examined through a black—white binary. In essence, the Relocation Program contributed to the racialized white/nonwhite, urban/suburban divide, if not deliberately then as a by-product of postwar housing policies that were increasingly marked by race. As I discuss, the GI Bill operated as a racialized housing policy precisely because of the limitations American Indians and other servicemen and -women of color faced when they attempted to access its home loan benefit, and because (white) veterans who were able to make use of it benefited from racially restrictive covenants while simultaneously contributing to white flight.

In this article I pay close attention to the contradictory nature of federal housing policies begun in the 1930s and underscore the mid-century history of unequal access to homeownership for American Indian people. Through my examination of primary documents and secondary literature, I argue the Relocation Program, as a housing program for American Indians, is directly opposite the home loan benefit of the GI Bill. Further, American Indian veterans were faced with a bureaucratic nightmare as they worked to navigate both the VA and the BIA to access entitlement programs in the wake of WWII. The arguments I make throughout are significant because of the long-term and lasting influences of both the GI Bill and Relocation on veterans and American Indians. As I demonstrate, the GI Bill continued the exclusionary nature of home loan programs and prevented an indeterminable number of Indian people from moving to suburban areas to pursue homeownership. Instead, Relocation influenced the urban neighborhoods to which Indian people migrated—areas that have remained Indian-concentrated, including today's Phillips neighborhood in Minneapolis, with continuous unequal access to homeownership.[8] It is the significance of homeownership that plagues this race-based, unequal access. Home equity, generational wealth, and policies that "reward" homeowners via property tax deductions are all

directly associated with homeownership, while secondary benefits like better schools, roads, and public services must also be remembered when examining the lasting legacies of inconsistent and unfair housing policies marked
by race.

I base my analysis on archival materials that document American Indian
veteran experiences with urbanization and suburbanization through the lens
of federal housing policies, specifically the GI Bill and the Relocation Program. In my effort to understand better how Relocation and the GI Bill operated, I supplement my research with secondary literature that has largely
ignored American Indian peoples' engagements with housing programs and
policies. My use of primary source material includes numerous pieces of legislation, such as the text of the GI Bill of 1944 and the Indian Relocation Act of
1956, as well as related government reports produced by such agencies as the
BIA, the FHA, and the VA.[9] I also analyze the rich and underutilized archives
of the Bureau of Indian Affairs, in particular the Relocation records of the
Minneapolis-area office established in 1949, including personal narratives of
those who were relocated.[10] I expand my analysis of how the Relocation Program worked on the ground in Minnesota with an examination of additional
Relocation records for the Chicago area. The reason for this is twofold. First,
despite the fact that hundreds, perhaps even thousands, of Indian people
chose to relocate to the Twin Cities and received BIA monies and employee
support to do so, it was not technically considered a Relocation destination
and as such there are perhaps fewer records for Minneapolis / St. Paul. It
is also likely that the records for persons who relocated to the Twin Cities
are housed in the archives that correspond to their home state (e.g., Relocation records of persons from North and South Dakota are held at the Denver
branch of the National Archives). Second, the Newberry Library in Chicago
houses primary source Relocation records that I examined and incorporate
because these records are publicly accessible and lack the privacy restrictions
and security clearance required to access individual Relocation records at the
National Archives. Further, Chicago offers a complementary comparison to
the Twin Cities because of their geographic proximity and because many of
the relocatees to each destination were from the same areas (northern Minnesota and Wisconsin). Finally, I examine local, Minneapolis and St. Paul area
newspapers and housing reports as primary documents to underscore public
interpretation and reaction to the housing programs of the mid-twentieth
century that influenced the movement and relocation of Indian people. I
bring together primary source material that spans the text of federal legislation, protected archival material housed in the National Archives, donated
material in private collections at the Newberry Library, and local newspapers
and reports to make clear the ways the GI Bill and the Relocation Program

served as carefully organized housing programs that served to move different peoples, marked by race, to very different locations.

While there has been a recent growth in scholarship on alternative narratives of suburbanization and suburban homeownership, particularly for communities of color, in American studies and urban studies literature, no one has put American Indians or federal Indian policy at the center of their analysis. In the field of American Indian and Indigenous studies, scholars have begun to reframe the processes of twentieth-century urbanization across the United States and Canada, including a more thorough interrogation of the Relocation Program. In this article I begin to address the absence of a concise analysis of American Indian housing policies and the effects of mid-century U.S. housing policies on Indians. No existing scholarship examines the policy of relocation as an Indian-specific, race-based housing policy. Instead, much focus has been given to the employment and vocational training/education aspects of the policy and to critiques of the program's short-term housing and preparation of relocatees.

I draw on early Indian urbanization literature and on the scant literature that examines Indian housing policies. My work expands on the scholarship of Elaine M. Neils, Donald Fixico, and Kenneth R. Philp through an examination of American Indian housing programs and policies during the termination and relocation era and relies on the scholarship of legal scholar Virginia Davis as a starting point from which to offer such critique.[11] *American Indians and the Urban Experience*, edited by Susan Lobo and Kurt Peters, provides key Native perspectives on the processes of urbanization during the mid-twentieth century and serves as a framework to understand better urbanization through historical, cultural, sociological, and literary lenses.[12] My work builds on this, as well as the scholarship of James B. LaGrand, Coll Thrush, Renya Ramirez, and Nicholas Rosenthal, each of whom provides significant and localized analysis of the processes and history of Indian urbanization in Chicago, Seattle, the Bay Area, and Los Angeles, respectively. I extend LaGrand's examination of Relocation in particular through my examination of primary source materials to understand better the critiques of relocatees from Minnesota. LaGrand also opens an opportunity for dialog into housing and American Indian suburbanization.[13] My scholarship emphasizes the significance of Native people in the metropolitan areas of Minneapolis and St. Paul, similar to Thrush's *Native Seattle*, but also underscores the significance of Native people in the housing market. This is particularly significant given the obstacles American Indians faced as they sought access to home ownership and suburbia.[14] Ramirez's *Native Hubs* provides a critical framework to think about how family, friends, and kin have served as liaisons and support networks for new relocatees and the significant roles they play in migration and movement to specific Relocation destinations.[15] Rosenthal's *Reimagining Indian Country* reminds us that Indian urbanization occurred long before the 1950s and that many Native people worked in concert with one another to produce a new kind of Indian community, echoing Ramirez.[16] The groundbreaking *Indigenous in the City*, edited by Evelyn Peters and Chris Andersen, offers critical international perspectives on Indigenous urbanization.[17] Peters and Andersen incorporate international scholarship from Native studies scholars in the United States, Australia, and New Zealand that provides a thought-provoking analysis of the systematic colonialism of Indigenous people during the twentieth century across these continents. Their text offers a comparative and historical critique of Indigenous urbanization, in particular the ways urbanization intersects with identity for Native people. More, Peters, and Andersen examine localized and community responses to increasing Indigenous urbanization.

I put this scholarship into conversation with the work of scholars of urban studies and American studies who examine race relations in twentieth-century American suburbs, particularly those scholars who examine African American suburbanization, housing discrimination, redlining and segregation, and postwar ideals of home and property ownership, domesticity, and whiteness.[18] For example, in Kenneth Jackson's *Crabgrass Frontier* he argues that suburbanization has been largely racially (and economically) motivated, particularly after WWII. Though he keeps most of his attention on African American discrimination and housing market exclusion in the postwar era, I argue that American Indians endured similar challenges.[19] Significantly, Arnold R. Hirsch argues that blacks were intentionally kept out of postwar suburbs and forced into "second ghettos" through the apparatus of a "two-tiered federal housing policy" designed to promote racial (and economic) segregation, a sentiment that was also at play in regard to American Indian housing policy and homeownership opportunities.[20] In *Places of Their Own* Andrew Wiese examines African American suburbanization throughout the twentieth century and describes the ways a move to the suburbs provided economic opportunity and equality.[21] Unlike the case with American Indian veterans, however, Wiese notes that suburban housing advertisement specifically targeted African American veterans, though this was no guarantee of antiblack racial backlash.[22] I use Robert O. Self's *American Babylon*, a study of African American suburbanization in postwar Oakland through grassroots politics and activism, to think about American Indian suburbanization efforts despite policies that worked against them.[23] I extend David M. P. Freund's examination of language and housing policies from *Colored Property* to the case of American Indians to demonstrate how American Indian veterans were excluded from the GI Bill.[24] The works in each of these fields provide a framework from which to begin thinking about Indian policies and housing policies of the mid-twentieth century as I investigate further American Indians in suburbs as well as their absence as homeowners.

The New Deal

Eager to secure a stable economy following the Great Depression, Franklin D. Roosevelt during the first term of his presidency has been noted by scholars and citizens for his efforts at relief, recovery, and reform. Despite the federal government's attempts to stimulate the economy and the well-documented history of urban slums and tenement housing in the country's early industrial cities, the government did not make a formal or significant intervention into the housing sector until the early 1930s.[25] At the same time, the federal government made a dramatic shift in its Indian policy, largely to address the horrific findings of the Meriam Report.[26]

More significantly, in 1934 the federal government passed the National Housing Act of 1934, which created the Federal Housing Administration. The FHA, the main federal agency that handles mortgage insurance, also created a national mortgage association that provides a market for home mortgages to be bought and sold by banks and investors, thus increasing the availability of money and potential for lender profit.[27] Intended to make home loans more accessible and affordable for most Americans, the policies of the FHA did little to assist lower-income people, including many people of color, attain home loans. Despite its promises, the FHA actually contributed to a major aspect of racial discrimination in the housing market as a direct result of its *Underwriting Manual*, which created the process of redlining.[28] In order to determine the properties for which it would approve mortgages, the FHA used a series of "quality standards" including physical characteristics, location, and racial/ethnic makeup of the neighborhood. These "quality standards" corresponded to a series of color-coded maps where neighborhoods ranged in color from green (most desirable) to red (least desirable, namely, black and lower-income neighborhoods deemed most risky for lending), cementing the term and process of redlining.[29] Edina, an inner-ring suburb on the southwestern fringe of Minneapolis, is a frequently cited example of redlining. As James W. Loewen points out in *Sundown Towns*, the Country Club district of Edina is a well-known case where racially restrictive covenants were built into the deeds of many homes and attempted to ban "any person other than the one of the white or Caucasian race" from owning a home in the area.[30]

To address the inherent racism and segregation in the housing market, Congress passed the Housing Act of 1937 to establish the Public Housing Program. Intended to assist "lower-income families," the Public Housing

Authority (PHA) authorized loans to local, public housing agencies for low-rent housing projects.[31] Sumner Field Homes, Minnesota's first public housing project, opened in Near North, Minneapolis, in 1938. The development, built with competitive federal public housing funds, was intentionally segregated by race. Developers demolished a historically African American neighborhood that grew on the heels of an earlier Jewish settlement to make room for the complex. During the first half of the twentieth century the Twin Cities was known as a bastion of anti-Semitism, and Jewish people (along with people of color) frequently endured discrimination in the housing market.

Though the FHA stipulated reasonable finance terms to make home loans more accessible, it directed a majority of loan monies to white families during the mid-twentieth century.[32] The FHA's effort to provide affordable housing was closely followed by the VA, which administered the GI Bill of 1944; in fact, the "two programs can be considered as a single effort" at white suburbanization.[33] As argued by numerous scholars, including George Lipsitz, "by channeling money away from older inner-city neighborhoods and toward white home buyers moving into segregated suburbs, the FHA and private lenders after World War II aided and abetted the growth and development of increased segregation in U.S. residential neighborhoods."[34] Though the FHA and VA did not build the houses or design the suburbs, they did determine who was able to receive a government-backed loan with lower down payments and longer repayment terms.

Just days before the passage of the National Housing Act, June 1934 also saw the passage of the Indian Reorganization Act (IRA). Recognized widely as the Indian New Deal, the centerpiece of the IRA was to end the process of allotment that began under the 1887 Dawes Act.[35] The IRA was intended to put tribal governments in control of tribal affairs and to allow tribes to exercise their inherent sovereignty, but the IRA did not live up to its goals. Though many tribes did benefit from increasing levels of self-determination and the more complete exercise of tribal sovereignty, others quickly lost their self-determination and even legal recognition as the BIA began to shift its Indian policy toward relocation and termination in the late 1940s.

The first months of Roosevelt's presidency were a period of transition. For most, the New Deal symbolized a progression from economic instability to stability; for Indian people the IRA ushered in an era of increased tribal authority and put an end to allotment. But New Deal housing programs must also be viewed as efforts by the federal government to move specific groups of people to differing residential locations with unequal access to home ownership. These efforts became increasingly divergent during the post-WWII housing boom when WWII veterans were entitled to the GI Bill and promises of suburban home ownership, while Indian people were limited to relocation to urban areas and temporary housing. The juxtaposition of the GI Bill and Indian relocation policy, which stand in direct opposition to each other during the same temporal moment, demonstrates the power of the federal government to determine who should live where and that these policies were also based on race.

The GI Bill and Indian Relocation

After army veteran Damon James and his family moved to Minneapolis on Relocation in the early 1950s they soon learned that the promises of "adequate" housing left much to be desired. The Jameses, who were from the Mille Lacs Reservation in north-central Minnesota, chose to move to Minneapolis because Mr. James already had a cousin in the city. Initially they lived with Mr. James's cousin in "rather crowded quarters in South Minneapolis," but were "quite anxious to find housing of their own and [were] moving into other quarters as soon as the [Relocation] checks are received covering their relocation grant."[36] Similarly, Gerald Owens, an Ojibwe man from the White Earth Reservation in northern Minnesota and an army veteran, also moved his family to Minneapolis in the early 1950s on Relocation. Though Mr. Owens was employed, his family "had a problem with securing adequate housing" and was "living in rather crowded quarters."[37] Indeed, the lure of opportunity continued to bring Native families to the Twin Cities.

The federal government's by now decades-long intervention into the housing sector certainly contributed to the movement of many Native families to Minneapolis and St. Paul. However, rather than provide relocated Indian individuals and families with stable housing, the policy, as an arm of termination, worked to sever government responsibilities to Indian tribes and to the individual Indian people who relocated to urban areas.[38] As I argue, relocation was an Indian-specific housing policy; I juxtapose it with the GI Bill to make visible the deliberate and ongoing attempts of the federal government to move certain racialized groups of people, in this case white Americans and American Indians, to different residential locations, suburban and urban. The historical legacies of the GI Bill and relocation, as housing policies, are easily observed today in the concentrated urban Indian neighborhoods that dot the cities Indian people were encouraged to move to, including Minneapolis and St. Paul. Most urban Indians in the Twin Cities today continue to rent and have little chance of home ownership. As noted on the opening page of a recently published report by the Institute on Metropolitan Opportunity, "Toxic subprime loans were deeply embedded in the mortgage market in the Twin Cities and were highly targeted towards communities of color." The report goes on to examine the low rates of home ownership in the Phillips neighborhood, a largely American Indian community.[39] At the same time, individuals and families who benefited from the GI Bill's home loan provision have also generationally benefited from home equity and the ensuing upward mobility, better suburban schools, and home stability. Finally, and perhaps most significant to this research, there are the individuals whose dedicated military service qualified them for participation in both the VA and BIA programs—American Indian veterans of WWII like Damon James and Gerald Owens—many of whom were never given the opportunity of home ownership through the GI Bill.

The strain placed on reservation economies by WWII-related activities was enormous. Over sixty-five thousand Indian people moved away from their reservations for war-related activities and employment while congressional appropriations to individual tribes and the operating budget of BIA were dramatically reduced to fund the war effort.[40] By 1940 the BIA, still under John Collier's leadership, issued a memorandum that recommended tribal resources be placed under government control for future war use, including the free use of Indian land, which led to economic burdens for Indian people and reservation communities.[41]

The federal government had firm plans to push for the "full integration" of Indian people into the dominant white society prior to U.S. involvement in WWII. By the late 1930s government appropriations to the BIA for the IRA were already under scrutiny and viewed as a waste of government funds. Some members of Congress, going against the wishes of Commissioner of Indian Affairs John Collier, thought BIA money should be redirected. The assimilation of Indian people again became the goal of Indian policy.[42] After the attack on Pearl Harbor the federal government committed to trimming the budget and reducing obligations, and American Indian programming became a target for federal cutbacks. The American Indian men and women who participated in the war effort, in war-related industries, and through military service were in a precarious situation at war's end—forced to decide if they wanted to (with the ability and means) return to reservations or opt for life in increasingly white-dominated metropolitan areas. As Alison R. Bernstein argues:

> [Indian] participation in the war, however, placed [Indian people] at the proverbial crossroads. Having been so closely associated with white society during the war, viewed and treated as equals, often trained in skills transferable to urban employment, exposed to a much larger world than that from which they came, and molded by a war unparalleled in history, each veteran confronted a choice—to return to reservations and continue tribal revitalization efforts with an emphasis on one's Indian identity, or make the move into white society. The same choice confronted those Indian men and women who remained on the home front.[43]

Yet, for many Indian veterans of the war, the choice was not so simple. By the late 1940s the federal government was not so much interested in "tribal revitalization efforts" as it was termination, and the move into "white society" for Indian people was not easy, swift, or direct.

Over twenty-five thousand American Indians served during WWII and another forty thousand Indian civilians were employed in war industries throughout the duration of the war on the home front. According to Bernstein, "The movement of American Indians from reservations to either the armed forces or urban areas during World War II totaled one-third of the entire Indian population and represented the first mass exodus of Indians from reservations to the surrounding white world."[44] As U.S. efforts and involvement in the war amplified, increasing numbers of American Indians relocated to urban areas for the guarantee of steady employment. One-half of Indian men and over one-fifth of Indian women relocated to urban areas by war's end for war-related employment.[45] Although these levels of employment may sound optimistic, just before the war ended in 1944 American Indian people were earning only 25 percent of what whites were earning.[46] The incomes of those on the home front, including thousands of American Indians who had relocated to find employment, were severely curtailed at the end of WWII as many white veterans returned to their old jobs, which many American Indians filled during the war, and the need for war-related employment dropped.[47]

When the war ended, the bulk of Indian servicemen returned to their home reservation communities; later, many would go on to apply for the Relocation Program.[48] The sudden influx of people on reservation communities, both veterans and war-industry-employed urban Indians, placed further strain on reservation economies already suffering from WWII-era policies and federal cutbacks. For Indian people who decided to remain in the city after returning home from military deployment, steady employment was no guarantee. Less than 10 percent of the two thousand Ojibwe, Winnebago, Dakota, and Menominee Indians in Minneapolis and St. Paul were able to find permanent employment after the war.[49]

Before war's end, the Serviceman's Readjustment Act of 1944 became law on June 22, nearly one decade to the day after the FHA was created. The American Legion, seeking to streamline veteran benefits and to avoid the confusions that followed WWI, pushed Roosevelt for a designated and accessible program to administer veterans' benefits earned during wartime. Included among the many benefits and entitlement programs available to veterans of WWII through the Serviceman's Readjustment Act was a low-interest, government-insured home loan program. Later, the home loan benefit of the GI Bill would be compared to the Homestead Act of 1862 in its ability to dramatically alter the landscape through the expansion and growth of new settlement and housing.[50] While it is impossible to know when and with what speed postwar suburbs would have developed and grown without the GI Bill, it certainly sped up and promoted the process.

The GI Bill was an extensive and expensive strategy to reintegrate WWII veterans. The $14 billion spent on the GI Bill of 1944 was to provide medical, education, temporary cash assistance, and home loan programs to military veterans— the most expansive returning veteran benefits package to date. By 1955, 4.3 million homes—20 percent of all new home construction— were built using the GI Bill's home loan guarantee for new construction or purchase, worth a combined market value of $33 million.[51] Within the terms of the GI Bill home loan guarantee, the government assumed responsibility for the first year of interest, stipulated that the interest rate of the loan was not to exceed 4 percent, allowed for a twenty-year repayment period, and required only 10 percent down. Almost one-third of WWII veterans took advantage of the GI Bill home loan program. As suburbs became desirable sites for new homes, the VA and FHA preferred the construction of suburban homes rather than make improvements on older structures in urban areas.[52] As pointed out by Michael J. Bennett, 85 percent of the nation's growth after World War II occurred in suburbs: "Starting in 1950, almost all of the nation's cities lost population while the suburbs gained 60 million new residents. The [GI] bill, like all laws, had unintended consequences; in this instance, it helped accelerate the concentration of blacks and minorities in the cities. If people were leaving the cities to find a better life, they were also fleeing them to avoid shadows cast by urban blight—and people of darker skin."[53] Though the GI Bill promoted and supported home ownership for all veterans, it also bolstered already occurring white flight to the suburban fringe while limiting housing options for veterans of color.

Homeownership for African Americans was not necessarily bolstered by the Housing Act of 1949, which had the stated goal of providing "a decent home and suitable living environment for every American family."[54] The pillars of the Act were federal funding for "slum clearance" (Title I), increased authorization for FHA mortgage insurance (Title II), and extended federal funding to build over eight hundred thousand public housing units (Title III). As scholars of U.S. housing policies have pointed out, the legislation of the Housing Act of 1949 was inherently contradictory.[55] Designed to alleviate housing shortages, particularly for lower-income people, the Housing Act of 1949 placed the burden of finding adequate and affordable housing most acutely on people of color, specifically African Americans. To be sure, in the midst of the postwar environment "massive white suburbanization [and] federal housing policy provided the framework within which national agencies and state and local authorities could accommodate demographic change, a budding civil rights revolution, and majoritarian racial sensibilities all at the same time" and thereby create a "second ghetto."[56] Indeed, urban African Americans were often caught up in the "historical inertia supporting segregation," forced to decide between the push of urban renewal efforts and the pull to move to public housing projects rather than to integrate truly into growing, white suburbs.[57]

Even after the 1948 Supreme Court case *Shelley v. Kraemer*, residential discrimination in the form of racially biased deed restrictions and racial covenants, commonplace in housing programs throughout the twentieth century, including communities in Minnesota, went largely unchallenged.[58] In 1954, Minnesota became one of the first states in the nation to pass a law that specifically banned racially restrictive covenants; however, as with case of the earlier Supreme Court ruling, informal segregation and discriminatory attitudes remained largely unchanged. In Minnesota, the 1948 Supreme Court ruling and the 1954 bill signed by Governor Elmer C. Anderson came decades too late to protect at least one African American family. After they purchased a home in a predominately white neighborhood in southern Minneapolis during the summer of 1931, Arthur and Edith Lee soon faced a mob of nearly four thousand people who protested their move to the neighborhood.[59] Though African Americans were the most common victims of this form of racism, American Indians also felt the burden of the color line. In 1940 Helen Lightfoot, a twenty-nine-year-old Indian woman from South Dakota, worked as a live-in maid for a white family in Edina. Though the neighborhood's racially restrictive covenant prevented anyone other than "one of the white or Caucasian race" from purchasing or renting a home in the community, the covenant did allow people of color to "[serve] as domestics for the owner or tenant of said lot."[60] This caveat was in line with neighborhood deeds that sought to "maintain a high class, restricted, residential district, free from objectionable or value destroying features" by prohibiting livestock, "objectionable trees or shrubbery," and keeping all garbage and waste hidden from view.

While the VA worked diligently to determine the exact benefits veterans of WWII would receive through the GI Bill, Congress, the Hoover Commission, and Republican leaders in Washington considered eliminating the BIA, optimistically described as a way to save the federal government millions of dollars. Similar to the GI Bill, the Indian policy of relocation was also touted as a way to (re)integrate Indian people into mainstream society, particularly veterans who were deemed more "prepared" for "full integration." Two key questions applicants for Relocation were asked on their application materials pertained to their military service and "previous experience away from the Reservation," which often signified to the Relocation officers their potential ability to adapt to urban life.[61] As Kenneth R. Philp asserts, the government strove to maintain American idealism "reflected [in] Cold War beliefs about the superiority of Euro-American civilization and political ideology."[62] As government policies, then, relocation and termination offered "emancipation" from federal wardship, a marker of the degree of "civilization" American Indians had finally attained. It is precisely this liberatory language, intentionally and deliberately used by policy makers, that allowed for the seemingly opportunistic and "freeing" Indian policies of relocation and termination to move forward in such a positive light.[63]

In retrospect, if the federal government strove for the full integration of Indian people into mainstream society, the BIA's housing policy, in the form of Relocation, would have more closely followed the VA's GI Bill home loan program. Instead of moving Indian people to short-term rental housing, the federal government would have supported and sponsored homeownership programs for Indian people. Instead of moving Indian people to urban areas many whites were leaving, the federal government would have encouraged relocating Indians to move to the suburbs. Instead of denying Relocation opportunities to many Indian families due to higher associated costs, the federal government would have allowed for the maintenance and stability of nuclear families. Indeed, the GI Bill and Relocation were the government's way of putting people where they were deemed to belong.

Ending the government's guardian—ward relationship with Indian people was viewed by many conservative politicians, including Secretary of the Interior Julius A. Krug, Senator Author Watkins, and the Senate Civil Service Committee of 1946—47, as the final necessary step for Indians to assimilate fully and "enjoy" the benefits of American citizenry.[64] In 1953, Congress passed House Concurrent Resolution 108, announcing an official start to termination. Termination was intended to sever all ties between the federal government and sovereign tribal nations. This comprised all treaty-negotiated responsibilities of the federal government, including promised federal aid, services (e.g., health care and education), and protections (i.e., sovereignty). Perhaps most significantly, termination eliminated the trust status of reservation land under the protection of the federal government. In order to determine if a tribe was "ready" for termination (portrayed as a "freeing" of Indian people from the confines of government supervision), Congress looked to the degree of intermarriage, assimilation to white customs, literacy rates, and *military participation* of tribal members.[65] Termination policy had devastating effects on American Indian people: while most have been restored to a federally recognized status, between 1953 and 1964 109 tribes lost their status as federally recognized tribal nations, a severe blow to tribal sovereignty.[66] Assimilation, the government and numerous supporters believed, had been the ultimate goal of Indian policy since the mid-eighteenth century.

Essentially, by way of termination, Indian people would be forced to give up their tribal identity, which would legally no longer exist, and "[conform] to the values and attitudes of mainstream, Anglo-American society."[67] Undergirding termination policy was the hope that Indian people would move away from reservations, which legally no longer existed, to a more metropolitan area to assimilate and integrate further. For those Indian people who, upon tribal termination, did not relocate, they were no longer reservation Indians, but rather "Indians" with no formal recognition, rights, or sovereignty.

As LaGrand and Rosenthal point out, movement away from reservations and toward more urban areas had been a practice of many American Indians long before the 1950s. There were waves of migration to California in particular in the wake of the Dust Bowl of the 1930s; moreover, if we consider the history of seasonal rounds, Indian people have virtually always been migrating.[68] Similarly, in both Ramirez's text *Native Hubs* and in the introduction to Peters and Andersen's *Indigenous in the City*, we are reminded of the significant role family and kin play in the migrations and movements of Native people to more metropolitan areas and the importance of these connections once new relocatees arrive in the city.[69] Despite this, most attention on Indian urbanization has largely remained on the Relocation Program.

It was not until the late 1940s that federal and local support (financially and administratively) for Indian relocation to urban areas began, though not formally enacted as law until the 1956 Indian Relocation Act.[70] American Indians who participated in the voluntary Relocation Program, later to coincide with the Adult Vocational Training or AVT Program, were provided a one-way bus ticket to a designated urban relocation area, such as Chicago, Dallas, New York, Los Angeles, Chicago, or Oklahoma City.[71] Though Minneapolis was not a designated Relocation location, it was a major destination for many Ojibwe individuals and families from northern Minnesota and Wisconsin. As many of the applications for Relocation assistance demonstrate, frequently the relocatees to the Twin Cities had familial connections or close friends already in the city, and these sorts of connections bolstered many relocatees' decisions on where to move. Further, many of the Ojibwe who came to Minneapolis and St. Paul on Relocation chose to stay relatively local so they would be able to travel back to their home reservation.[72] Regardless of the Relocation destination they chose, the relocated Indians, and sometimes entire families, were provided short-term financial support and temporary housing in a rental unit in the city; in Chicago this included $10.10 per week for "temporary shelter," possibly at the YMCA.[73] Although voluntary, the BIA marketed the Relocation Program to Indian people using images of single-family homes, "with shutters in suburban America," that would entice women and families into relocating to cities.[74]

FIGURE 1. From the Newberry collection of promotional Relocation photos depicting a "suburban" home with shutters and Indian men and women out front. Photo courtesy of the Newberry Library, Chicago. Call number: Ayer MMS BIA Relocation, Box 2, Folder 26.

This stands in stark contrast to what they actually received.

Government housing reports of Minneapolis state that, in reality, relocated Indians occupied semipermanent rental units that were overpriced, regularly overcrowded, often accommodating extended families, and in disrepair, both inside and out, lacking adequate plumbing and electrical features.[75] According to a 1947 report out of Minnesota, "recent migrants to the cities were crowded into homes in blighted areas" and "in at least one instance the multiple structure into which families have moved [has] been condemned."[76] In 1947 Minnesota also saw two major developments in the housing sector. The Minnesota Legislature passed the Municipal Housing and Redevelopment Act that required local jurisdictions to establish their own public housing and community development agencies, which opened the door for localized public housing programs, including those in suburbs.[77] Second, in 1947 Minneapolis mayor Hubert H. Humphrey (later U.S. senator and vice president) did just that when he created the Minneapolis Housing and Redevelopment Authority, the city's first public housing program. Less than a decade passed before American Indians arrived in the city on Relocation and were moved into housing that was often dilapidated.[78] As Donald

Fixico argues in his examination of urban Indians, although government "officials envisioned relocation as a reform effort to assist American Indians in finding jobs and housing . . . it was again Indian removal like in the 1830s."[79] Relocation was largely unsuccessful, particularly in regard to housing. Of all relocated Indians across the country, an estimated 30 percent eventually returned to the reservation (though this estimate is conservative, and others suggest the return rate was closer to 60 percent).[80]

The GI Bill and Relocation as Racialized Housing Policies

In February 1955, at the age of thirty-six, David Dowd, an Ojibwe man from Bemidji, Minnesota, applied for Relocation services to move his wife and himself to Oakland, California. Dowd had significant work experience as a laborer doing road construction and electrical work. Mrs. Dowd was also interested in work, though she preferred employment in the garment-making industry. The Dowds had previously used the Relocation Program to relocate to Longview, Washington, where Mr. Dowd was employed at a sawmill. They were forced to return to Minnesota due to illness in the family. Since neither Mr. nor Mrs. Dowd drank, and because both fit the picture of "an ideal" Relocation candidate, their second Relocation request was approved and they soon moved to Oakland.[81]

Unlike Relocation, the GI Bill, significantly influenced by the early goals of the FHA, provided federally insured funding for the construction or purchase of single-family homes, and increasingly these homes were in suburbs. By overlaying the GI Bill and Indian relocation, both federal policies of the postwar era, the inherent contradictions between federal housing policies and federal Indian policies, and the government's desire to put certain groups of people in certain places, becomes quite clear. On the one hand, the government worked to provide (white) military veterans with substantial readjustment benefits, including unheard-of home loan terms. Of the sixteen million military veterans who were eligible for the GI Bill, five million eventually bought a home in suburbia.[82] White veterans were encouraged and supported in the process of becoming property owners in developing suburbs, aided and protected by the government; this was not the case for American Indians. Instead, relocation, as an Indian-specific housing policy, was a way for the federal government to reduce further its treaty obligations to Indian people, and instead gradually sever its relationship to Indian people while moving them to urban areas where they were expected to assimilate and integrate. Rather than address the unique set of challenges many American Indian people faced in the housing market, the U.S. government promoted Relocation as a new opportunity in a metropolitan area.[83]

Relocation must be thought of as a racialized housing policy with a lengthy

FIGURE 2. Promotional bulletin used by the Bureau of Indian Affairs—Chicago that shows Indian women in a suburban home. Photo courtesy of the Newberry Library, Chicago. Call number: Ayer MMS BIA Relocation, Box 2, Folder 26.

history, not simply as a federal initiative that provided job training and employment opportunities in urban environments throughout the 1950s. This Indian-specific policy was premised on techniques used throughout WWII as the War Relocation Authority (WRA) interned over 110,000 noncitizen Japanese and Japanese Americans along the Pacific coast. Dillon S. Meyer, appointed as director of the WRA in 1942, would go on to lead the FHA for a short time before being appointed commissioner of the BIA in 1950. While leading the WRA program during WWII Meyer initiated a program that moved Japanese individuals and families from the relocation centers to jobs and homes outside the Japanese exclusion areas. The WRA internment of the Japanese further complicates the history of race-specific housing policy and adds to this complexity another layer, as several Japanese Relocation centers were located on Indian reservations, including the Gila River War Relocation Center on the Gila River Reservation and the Poston War Relocation Center on the Colorado River Reservation. Perhaps it is not so surprising, then, that the WRA was used as a model for the Indian Relocation Program only a few years later.

By 1948 the BIA conducted its inaugural relocation on the Hopi and Navajo Reservations. The harsh winter of 1947–48 compounded the lack of reservation resources for the two Southwest tribes. The BIA sought to relocate tribal members to the urban areas of Denver, Salt Lake City, and Los Angeles for expanded employment opportunities, akin the relocation of interned Japanese persons outside of internments camps during WWII. When Meyer became the commissioner of Indian Affairs in 1950 he suggested expanding the Relocation Program of the Hopi and Navajo tribes to include all reservation Indians. The Indian Relocation Program, then, has a significant history as a housing policy that stems from WWII when viewed with an eye on the government's deliberate movement of racialized people, both Japanese and American Indians, to specific areas. The Japanese during WWII were moved to isolated areas, including reservations, where they were no longer perceived of as a "threat" and were perhaps even seen as docile bodies, as reservation Indians had also been viewed. Later, the choreographed movement of American Indians to urban areas was intended to complete their assimilation, by removing them from their culture and reservations, and eventually to eliminate the need for reservations through termination policy.

Historically entrenched lending procedures and racial discrimination added another layer of complexity to the deliberate movement of certain racialized groups to urban and suburban areas. The home loan portion of the GI Bill, based on earlier FHA lending policies and programs, continued to allow for racially discriminatory covenants that prevented people of color from purchasing homes in increasingly white suburban developments. *Shelley v. Kraemer* (1948) held that racial covenants which prevented "people of the Negro or Mongolian race" from owning property were legally unenforceable. However, in its ruling the Supreme Court also asserted the validity of race-based covenants as a freedom of private parties guaranteed under the Fourteenth Amendment. Yet the racial covenants were ruled judicially unenforceable due to the equal protection clause within the Fourteenth Amendment. Race-based covenants certainly curtailed American Indians' freedom to purchase property. In 1948 a second case concerning the legality of race-based covenants, *Hurd v. Hodge*, reached the Supreme Court. At issue in this case from a Washington, D.C., neighborhood was a racially restrictive covenant that stated, "Said lot shall never be rented, leased, sold, transferred or conveyed unto any Negro or colored person, under a penalty of Two Thousand Dollars."[84] The defendant in this case, James M. Hurd, is described as a "Negro" in the legal commentary on the case; however, as emphasized by Alison Bernstein and buried in the footnotes of the case, Hurd was actually a Mohawk Indian.[85] Even with the court cases settled, throughout much of the country segregation remained legal and discrimination remained active in the housing and employment sectors.[86]

Certainly there were covenants that specifically precluded Indian occupancy, while others considered American Indians as "Negro" precisely for the purposes of exclusion. These racially restrictive covenants added to the burden of finding adequate housing for many Indians, particularly those in metropolitan areas, including across the Twin Cities, by further limiting their options.[87] Nearly all major metropolitan areas of the 1940s, including new suburban developments and existing urban rental properties, imposed a version of racially restrictive housing ordinances. Both 1948 court cases make explicit the blurring of the color line and the efforts homeowners and neighborhood organizations made to maintain their "whiteness." Although the Supreme Court struck down the enforcement of race-based restrictive covenants, it did not prevent them from being carried out undetected and uncontested. Racially restrictive property covenants have carved out a lasting legacy across many of America's communities by preventing people of color, including American Indians, from purchasing property and becoming residents of suburban areas that were increasingly white and homogenous. Even today subprime lending continues to be directed toward communities of color; in Minneapolis this includes the historically and largely American Indian Phillips neighborhood, where 38 percent of all home loans between 2004 and 2006 were subprime. In the same neighborhood that grew out of postwar Indian urbanization and Relocation, 63 percent of home loan applicants of color were denied mortgage financing, compared to 54 percent of whites of the same income levels.[88]

The Indian Relocation Program, designed and widely promoted as a method to integrate Indian people into the mainstream, dominant, white society, actually did the opposite. Relocation provided short-term housing to its participants, exclusively in urban areas. These were the very same places many white families were fleeing—many on the GI Bill, but many more through the benefit of ongoing lending practices and policies of the FHA available to white Americans since the 1930s. According to a Chicago-area Relocation report, Relocation actually spurred "white flight" as many "white residents of neighborhoods" in Chicago that were "becoming mixed" with Indians "[reported] panic selling."[89] If Relocation was viewed as a tool to integrate Indian people, then why were Indian people not also provided with home loans and encouraged to relocate to *suburban* areas, instead of urban residences commonly described as "predictably dreary"? This question becomes particularly significant when numerous American Indian veterans inquired about VA loans to purchase homes, often specifically asking about buying in suburban areas. After moving nearly twenty miles north of the Twin Cities to a home under contract in Ham Lake, Gerald Owens expressed to the Relocation officer that he was "interested in securing a VA loan to improve the place." The officer simply referred him to the Loan Division of the VA at Fort Snelling.[90] Similarly, David Dowd, who was from Bemidji, contacted the Minnesota Chippewa

Agency Relocation Department about down payment assistance after relocating to Oakland. In his August 1956 letter Mr. Dowd writes:

> I am writing in regards to information on the bill that was passed for down payment assistance on houses for relocated Indians. The Indian office in San Francisco will not give us any information. They told us to write your office to see if we are entitled [to] a down payment. It is very hard to find places to live, and rent is very high. Will you please let us know as soon as possible. We've been out here a year and a half, and would like to know if we are entitled to this. Have worked steady since we've been out here.[91]

In response the Relocation officer wrote, "As I understand it, there has been no full procedure set up for this program," and that regardless, Mr. Dowd would in fact have to contact and work with the local San Francisco Office. Despite their best efforts, American Indian people on Relocation never had the same opportunity for suburban home ownership that many on the GI Bill had.

Lenders and builders in the postwar years were heirs to millions of dollars funneled their way by the GI Bill and preferred new construction in developing suburbs; Relocated Indians, on the other hand, were almost always relegated to cramped quarters in the urban core. A 1956 report on Relocation describes the typical housing available to Indian people as "passable to working-class standards, inadequate according to middle-class standards," where "the rooms [are] shabbily but not wretchedly furnished," with the hope for "improvement" coming "as more relocated families find their way into the racially mixed public housing developments."[92] As Kenneth Philp notes, "Relocation officials could not always keep their promise of finding adequate housing for the Indians. After 1945 most of the new housing stock was located in middle-class suburbs. Desirable rental property often cost too much for low-paid, unskilled Indian workers who faced frequent layoffs. Consequently, Indians usually had to move into public housing projects or shabby unfurnished ghetto apartments in lower-class neighborhoods where slum landlords charged excessive rent."[93] As stated in a report by the Association of American Indian Affairs, access to housing at mid-century, for differing racialized groups, makes clear the intentions of the federal government through its organized and funded efforts to move white and nonwhite people: "Much good housing at reasonable cost will never be easily found. It is not here. This is a community problem and the Relocation Office cannot solve it."[94] This was also true of the housing available in the Twin Cities. Like most other metropolitan areas across the country, Minneapolis and St. Paul saw a severe shortage in adequate housing in the wake of WWII. During the early to mid-1950s, and in the midst of urban renewal, there had not yet been enough public housing units constructed, and most developers were focused on new home construction in the inner-ring suburbs around Minneapolis and St. Paul.

As new suburban home construction soared in the postwar years, and the GI Bill created an opportunity for homeownership for many veterans, American Indian veterans were largely prohibited from accessing the home loan benefit. For many American Indian veterans, the GI Bill was not the same guarantee of homeownership it was for white veterans. The home loan benefit of the GI Bill was not applicable on reservation land, which is held in trust by the federal government.[95] Since trust land cannot be used as collateral in case of mortgage default, it has and continues to limit the availability and accessibility of home loans for Indian people who live on reservations.[96] Though thousands of Indian veterans were entitled to the GI Bill, the home loan benefit was out of reach for Indian people who returned to their reservation communities after the war. The majority of Indian veterans were virtually unable to access and essentially ineligible for the federally insured home loans. The trust status of Indian land works as a double-edged sword, protecting Indian land from outside purchase but also preventing Indian people from taking individual ownership of it. However, as early as 1947, members of Congress sought ways to "assist" and "emancipate" Indian veterans from "government control." In February 1947, House Resolution 2165 was introduced to allow Indian veterans of WWII to access the home loan benefit of the GI Bill by lifting the trust restrictions on their properties, though it was never passed.[97] Seemingly the federal government recognized the problem of home ownership for Indian people on reservations, including veterans, but chose not to address directly the complicated nature of trust land and loan collateral. The federal government pursued relocation and termination as a way to end all government responsibilities to Indian people, rather than fulfill them, and to move Indian people off reservations.

At the same time, Relocation added to the difficulty and confusion many American Indian veterans faced as they worked to become homeowners but instead were encouraged to move to short-term accommodations in urban areas and were provided no clear or direct chance of home ownership. Viewed as the "most likely to succeed" Relocation participants due to their military service and travel, 55 percent of all Relocation participants between 1953 and 1956 were American Indian veterans.[98] Yet, as the stories of Jerry Flute, Damon James, and Gerald Owens demonstrate, many Indian veterans faced difficulty accessing VA benefits; the VA regularly insisted that Indian veterans instead go to the BIA for their housing needs, while the BIA told them to go to the VA to access home loans.[99] Other urban Indians echoed the plight of Flute, James, and Owens as they worked to access BIA programs. Many people, both Indian and non-Native, believed American Indians were not "entitled" to BIA programs once they moved to the city, while others described the BIA program as "illogical" since it "[assisted] only those urban Indians who have come to the cities under the formal BIA relocation program," but not others or those who already lived there. In summary, "life with the bureau [of Indian Affairs] seldom has been a happy medium."[100]

The demobilization of military veterans sharply reduced the need for labor, and as white veterans often received preferential treatment by employers, American Indians lost jobs to white veterans.[101] A Mankato, Minnesota, newspaper article that discussed the service of Native people stated, "Navajos claim that veterans benefits available to other U.S. veterans are practically nonexistent on the reservation. Many claim they can't get VA financing to buy a home. The Navajos say they want the government to build a veterans hospital on the reservation. But most of all, they say they want more jobs."[102] Not only was the VA difficult to navigate for many Indian people, the VA and other local banks would not offer loans to Indian people because they assumed that the government already provided support for Indian "wards."[103] In essence, while the federal government's housing policies, specifically FHA lending practices and the GI Bill, worked to populate newly developed and growing suburbs with specific kinds of people—whites, middle- and upper-income individuals, and nuclear families—they also prevented Indian residency, including Indian veterans who had served the country through war and earned GI Bill benefits.

Conclusion

As scholars have argued, the GI Bill, and the FHA loan programs that predate it, were strategically designed to foster suburban development while mass-home construction firms benefited from the GI Bill and guaranteed low-interest rates took the financial fears out of buying. Suburbs, envisioned as the "new frontier," were defined by home ownership and widely promoted by a growing body of real-estate developers.[104] However, in the postwar age of prosperity and suburbanization, not all people were allowed participation. For Indian people who made the difficult choice to return to reservation life after wartime employment or service, the federal Indian policies of relocation and termination dominated tribal affairs for well over a decade. While the GI Bill and FHA loans promoted an idyllic (white) suburban America, Relocation prompted a new generation of short-term urban residence in the least desirable rental units for American Indians. The GI Bill worked to prevent another Great Depression by offering employment, education, loans, and cash assistance to military veterans, but many Indian veterans were denied these benefits and continued to face discrimination in the workforce, housing, and financial sectors.

In the government's efforts to avoid financial crisis and promote the growth of capitalism, the patriotism and military service of many American Indian people during WWII went unacknowledged—arguably, they were betrayed. Approximately one-third of all Indian men were inducted into military service, a rate higher than any other racial group, yet many were unable to access earned benefits of their service the way white veterans did.[105] As individual tribal communities contributed vital resources to the war effort, Indian people continued to be viewed along racial lines. Federal housing policies specifically contributed to white suburbanization while preventing Indian people from residing in these same areas. Relocation policy did not consider suburbs as residential options for Indian people. The contrasting policies of the GI Bill and relocation during the same political time are astounding. As Kenneth Jackson discusses, the effect of FHA mortgage funding after WWII was to hasten "the decay of inner-city neighborhoods by stripping them of much of their middle-class constituency" and contributing to the "neglect of core cities"—and these were the precise areas Indians were placed during Relocation.[106] Interestingly, the government viewed Indian involvement in WWII as a sign they were ready to leave reservations for good and to assimilate into white society, yet many were never given the opportunity to move to the suburban areas whites flocked to in the postwar environment. Instead, Indian people were encouraged and supported by the federal government to move into urban areas, which in certain cases were designated as "urban slums" needing "revitalization." Donald Fixico notes that Indian Relocation was less about opportunity and more about control and containment, directly opposite the goals of the GI Bill.[107] The work of making suburbs into predominately white places after WWII entailed the active disregard of people of color and lower-income people, including American Indians in federal housing and Indian policies. As I propose here, if we consider postwar suburbanization as an example of a relatively new form of long-term, white "settlement," Indians have again been erased by the dramatic increase of non-Natives in the suburban housing boom.[108]

Though it must be examined alongside other forms of residential discrimination in the postwar era, including historically entrenched Jim Crow laws, white flight, and redlining, relocation is inherently different because it was an *Indian*-specific housing policy. Due to American Indian peoples' history of treaty making with the federal government, Indian people have a distinct political and legal relationship with the federal government, a space no other race or ethnic group occupies.[109] I follow the lead of legal scholar Virginia Davis, then, to demonstrate how Relocation follows from the historical obligations of the federal government to Indian people.[110] It is in this vein that I view Relocation as a racialized housing program meant to deter Indian people away from suburbs *and* reservations and into urban areas through federal

Indian policy that largely remained beyond the purview of federal housing policy. Though numerous scholars have examined African American suburbanization and the access of low-income persons to suburbia at mid-century, creating a valuable body of scholarship on postwar suburbanization and race relations, the interaction between the federal government and Indian people, via Relocation, is inherently different.[111] Relocation policy was crafted and carried out through the Bureau of Indian Affairs, not the Housing and Home Finance Agency (as other housing policies and programs were).[112]

Yet both the GI Bill and Relocation were intended, or at least promoted, as ways to reintegrate military veterans of WWII into mainstream society. Although the two programs were designed to achieve the same goal, they used very different methods, and different governmental agencies, for presumably very different populations. The GI Bill, framed around the bleak reality returning veterans of WWI faced and the prevention of another depression, was negotiated well before war's end. Likewise, Relocation, as an effort to fully integrated Indian people into mainstream white society, was also being carefully negotiated prior to the war's end. Relocation, as an American Indian–specific housing policy, focused on Native veterans and was regularly portrayed as an opportunity for employment and urban residency, but it was also based on the racialized internment and job placement of ethnically Japanese persons during WWII. The stated and funded goals of Relocation then stands in direct contrast to the goals of the GI Bill as a housing policy for (white) military veterans. This is particularly disconcerting as both programs supposedly worked to reintegrate war veterans while clearly distinguishing between American Indian veterans and white veterans.

Federal Indian policy at mid-century, when viewed alongside federal housing policy of the same postwar era, allows us to understand the choreographed nature of suburbanization. Rather than view American Indian people as absent from or invisible in suburbs, it must be remembered that they were prevented by both federal Indian policies and federal housing policies throughout the mid-twentieth century from moving to new, increasingly white, suburban developments and instead were encouraged to move to shorter-term rental housing in urban areas. The deliberate movement of people, white veterans and American Indians, to specific residential locations, suburban and urban, becomes clear when the Indian policy of relocation is examined alongside the GI Bill and earlier housing policies of the FHA.

KASEY KEELER (Citizen Potawatomi Nation and Tuolumne Band of Me-Wuk) is the Native American studies postdoctoral fellow at the University of Virginia.

Appendix:
Key Pieces of Legislation, Including Government Reports and Supreme Court Cases

1862. Homestead Act of 1862: Signed by President Lincoln, made eligible anyone over the age of twenty-one or the head of family to file an application to claim a federal land grant

1887. Dawes Act: Authorized Congress to survey and divide tribally held Indian land into individual allotments

1924. Indian Citizenship Act: Signed by President Coolidge, grants U.S. citizenship to Indian people who were not yet citizens

1928. Meriam Report: 847-page report documenting overall conditions of Indian reservations and Indian boarding schools; leads to the IRA

1932. Federal Home Loan Bank Act: Passed under President Hoover, intended to lower the cost of home ownership; establishes Federal Home Loan Banks

1932. Reconstruction Finance Corporation: A corporation of the federal government that provided financial support to provide loans at state and local level

1934. Indian Reorganization Act (IRA): Designed to end allotment policy, restore Indian control of Indian assets, and end forced assimilation

1934. National Housing Act: A component of the New Deal; worked to make housing and home loans more affordable and created the FHA

1934. Policy of Redlining: Begun with the creation of the FHA and the underwriters manual; a practice of denying loans to areas based on race

1937. United States Housing Act: Created subsidies for local housing agencies to create public housing programs

1942. Executive Order 9102: Creates the War Relocation Authority, that is, Japanese American internment during WWII

1944. GI Bill of 1944: Also known as the Serviceman's Readjustment Act, provided education, housing, and unemployment benefits for veterans of WWII

1948. Relocation of the Hopi and Navajo: BIA off-reservation employment program that served as basis for later Relocation Program

1948. *Shelley v. Kraemer*: Landmark Supreme Court case which held that racially restrictive covenants were unenforceable

1948. *Hurd v. Hodge*: Companion case to *Shelley v. Kraemer* from the District of Columbia; upholds *Shelley v. Kraemer*

1953. House Concurrent Resolution 108: Official start to Termination, Congress seeks to end federal "supervision" of tribes and terminates sovereign status

1956. Indian Relocation Act: Official start to Relocation though de facto Relocation was long underway, federal program to move Indians to urban areas

1958. Adult Vocational Training Program: A continuation of the Relocation Program that promoted job training and placement

Notes

1. Alvin M. Josephy, 1915–2005, Alvin M. Josephy, Jr., Sioux Indian Interview Cassettes, 1982–1983, Tape 36, Ayer Modern MS Collection, Newberry Library, Chicago. Based on the archival materials available, the exact dates of Flute's military service are unclear.

2. Kenneth R. Philp, "Stride toward Freedom: The Relocation of Indians to Cities, 1952–1960," *Western Historical Quarterly* 16, no. 2 (1985): 175–90; and individual case files from Department of the Interior, Bureau of Indian Affairs, Minneapolis Area Office, Minnesota Agency National Archives at Kansas City, Record Group 75, Series 5.

3. African Americans also faced difficulties in accessing GI Bill benefits, namely, in the form of racism. However, this differed for American Indians, whose legal and political status, and that of Indian land/reservations, is unique.

4. For example, the text of the GI Bill includes such language as "loans for the purchase or construction of homes," "interest for the first year on that part of the loan guarantee by the Administrator shall be paid by the Administrator out of available appropriations," and "the guarantee of a loan to be used in purchasing residential property or in constructing a dwelling on unimproved property," which clearly delineates the purposes of the GI Bill home loan benefit. Public Law 346, Chapter 268, January 10, 1944, Chapter V: General Provisions for Loans. Relocation records demonstrate the temporary assistance relocated individuals and families received, often limited to two weeks of assistance. For example, each member of the Jones family, who relocated from Bemidji, Minnesota to Minneapolis, were allowed twenty dollars a week for each family member in addition to the head of household, who was given thirty dollars a week. If relocatees required more assistance they would generally have to reapply and seek it out. Similarly, rent for relocatees in Minneapolis or St. Paul was generally covered for only ten to fourteen days if they were not living with a family member already there.

5. For more information on urban renewal in Minneapolis and St. Paul see Judith A. Martin and Anthony Goddard, "Past Choices/Present Landscapes: The Impact of Urban Renewal on the Twin Cities," a report published in 1989 by the Center for Urban and Regional Affairs, Hubert H. Humphrey Center, Minneapolis.

6. The Relocation Act of 1956, Public Law 959, Chapter 930, August 3, 1956 (S. 3416). Although Relocation as an Indian policy fell under the larger and more dominant Termination umbrella of the 1950s, it began as an expansion of the Hopi–Navajo Relocation. However, in this article I focus specifically on Relocation as an Indian-specific housing policy. For more on Termination Policy please see Kenneth R. Philp, *Termination Revisited: American Indians on the Trail to Self-Determination, 1933–1953* (Lincoln: University of Nebraska Press, 2002); Donald Fixico, *Termination and Relocation: Federal Indian Policy, 1945–1960* (Albuquerque: University of New Mexico Press, 1990); and Brian Hosmer, ed., *The Native American Legacy of Harry S. Truman* (Kirksville, Mo.: Truman State University Press, 2010).

7. A more in-depth description of the process of redlining can be found in the next section of this article.

8. Myron Orfield, Thomas F. Luce, Jr., and Eric Myott, "Twin Cities in Crisis: Unequal Treatment of Communities of Color in Mortgage Lending," published in April 2014 by the Institute on Metropolitan Opportunity, University of Minnesota Law School.

9. See the appendix for a list of legislation. I focus on the Relocation Act of 1956, Public Law 959, Chapter 930, August 3, 1956 (S. 3416); and the GI Bill, Public Law 346, Chapter 268, January 10, 1944. My critique also pays particular attention to the predecessor of the Relocation Act, the Navajo-Hopi Law, Public Law 474, Chapter 92. April 19, 1950 (64 Stat. 44), which was quickly expanded to include all Indian people and the gradual opening of Relocation offices around the country by the mid-1950s.

10. These are restricted records and are federally protected until no less than seventy years has passed from the date of the last record/file contained within each box and or series. I was able to access these records at the Kansas City branch of the National Archive and Records Administration after applying for and receiving approval for a social science research exemption request. The names of each of the individuals and families whose records I accessed and are included in this article have been changed to protect their identity and to adhere to the specific conditions of my research exemption.

11. Elaine M. Neils, *Reservation to the City: Indian Migration and Federal Relocation* (Chicago: University of Chicago Press, 1971); Fixico, *Termination and Relocation*; Philp, *Termination Revisited*; and Virginia Davis, "A Discovery of Sorts: Reexamining the Origins of the Federal Indian Housing Obligation," *Harvard BlackLetter Law Journal* 18 (Spring 2002): 215–23.

12. Susan Lobo and Kurt Peters, eds., *American Indians and the Urban Experience* (Walnut Creek, Calif.: AltaMira Press, 2001).

13. James B. LaGrand, *Indian Metropolis: Native Americans in Chicago, 1945–1975* (Urbana: University of Illinois Press, 2002).

14. Coll Thrush, *Native Seattle: Histories from the Crossing-Over Place* (Seattle: University of Washington Press, 2008).

15. Renya K. Ramirez, *Native Hubs: Culture, Community, and Belonging in Silicon Valley and Beyond* (Durham, N.C.: Duke University Press, 2007).

16. Nicholas Rosenthal, *Reimagining Indian Country: Native American Migration and Identity in Twentieth-Century Los Angeles* (Chapel Hill: University of North Carolina Press, 2012).

17. Evelyn Peters and Chris Andersen, eds., *Indigenous in the City. Contemporary Identities and Cultural Innovation* (Vancouver: University of British Columbia Press, 2013).

18. This scholarship includes Arnold R. Hirsch, *Making the Second Ghetto: Race and Housing in Chicago, 1940–1960* (Chicago: University of Chicago Press, 2009); Becky M. Nicolaides, *My Blue Heaven: Life and Politics in the Working-Class Suburbs of Los Angeles, 1920–1965* (Chicago: University of Chicago Press, 2002); Elaine Tyler May, *Homeward Bound: American Families in the Cold War Era* (New York: Basic Books, 2008); Preston H. Smith, *Racial Democracy and the Black*

Metropolis: Housing Policy in Postwar Chicago (Minneapolis: University of Minnesota Press, 2012); and Thomas J. Sugrue, *The Origins of the Urban Crisis: Race and Inequality in Postwar Detroit* (Princeton, N.J.: Princeton University Press, 2005).

19. Kenneth T. Jackson, *Crabgrass Frontier: The Suburbanization of the United States* (New York: Oxford University Press, 1987), 133, 241, 287–90.

20. Arnold R. Hirsch, "Less Than *Plessy*: The Inner City, Suburbs, and State-Sanctioned Residential Segregation in the Age of *Brown*," in *The New Suburban History*, ed. Kevin M. Kruse and Thomas J. Sugrue (Chicago: University of Chicago Press, 2006), 35–36.

21. Andrew Wiese, *Places of Their Own: African American Suburbanization in the Twentieth Century* (Chicago: University of Chicago Press, 2005); see also Wiese, "'The House I Lived In': Race, Class, and African American Suburban Dreams in the Postwar United States," in *The New Suburban History*, ed. Kevin M. Kruse and Thomas J. Sugrue (Chicago: University of Chicago Press, 2006), 99–119.

22. Wiese, *Places of Their Own*, 145–59.

23. Robert O. Self, *American Babylon: Race and the Struggle for Postwar Oakland* (Princeton, N.J.: Princeton University Press, 2003).

24. David M. P. Freund, *Colored Property: State Policy and White Racial Politics in Suburban America* (Chicago: University of Chicago Press, 2010).

25. Primarily through the Federal Home Loan Bank Act (see Federal Home Loan Bank Act, Public Law 72-304, Chapter 522, July 22, 1932, 47 Stat. 725) and the Reconstruction Finance Corporation and Federal Home Loan Bank Board of 1932. In operation between 1932 and 1957, the Reconstruction Finance Corporation made loans and provided financial support to business, railroads, and financial institutions in the wake of the Great Depression. The Federal Home Loan Bank Board of 1932 served to make home ownership more affordable by creating the Federal Home Loan Bank Board and Federal Home Loan Banks, which worked to create credit reserves and increase the supply of credit in the housing market.

26. Lewis Meriam, *The Problem of Indian Administration* (Baltimore: Johns Hopkins University Press, 1928). Chief among the findings of the scathing 850-page report were the high rates of disease and death among Indian people who lived on reservations and the rampant poverty that plagued reservations post-allotment.

27. The National Housing Act of 1934, Public Law 73-479, 73rd Congress, H.R. 9620, June 27, 1934.

28. See the United States Federal Housing Administration, *Underwriting Manual: Underwriting and Valuation Procedure under Title II of the National Housing Act* (Washington, D.C.: Government Printing Office, 1936).

29. For more information on FHA lending practices and redlining see Jackson, *Crabgrass Frontier*.

30. James W. Loewen, *Sundown Towns: A Hidden Dimension of American Racism* (New York: Touchstone, 2005), 7, 23, 116. Also see Hennepin County Government Center, Minneapolis, Hennepin County Deed Book 1235, p. 261, November 21, 1930.

31. The United States Housing Act of 1937, Public Law 75-412, Chapter 896, September 1, 1937, 50 Stat. 888.

32. Jackson, *Crabgrass Frontier*, 203.

33. Ibid., 204.

34. George Lipsitz, *The Possessive Investment in Whiteness: How People Profit from Identity Politics*, rev. ed. (Philadelphia: Temple University Press, 2006), 373.

35. The Indian Reorganization Act, 48 Stat. 984, 25th U.S. Congress, June 18, 1934. The Dawes Act, also commonly known as the General Allotment Act, enacted in 1887, authorized the president to survey and divide reservation land. Traditionally and historically, Indian land was held in common, not as individual property; allotment broke up Indian land into individual allotments, generally of 80 or 160 acres. After reservation land was allotted, the federal government then purchased "excess" land at a nominal price. This land was then sold to white settlers. It was hoped that the process of allotment would speed up the assimilation process of Indian people and lead to citizenship for Indian people who maintained their allotment for a set amount of years. In reality, allotment led to the dramatic and rapid loss of Indian land and put an end to communal land holdings for Indian tribes. Furthermore, allotment allowed non-tribal members, generally white settlers, to own property within the borders of a reservation, further complicating jurisdictional and tax issues. Today most reservations are still dealing with allotment in the form of fractionalization in which the original owner of an allotment dies and the heirs receive equal interests in said allotment; this has occurred over several generations, and today fractionated reservation land is virtually worthless because many times individuals do not know they are heirs to the land or not all heirs agree to the sale of the individual allotment.

36. Department of the Interior, Bureau of Indian Affairs. Minneapolis Area Office, Minnesota Agency National Archives at Kansas City, Record Group 75, Series 5.

37. Ibid.

38. Ibid.

39. Orfield, Luce, and Myott, "Twin Cities in Crisis."

40. Kenneth William Townsend, *World War II and the American Indian* (Albuquerque: University of New Mexico Press, 2002), 173.

41. Alison R. Bernstein, *American Indians and World War II: Toward a New Era in Indian Affairs* (Norman: University of Oklahoma Press, 1999), 64.

42. Ibid., 195.

43. Ibid., 150.

44. Ibid., 180.

45. Ibid., 64.

46. Ibid., 59.

47. Christopher P. Loss, *Between Citizens and the State: The Politics of American Higher Education in the 20th Century* (Princeton, N.J.: Princeton University Press, 2012). Excerpt accessed online at Vanderbilt University's *Peabody Reflector*, http://www.vanderbilt.edu/magazines/peabody-reflector/2012/12/democracys-proving-ground/.

48. Department of the Interior, Bureau of Indian Affairs, Minneapolis Area Office, Minnesota Agency National Archives at Kansas City, Record Group 75, Series 5.

49. Bernstein, *American Indians and World War II*, 150.

50. Ibid., 24.

51. The Servicemen's Readjustment Act of 1944, https://www.ourdocuments .gov/doc.php?flash=true&doc=76.

52. Thomas W. Hanchett, "The Other 'Subsidized Housing,'" *Journal of Housing and Community Development* 58, no. 2 (2001): 18–49.

53. Michael J. Bennett, *When Dreams Came True: The GI Bill and the Making of Modern America* (Dulles, Va.: Potomac Books, 1999), 26.

54. The Public Housing Program was created by the Housing Act of 1937. See *Housing Act of 1949: Summary of the Provisions of the National Housing Act of 1949*, https://bulk.resource.org/gao.gov/81-171/00002FD7.pdf.

55. Alexander von Hoffman, "A Study in Contradictions: The Origins and Legacy of the Housing Act of 1949," *Housing Policy Debate* 11, no. 2 (2000): 299.

56. Arnold R. Hirsch, "'Containment' on the Home Front: Race and Federal Housing Policy from the New Deal to the Cold War," *Journal of Urban History* 26, no. 2 (2000): 159.

57. Ibid., 163.

58. See *Shelley v. Kraemer*, 334 U.S. 1 (U.S. Supreme Court, 1948).

59. "Accord within Day Is Seen in Fight on Negro: Ministers Urge Arbitration in Order to Avoid Violence," *Minneapolis Star*, July 17, 1931; "Negro Insist He'll Not Move Now or Later: Engages Woman Attorney Who Declares Police Protection Assured," *Minneapolis Star*, July, 20, 1931.

60. *1940 United States Federal Census*, Ancestry.com, Provo, Utah, USA, 2012. See also Hennepin County Deed Book 1235, p. 261, November 21, 1930, Hennepin County Government Center, Minneapolis.

61. Department of the Interior, Bureau of Indian Affairs, Minneapolis Area Office, Minnesota Agency National Archives at Kansas City, Record Group 75, Series 5. Individual case files contained within this series repeatedly and thoroughly discuss an applicant's veteran status and "urban experience." Military service was often listed as "previous experience in living away from the Reservation" and played a role in the Relocation officer's decision whether to approve an application for Relocation.

62. Philp, *Termination Revisited*, 68. See also Ned Blackhawk, "I Can Carry on from Here," *Wicazo Sa Revew* 11, no. 2 (1995): 16–30, for discussion of McCarthy-era emphasis on conformity.

63. See 1953 Termination Bill, House Concurrent Resolution 108, 67 Stat. B122, 83rd Congress, August 1, 1953; and Relocation Act of 1956, Public Law 959, Chapter 930, August 3, 1956 (S. 3416). Specific excerpts from the Termination Bill include the following: "It is the policy of Congress, as rapidly as possible, to make Indians within the territorial limits of the United States subject to the same laws and *entitled to the same privileges . . . to end their status as wards of the United States, and to grant them all of the rights and prerogatives* pertaining to American citizenship" (emphasis added). The Bill goes on to state that tribes

deemed "ready" for Termination "should be *freed from Federal supervision and control*" (emphasis added).

64. 1953 Termination Bill, 68; and Vine Deloria, Jr., and Clifford M. Lytle, *The Nations Within: The Past and Future of American Indian Sovereignty* (Austin: University of Texas Press, 2006), 192.

65. 1953 Termination Bill, House Concurrent Resolution 108, 67 Stat. B122, 83rd Congress, August 1, 1953.

66. For more information on Termination Policy see Philp, *Termination Revisited*; Fixico, *Termination and Relocation*; and Brian Hosmer, ed., *The Native American Legacy of Harry S. Truman* (Kirksville, Mo.: Truman State University Press, 2010).

67. Blackhawk, "I Can Carry on from Here," 18.

68. LaGrand, *Indian Metropolis*, 19–40, 77; and Rosenthal, *Reimagining Indian Country*, 11–30. For more information on seasonal rounds please see Chantal Norrgard, *Seasons of Change: Labor, Treaty Rights, and Ojibwe Nationhood* (Chapel Hill: University of North Carolina Press, 2014); and William Cronon, *Changes in the Land: Indians, Colonists, and the Ecology of New England* (New York: Hill and Wang, 2003).

69. Ramirez, *Native Hubs*, 58–83; and Peters and Andersen, "Introduction," in *Indigenous in the City*, 7–9.

70. Also known as Public Law 959 or the Adult Vocational Training Program (AVTP).

71. The Relocation Program was formally adopted as policy and expanded to include the AVTP in 1956. Relocation Field Offices were located in Chicago, Los Angeles, Dallas, San Francisco, Denver, San Jose, Cleveland, St. Louis, and Cincinnati.

72. Department of the Interior, Bureau of Indian Affairs, Minneapolis Area Office, Minnesota Agency National Archives at Kansas City, Record Group 75, Series 5.

73. Chicago Field Employment Assistance Office, Records on Employment Assistance, 1951–1958, National Archives, Chicago, Folder 1, Placement Statistical Report, February 1952.

74. Donald Fixico, *The Urban Indian Experience in America* (Albuquerque: New Mexico, 2000), 13.

75. Gregory W. Craig, Arthur M. Harkins, and Richard G. Woods, *Indian Housing in Minneapolis and St. Paul* (Minneapolis: University of Minnesota, 1969).

76. "The Indian in Minnesota: A Report to Governor Luther W. Youngdahl of Minnesota by the Governor's Interracial Commission," April 1, 1947.

77. Municipal Housing and Redevelopment Act, Chapter 487, Laws of Minnesota for 1947, approved April 23, 1947.

78. In addition to American Indians' unequal opportunity to access suburban housing akin to those on the GI Bill, many Indians also arrived in urban environments on the cusp of urban renewal programs and at a time when many cities were just beginning to provide/expand public housing opportunities.

79. Fixico, *Urban Indian Experience in America*, 4.

80. Bernstein, *American Indians and World War II*, 169.

81. Department of the Interior, Bureau of Indian Affairs, Minneapolis Area Office, Minnesota Agency National Archives at Kansas City, Record Group 75, Series 5.

82. Bennett, *When Dreams Came True*, 279.

83. Here I am specifically referring to land held in trust on reservation and the inability to use that land as collateral to secure a home loan.

84. *Hurd v. Hodge*, 334 U.S. 24 (U.S. Supreme Court, 1948).

85. Bernstein, *American Indians and World War II*, 164. See also *Hurd v. Hodge*, note 76.

86. Suzanne Mettler, *Soldiers to Citizens: The GI Bill and the Making of the Greatest Generation* (New York: Oxford University Press, 2007), cited by Patricia Kelly Hall in "Privileged Moves: Migration, Race, and Veteran Status in Post–World War II America" (Ph.D. diss., University of Minnesota, 2009).

87. For an example of a restrictive covenant, see Hennepin County Deed Book 1235, p. 261, November 21, 1930, Hennepin County Government Center, Minneapolis.

88. Orfield, Luce, and Myott, "Twin Cities in Crisis."

89. "The American Indian Relocation Program: A Report Undertaken with the Assistance of the Field Foundation, Inc.," published in December 1956 by the Association on American Indian Affairs.

90. Department of the Interior, Bureau of Indian Affairs, Minneapolis Area Office, Minnesota Agency National Archives at Kansas City, Record Group 75, Series 5.

91. Ibid.

92. Association on American Indian Affairs, "American Indian Relocation Program."

93. Philp, "Stride toward Freedom," 185–86.

94. Association on American Indian Affairs, "American Indian Relocation Program."

95. In 1992 the VA worked to remedy this situation and created the Native American Direct Loan that can be used by American Indian veterans on trust land. At the time this program was inaugurated, "VA housing assistance to Native American veterans was minimal. In fact, the Advisory Committee on Native American Veterans had been unable to find a single instance of a Native American veteran benefiting from the loan guarantee program" because of the unique status of tribal land. See the Congressional Research Service Report from April 24, 2012, by Libby Perl, "VA Housing: Guaranteed Loans, Direct Loans, and Specially Adapted Housing Grants."

96. Bernstein, *American Indians and World War II*, 143.

97. U.S. Congress, House Committee on Public Land, "Providing for the Removal of Restrictions on Property of Indians Who Served in the Armed Forces," House Report, 80th Congress, 1st Session, 1947.

98. Douglas K. Miller, "Willing Workers: Urban Relocation and American Indian Initiative, 1940s–1960s," *Ethnohistory* 60, no. 1 (2013): 51–76.

99. For examples please see individual case files and Relocation records for the Department of the Interior, Bureau of Indian Affairs, Minneapolis Area

Office, Minnesota Agency National Archives at Kansas City, Record Group 75, Series 5; and Alvin M. Josephy, 1915–2005, Alvin M. Josephy, Jr., Sioux Indian Interview Cassettes, 1982–1983, Tape 36, Ayer Modern MS Collection, Newberry Library, Chicago.

100. "U.S. Indians' Big Brother: The BIA," *Minneapolis Tribune*, May 10, 1970; and "An Urban Indian Thrust for the BIA," *Minneapolis Tribune*, March 25, 1971, found in the Michael Scullin Collection, Ayer Modern MS Collection, Newspaper Clippings—Audio Cassettes, Box 1, Folder 1, Newberry Library, Chicago.

101. Townsend, *World War II and the American Indian*, 216–17.

102. Article from *Free Press*, Mankato, Minnesota, July 27, 1974, Michael Scullin Collection, Ayer Modern MS Scullin, Newspaper Clippings—Audio Cassettes, Box 1, Folder 1, Newberry Library, Chicago.

103. Bernstein, *American Indians and World War II*, 145.

104. Bennett, *When Dreams Came True*, 24.

105. Townsend, *World War II and the American Indian*, 62.

106. Jackson, *Crabgrass Frontier*, 206.

107. Fixico, *Urban Indian Experience in America*.

108. For more about the erasure and replacement of Indian place histories see Thrush, *Native Seattle*.

109. David E. Wilkins and K. Tsianina Lomawaima, *Uneven Ground: American Indian Sovereignty and Federal Law* (Norman: University of Oklahoma Press, 2001), 5–9.

110. Davis, "A Discovery of Sorts."

111. See Freund, *Colored Property*; Hirsch, *Making the Second Ghetto*; see also Hirsch, "Less Than *Plessy*"; Jackson, *Crabgrass Frontier*; Loewen, *Sundown Towns*; Nicolaides, *My Blue Heaven*; May, *Homeward Bound*; Self, *American Babylon*; Smith, *Racial Democracy and the Black Metropolis*; Sugrue, *Origins of the Urban Crisis*; Wiese, *Places of Their Own*. See also Wiese, "The House I Lived In."

112. The Housing and Home Finance Agency was created in 1947 and was eventually superseded in 1965 by the Department of Housing and Urban Development.

DREW LOPENZINA

Letter from Barnstable Jail:
William Apess and the
"Memorial of the Mashpee Indians"

FROM MID-SEPTEMBER TO MID-OCTOBER OF 1833 the Pequot activist, writer, and Methodist minister William Apess served out a jail sentence of thirty days, having been found guilty of "inciting a riot" as a result of his attempts to advocate for the rights of the Mashpee Wampanoag at Mashpee on Cape Cod. Apess used his time in prison, among other things, to draft a detailed petition he would later submit to be read in the Boston Legislature. The petition, known as the "Memorial of the Marshpee Indians," was immediately circulated throughout the "plantation," where, in keeping with traditional processes, it was read to the assembled tribe, discussed, and amended where necessary, until a consensus was reached as to its overall language. The "Memorial" was signed or approved by well over half the residents of Mashpee and laid out the case for the Mashpee complaint, enumerating the unjust and opportunistic means by which the tribe had been oppressed over roughly a century of colonial oversight.[1] As Apess observed, "There is not one enlightened and respectable Indian upon the plantation, that wants overseers or the present minister (Phineas Fish). We say that all our rulers . . . were placed here amongst us without our consent." He additionally reprimands the august rulers of the state of Massachusetts that, "while ye are filled with the fat of our father's land and enjoy your liberties without molestation will not this Honorable Body be as benevolent to us, poor Marshpee Indians, who are sighing and weeping under bondage, as ye are to the poor Cherokees?" The "Memorial" concluded with a general cry for release from bondage, exclaiming, "*Oh, White man! white man!* the blood of our fathers, spilt in the Revolutionary War, cries from the ground of our native soil, to break the chains of oppression, and let our children go *free.*"[2]

Apess's Mashpee "Memorial," although first published in *The Liberator* in 1834, has not, to my knowledge, been reprinted anywhere since. And yet it is a seminal contribution to Native American literature, written, as Apess would later attest to the Barton Commission in charge of investigating the affairs at Mashpee (and as recorded in the stenographer's clipped transcription), "as voice of people."[3] Although Indigenous prison protest literature as

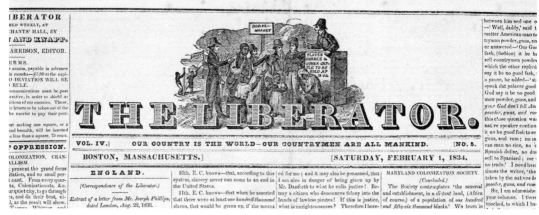

FIGURE 1. Masthead of *The Liberator* for February 1, 1834, in which the "Memorial of the Marshpee Indians" appears. Courtesy of the American Antiquarian Society.

a genre can be said to already have had a complex history in the colonies up to this point, including documents produced by the eighteenth-century Pequot bond servant Katherine Garrett, the Mohegan/Wampanoag Moses Paul, and arguably even the Sauk leader Black Hawk, Apess's petition stands as a centerpiece in the textualized struggle for Indigenous rights emerging from the heart of colonial containment. It highlights the manner in which Apess pioneered effective strategies of civil disobedience, including what I refer to hear as "negative work," marshaling the press, public opinion, religious sentiment, and nonviolent resistance to advocate for Native sovereignty in the first half of the nineteenth century, and thereby preparing the way for future movements for people of color in the United States.

The term "negative work" is lifted from the French philosopher Michel Foucault, who, in his *Archeology of Knowledge*, employed this interesting phrase to elaborate on the rhetorical reconfiguration of the genealogical pathways of knowledge he deemed essential to exposing entrenched operations of power.[4] The accrued knowledge of the Western world, in Foucault's estimation, was founded not in incontrovertible fact nudging its way forward from the milky origins of time, so much as an agreed-on series of inscribed traditions that were largely determined and canonized by dominant forces in the present moment. Foucault seems to imply that to contest these constructed formations of historical tradition required the exertion of an opposite, or negative, force, one equal to the task of tracing the nearly imperceptible flow of power even from within its coercive containments.

The relatively few published works of late eighteenth and early nineteenth-century Native American writers such as Samson Occom, Jane

Johnston Schoolcraft, David Cusick, Elias Boudinot, and William Apess demonstrate that for Natives to pick up the pen in this period was to run repeatedly against a formidable wall of history making. The frustrations and complexities of countering colonial histories often mandated taking on identity markers of only a slightly less destructive quality than those being forwarded in the dominant discourse of the times. As such, we find Native authors of this period invariably referring to themselves as "poor Indians," "children of nature," or "sons of the forest," found "sighing and weeping under bondage" to the white man, even while their overall rhetoric surely undercut the utility of such epithets. A major challenge these authors faced was the question of how to articulate the tradition of Natives and Europeans sharing space on this continent in a way that could envision alternative outcomes to the one already preordained and set in stone by colonial reporters. This often meant having to imagine and inscribe an alternative but historically coherent past, drawing heavily on consensual "truths" even while renegotiating the cognitive pathways along which such "truths" were traced by the dominant culture. Almost like taking apart an engine and putting it back together again in a newly imagined form, Native writers were left with the nearly impossible task of trying to reassemble the usable parts of dominant history in a manner that allowed for a more judicious reading of Native presence and agency. This challenge is perhaps best expressed in William Apess's 1836 historical address "Eulogy on King Philip," in which he proposes that "their own words, we presume, they will not deny."[5]

William Apess, for a brief moment in the first half of the nineteenth century, was a major purveyor of this kind of negative work, pushing against the grain of American literature by confronting directly the dominant narrative structures presented in legal statutes, histories, newspapers, novels, and countless other venues that constitute the discourse of settler-colonialism. As an Indigenous American, Apess stood precariously on the margins of early American nationhood, and as such was perfectly positioned to apprehend the fault lines running thick through the young nation's foundation, its self-congratulatory notions of enlightened democratic government, its fever visions of manifest destiny. However, that same marginalized subject position that enabled Native Americans to perceive these faults also typically left them powerless to confront or alter them. In this Apess proved an exception, a bold and radicalizing presence who insinuated himself into channels of mainstream speech and letters, exhorting America to reconsider the long line of cultural productions that served to rationalize and ameliorate the violent disenfranchisement of Native people across this continent.

Much has been written about Apess's involvement in what has come to be known as the 1833 Mashpee Revolt by scholars such as Barry O'Connell,

Robert Warrior, Lisa Brooks, Jean O'Brien, Maureen Konkle, and others, but new information allows us to build on these earlier interpretations and fill in valuable context.[6] I am particularly interested, in this article, about the extent to which we can see Apess pioneering strategies of civil resistance that will prove one of the more effective ways for a marginalized people to contest colonial power in the ensuing decades. Such strategies were, themselves, a species of negative work that aimed to subvert assertions of raw colonial power by contesting them through paradoxically peaceful means. And these strategies first came to fruition as Apess directed his path to the Mashpee Wampanoag Indians of Cape Cod in May 1833.

Loaded down with copies of his publication "The Experiences of Five Christian Indians," literally hot off the presses, the recently ordained Methodist minister made his way along the old Post Road from Boston to Barnstable, presiding over encouraging meetings in places like Scituate, Kingston, and Plymouth. Along the way he conversed with other reform-minded religious leaders and was adequately forewarned of the strained situation in Mashpee before arriving. The habitual disregard of Native rights on reservations was nothing new to Apess. As he observes in his 1835 tract "Indian Nullification," "I knew that no people on earth were more neglected; yet, whenever I attempted to supply their spiritual wants, I was opposed and obstructed by the whites around them, as was the practice of those who dwelt about my native tribe (the Pequots)."[7] Nevertheless, having managed to obtain proper letters of introduction from the ministers he had encountered en route, Apess now presented himself at the home of Phineas Fish, the white pastor assigned to Mashpee. With his canny eye for gaining whatever strategic political edge he could, Apess had already taken the precaution of broadcasting throughout the town his intention to preach at the Mashpee Indian church the very next day; Fish, having perhaps felt his hand forced, ceded Apess his pulpit.

The next morning Apess was brought by carriage to the old Mashpee meetinghouse. He looked upon the simple structure with reverence, appreciating the complex history of the hundred-year-old "sacred edifice" planted in the midst of a "noble forest."[8] The church had been erected in 1757 for the use of the Indians at Mashpee, a relic of the age-old colonial endeavor to bring light to "those poore Indians, who have ever sate in hellish darknesse."[9] No one understood better than Apess the double-edged nature of that mandate and the manner in which policies of presumed Christian benevolence were undergirded with schemes of colonial control and containment. And yet, as with the Pequot and other Native New England communities, the church still presented itself as a center of tradition, a place where the Indigenous community might anchor itself against the relentless tsunami of colonial assault.

Upon entering the meetinghouse, Apess claimed to be struck by the "hue of death" that sat upon the countenances of the congregation. Expecting to encounter, as he says, the "cheerful" aspect of his red brethren, he found instead a strange "paleness . . . upon all their faces." In this passage from "Indian Nullification," one can note Apess's performance of "negative work"—his rhetorical reversal of historical norms that works to position readers before his Indian's looking glass, wherein the pall of death, dislocation, and impermanence typically reserved for descriptions of Natives is strategically turned on its head and reflected outward instead, back at the dominant audience. For in place of the Mashpee Wampanoag he had come to address, Apess finds the meetinghouse usurped by whites, and it is this gathering that bears the twisted hue of impending mortality that he captures in his glass, shifting the scene one hundred and eighty degrees until it suggests a kind of inverted congregation, with the racial preconceptions of the reader becoming crossed in the process. In Apess's rendering, whites become Indians, Indians become whites, and the stereotypical traits commonly ascribed to each are hopelessly confounded. "I must do these Indians the justice," Apess quips, "to say that they performed their parts very well." When in his sermon Apess projects the inconsistency of an Indian meetinghouse devoid of Indians back at his congregation, however, he quickly discovers that "plain dealing was disagreeable to my white auditory."[10]

Following his address, Apess immediately set Fish further on his heels by determining, on the spot, to arrange for a second sermon at the meetinghouse, this time with the local Natives actually in attendance. When the appointed time for the gathering came, rather than offer a conventional sermon Apess opened up the floor for the Mashpee to voice concerns and grievances. He then read to them from his own work, probably relating choice sections from his "Experiences of Five Christian Indians," and in particular his "Indian's Looking Glass," to help illustrate similar abuses experienced in Mashantucket and elsewhere. His reading was met with cries of "truth, truth!" and Apess suddenly felt himself compelled to remain in Mashpee indefinitely to educate himself further on the dynamic there and strategize what might be done about it. As events will show, Apess had been giving a great deal of thought to the subject of Indian rights from both a civil and legal perspective.

Scholars have long marveled at the organizational skills Apess exhibited at Mashpee, but it is becoming more and more apparent how Apess, as an Indian exhorter and preacher, had been pushing the limits of rhetorical discourse and resistance in Native communities for well over a decade by this point. He had noted, directly following his war experiences, how the Haudenosaunee in Canada used tradition, ritual, and formal address within the protocols of wampum exchange to set themselves on even footing with the whites. At the age of nineteen he seems to have involved himself in efforts

FIGURE 2. Reconstructed Mashpee meetinghouse in Mashpee, Massachusetts. Photograph by the author.

to lobby for reform in Mashantucket, where the Pequot petitioned to gain control of the oversight process on their own reservation. As Maureen Konkle has argued, he lectured with the Cherokee and, through this encounter, collected new strategies for asserting nationhood and sovereignty.[11] He had also made inroads into the abolitionist communities of New York and Boston, placing himself in conversation with prominent black speakers of the period, such as David Walker and Maria Stewart, not simply by appropriating their rhetoric, as Anne Maria Dannenberg successfully argues, but because his own life, identity, and politics were so closely entwined with the issues that concerned black activism.[12] Immersing himself in the rhetorical struggle for black rights, he participated in temperance societies for "people of color" and preached on "the subject of slavery" in the same halls where the New England Anti-slavery Societies and anti-colonization agencies met.[13] He had faced oppression in the church and in the courts, had been threatened, libeled, attacked in his own home, and discouraged by countless other means; he had learned from community-level organizers like his Aunt Sally George and Hannah Caleb, but he had also made a study of the grand spiritual narratives of the Haudenosuanee Peacemaker and Christ, until he finally appears to have landed in Mashpee with a fully formed set of strategies that had been honed to perfection over a decade or more of struggle. Although the Mashpee, too, had long maintained legal and personal battles for political autonomy, Apess brought with him a body of knowledge and experience that broke new ground and created new opportunities for political advancement.[14]

Apess asserts in "Indian Nullification" that the causes of prevalent prejudice against his race had "been his study from his childhood upwards."[15] In other words, Apess's commitment to understanding and combating racism had been his lifelong passion, a broken and tormented riddle he had puzzled over since his maternal grandmother first confronted him as a child of four with the question "Do you hate me?"[16] Small wonder, then, that a full decade before Thoreau and the transcendentalists would fully hit upon this ideology, Apess apprehended how the resiliency and effectiveness of a marginalized resistance to power would have to be conducted through the acquired moral authority of directed nonviolent action or civil disobedience. As he continued to lecture the local circuit on the topic of "Indian Affairs," Apess noted, "Many of the advocates of oppression became clamorous, on hearing the truth from a simple Indian's lips, and a strong excitement took place in that quarter. Some feared that an insurrection might break out among the colored people, in which blood might be shed. Some called me an imposter, and others approved of my proceedings." Having already assessed the general temper of the region, Apess was fully aware that those who prophesized "savage" bloodshed were typically the ones most determined to provoke it.[17]

The so-called Mashpee Revolt of 1833 arose in response to the conditions of protectorship under which the Mashpee, like other Natives of New England, were reduced to serfdom on their own land. As elsewhere, the white overseers appointed to look after Mashpee interests had used their positions of authority and power to rent land, sell lumber (Apess estimated some 1,400 cords of wood a year), and parcel out other resources for personal gain. As Apess writes in the "Memorial," "We believe it is the design of the Overseers so to oppress us as to drive all our people from the plantation," and "If we say a word, we are then made out to be highway robbers, condemned, and hauled to the prison, and calumniated to the foulest extent by those very persons, who, we believe, have reaped the benefit of our property."[18] The Indigenous residents found themselves economically marginalized and stripped of all civil liberties, fully dependent on the overseers for nearly every necessity. As Benjamin Hallett, who would serve as counsel for the Mashpee before the Boston Legislature, later observed, the Mashpee overseers

> were vested with full power to regulate the police of the plantation; to establish rules for managing the affairs, interests, and concerns of the Indians and

inhabitants. They may improve and lease the lands . . . regulate their streams, ponds, and fisheries; mete out lots for their improvement; control and regulate absolutely their bargains, contracts, wages, and other dealings; take due care of their poor, and bind out their children to suitable persons, the parents having no voice in the disposition of their children, and there being no appeal, in any exercise of the above unlimited powers, from the overseers to any other tribunal.[19]

In other words, the overseers held power over the Indians equivalent to that of "overlords." If an Indian was deemed to be an "'idler" the overseers had the authority to forcibly bind them into service strictly based on their own arbitrary judgment, a power Hallett rightly characterized as "despotic." No small wonder then that the minister, Fish, might indiscriminately label the whole tribe a nation of idlers, as it gave himself and the overseers even greater authority in managing and suppressing Mashpee lives and ambitions.[20]

Nevertheless, the Mashpee had organized their own church, under the Wampanoag Baptist preacher Blind Jo Amos, in defiance of their appointed minister and had begun to agitate for political autonomy. When Apess arrived, he immediately seems to have *read* the situation and allied himself with Indigenous leaders of Mashpee such as Amos, Ezra Attaquin, and Isaac Coombs. Combining with these local leaders, Apess immediately set in motion a detailed plan to bring the situation at Mashpee to a highly publicized crisis. He began by assisting the Mashpee in the production of a number of formal resolutions, the first of which was to adopt Apess and his family into the tribe. Of his adoption, he explained, "If they wished me to assist them, it would be necessary for them to give me a right to act in their behalf. . . . They must be aware that all the evil reports calumny could invent would be put in circulation against me by the whites interested, and that no means to set them against me would be neglected."[21] A second resolution sent to the Massachusetts governor, the state legislature, and the Corporation of Harvard College, which held the Mashpee Lands in trust, declared the right of the tribe to rule itself given that all men were "born free and equal." It further announced the resolution that no white man would be permitted to cut or carry off wood or hay or any other resource from Mashpee. Anyone caught doing so would be removed from the "plantation." A third document was sent to the Harvard overseers to declare Mashpee dissatisfaction with Fish as their appointed minister. Fish had received tens of thousands of dollars in compensation over the years for preaching to the Indians, and yet had failed, according to the tribe, to administer this trust or convert even one Native.

Part of Apess's scheme was to make these resolutions public, openly proclaiming their intentions to the power structure that lorded over them and also to the press, which Apess had learned to manage so cannily in promoting his own various speaking campaigns. Therefore, sometime in mid-June, Apess and Blind Joe Amos traveled to Boston together to deliver their petition personally to the Massachusetts governor, Levi Lincoln. This done, Apess then notified William Lloyd Garrison, who, in the June 22 edition of *The Liberator*, announced to the world that the "Rev. Wm. Apes has requested us to publish the following resolutions, which he said were passed at a recent meeting of the tribe of Indians at Mashpee."[22] All in all, Apess had set in motion a sure-footed and surprisingly modern media campaign that forced all the issues at Mashpee to a head. Perhaps the most savvy component of Apess's plan, however, was that it established a firm deadline of July 1 for its resolutions to be put into effect. By implementing this time frame, no one could claim to be blindsided by ensuing events. The Mashpee provided themselves moral, though perhaps not legal, cover for their actions.

Apess returned to his newly adopted home at Mashpee around the eighteenth of June, and he and his allies immediately began to draft a constitution, elect representatives, and make other arrangements in preparation for the storm they knew to be coming. Clearly Apess was drawing a page from the handbook of the Cherokee (who had also drawn up their own constitution in a bid to reaffirm their sovereignty a few years prior) and was making a demonstration of Mashpee progress and modernity. Daniel Amos, the well-educated and successful owner of an oyster concern (Apess refers to it as a "coasting" or seafaring business), was recruited for the role of president. For the first time, Apess writes, a form of government, "suited to the spirit and capacity of freeborn sons of the forest," had been put in writing and, if it was modeled in some ways after "the pattern set us by our white brethren," there was one exception in that the Mashpee "were to be held free and equal, *in truth*, as well as in letter." The Mashpee constitution would be almost a negative of the U.S. Constitution, mirroring its language in some respects but reversing its intentionality. They also made public their resolution to keep all those who would deprive the Mashpee of their own resources, those who daily "degraded and robbed" them, off the reservation, noting that the Mashpee wanted "nothing but their rights betwixt man and man."[23]

What followed in the next few days set the local media on its feet for months to come and sent corresponding ripples throughout the national press. As Apess relates it, he was innocently walking through the woods on July 1, 1833, when he encountered two men preparing to haul off a wagonload of wood from the reservation. Of course, Apess did not just happen to be there by chance. July 1 was the date the Mashpee had set for their resolutions to go into effect. A "Nullifying Ordinance" composed in "good handwriting" had been posted at the meetinghouse, upon trees, and at various other places throughout the community, and undoubtedly the Mashpee had organized patrols along the paths leading in and out of the reservation, understanding full well that their assertion to self-governance would be immediately challenged.[24] Apess writes that he "mildly" informed the trespassers of the intentions and views of the tribe, noting it was not their design "to wrong or harm any man in the least," but that, until the matter was resolved with the overseers, all former practices of wood harvesting must cease. He remarks, "I begged them to desist, for the sake of peace; but it was to no purpose." What followed was undoubtedly a tense confrontation. Apess had been beaten back by blunt force in the past, but this time the Mashpee quickly came to his aid.[25] He is careful to note that he had "previously cautioned the Indians to do no bodily injury to any man, unless in their own defense, but to stand for their rights." The Mashpee proceeded to unload the wagon without so much as a "threat or an unkind word." Despite all this, the men, two brothers by the name of Sampson, "used very bitter language at being thus, for the first time, hindered from taking away what had always been as a lawful spoil to them hitherto."[26]

This action, given that it violated an essential privilege of white hegemony, seems to have erupted in precisely the way Apess anticipated it would, and in a matter of days the governor suddenly desired to appoint a time and place for the Mashpee to meet with an agent of the state. The Mashpee, however, quickly fired back a message of their own, insisting that the meeting be held on their own ground at the contested Mashpee meetinghouse, "there being no other place where we should like to see you for an interview."[27] Theresa Strouth Gaul has written that, "to the Mashpee, reclaiming the space of the meetinghouse from the whites became an important symbolic maneuver in their effort to gain the right of self-governance."[28] In effect, it shifted the very ground on which matters stood, converting the meetinghouse from a site of colonial control to a space of Native resistance. Therefore, on July 4, 1833, the two parties assembled, even though the Mashpee had to actually break into their own meetinghouse to gain access to it. This time it was not an inverted congregation seated before Apess, but the true people for whom the meetinghouse had originally been built. The governor's agent, J. J. Fiske, along with John Reed, the sheriff of Barnstable County, a local judge by the name of Marston, the press, and other curious onlookers, piled into a room that was already packed with a hundred or so of the Mashpee. At the insistence of the Natives, time was allowed to fetch the reservation's overseers to ensure that they, too, would hear the grievances to be aired out, and then, in the words of Apess, "they now heard preaching in our meetinghouse as they had never heard before."[29]

Apparently, prior to the meeting, the governor had considered calling out the militia due to hysterical reports by the Indian agent, Gideon Hawley, who insisted "that the Indians were in open rebellion and that blood was likely to be shed." Apess notes that the locals were expecting to encounter wild Indians, armed with "tomahawk and scalping knife; that death and destruction, and all the horrors of a savage war, were impending," and many were led to believe that white people had already been butchered.[30] The county had readied itself for some kind of full-on revolt and was prepared to defend itself with the force of its militia. But calmer heads ultimately prevailed, and the government agent patiently gave audience to the charges of the Mashpee over the course of the day. The surrounding white community conspired to ratchet the prevailing tensions to a kind of fevered pitch with a few, as Apess notes, still portending "bloodshed and murder." These claims of a barely averted riot would echo through the ensuing press reports for months to come, despite Apess's attempts to ridicule the notion of calling out some "fifty or sixty thousand militia; especially when the great strength and power of the Marshpee tribe was considered."[31] Three of the Mashpee Natives, coming in from hunting deer, had brought their broken-down rifles with them into the meetinghouse, and this was willfully interpreted by some as armed insurrection. Such false claims and provocations to violence demonstrate the efficacy of Apess's careful approach, his insistence on full transparency and peaceful means. The slightest gesture of aggression would have justified for the colonial powers every disproportionate countermeasure and was likely to have brought terrible reprisals down on the Natives at Mashpee. As it was, they had just barely averted a militarized crackdown.

One wonders if Apess not only precisely orchestrated the Mashpee resistance but actually planned for it all to come to a dramatic head on the day that America celebrated the birth of its democratic institutions. Having been told that their claims were illegal, Apess stood up to address the agents of state power, speaking "with an energy that alarmed some of the whites present considerably."[32] He reminded them that their laws were unconstitutional and stripped Native people of their rights as citizens. He reminded Massachusetts of its own revolutionary legacy—how, when faced with the crushing weight of an oppressive regime that refused to address their grievances, they at length "determined to try some other method." He recollected for his audience how their forefathers had thrown British tea into the harbor (dressed as Indians no less, though Apess leaves this detail aside) and ultimately fought a terrible war, "that your fathers sealed with their blood a covenant made with liberty." He also reminded those assembled that the Mashpee themselves had fought alongside the colonists in that long-ago war, furnishing them "with some of her bravest men to fight your battles. Yes, by the side of your fathers they fought and bled, and now their blood cries to you from the ground to restore that liberty so unjustly taken from us by their sons."[33] The result of

Mashpee loyalty and patriotism, Apess exhorted his listeners, had been imposed bondage, a people kept in darkness, ignorance, and vice. Rising to a rhetorical pitch, he exclaimed that, rather than set up schools, as was promised, the Mashpee children were "put out to service . . . Many of those who held them in servitude used them more like dogs than human beings, feeding them scantily, lodging them hard, and clothing them with rags." Apess's own childhood memories and traumas may have been rising to the fore—recollections of abuse and betrayal he had suffered as a bond servant intermingled with the threat of violence, the horrors of war. Bringing it all home, he continued, "Such, I believe, has always been the case about Indian reservations. I had a sister who was slavishly used and half starved; and I have not forgotten, nor can I ever forget, the abuse I received myself." Apess concluded by declaring to his audience that the Fourth of July was no day of celebration to the Indian, but a day of mourning and lamentation, a sore annual reminder of the ills Native peoples continued to suffer.[34]

No doubt, it was a fiery and disconcerting history lesson for the white people in attendance. For his troubles Apess was promptly arrested, and apparently some sort of examination was held that evening at the nearby Cotuit courthouse in which a hostile township gathered to ensure "justice" was done. Apess recalls that "excitement ran very high," and he intimated that if the white mob had its way, "I doubt not that I should have been ruined forever." In fact, had he not taken such meticulous preparations and precautions prior to his arrest, there can be little doubt that this (proto?)-lynching would have been carried out. Still, he went along peaceably, insisting, "I was glad they had taken me into custody, as it would lead to an investigation of the whole ground in dispute."[35] In a sense, Apess foresaw that jail time under these circumstances performed a valuable kind of negative work. It was one thing for such abuses of power to happen in isolation (as they so often did on Native reservations), safely out of view of the public eye, but for someone to be arrested on the Fourth of July before a large audience, with the press in attendance, for the crime of trespassing on one's own property no less, seemed to strain the very limits of nineteenth-century democratic discourse, even if the "trespasser" in question was an Indian. From his established position of moral high ground, Apess used his night in jail as a means of holding up American democracy itself before his Indian's looking glass, and the reflection ultimately proved unsettling to a number of people in relatively high places.[36]

Apess would have been obliged to spend many months in jail awaiting trial had his bail, which had been set at $200, not been paid by Lemuel Ewer, a white former treasurer of the tribe. Even this expediency seems to have been mapped out in advance by Apess, but the townspeople, still wanting blood, were blindsided by the event. Apess did not think it an exaggeration to claim that they "bellowed like mad bulls and spouted like whales gored mortally by harpoons" when they heard of his release. Sprung from prison, Apess was now, in the words of certain townspeople, "the leader of the Nullifiers at Mashpee [and] going about the plantation in full command of all its disposable force and treasure, ordering every white man he meets to quit, and not to touch a stick of wood, under penalty of being dealt with according to his Proclamation." Such a hyperbolic and unintentionally ironic account depicted Apess as a kind of Native Napoleon leading a sizeable force of combatants, rather than an ordained Methodist minister, lobbying for Indian use of Indian land through peaceful acts of resistance.[37] The local press, which stood in strident opposition to this assault on Barnstable's long-standing usages, was forced into untenable stances, complaining that somehow Native people were not entitled to the use of their own property, their own resources or "treasure." The inherent stinginess of such claims proved additional fodder for Apess, who happily published many of these tirades in the friendly *Boston*

FIGURE 3. Illustration of the Barnstable County Courthouse in mid-1800s, which hangs in the present-day courthouse in Barnstable, Massachusetts. Photograph by the author.

Advocate (and later in his "Indian Nullification"), gently alluding to the lack of both Christian and democratic principles in such rantings.

Nevertheless, the majority of newspapers ran alarming headlines declaring "Hostilities Commenced in Mashpee," "Indian War in Massachusetts!" and "Trouble in the Wigwam."[38] It would be easy to understand how people removed from the actual situation might think a minor Indian revolt had flared up, and the eagerly hyperbolic nature of such headlines speaks volumes to the type of reporting that would be generated by the struggles of Western Indigenous nations in years to come. A New Jersey paper, getting wind of the story, suggested that Apess, "a half-breed . . . who sometime since went about the country in the character of a preacher . . . wishes to be made Governor of his nation. He has stirred his people up to commit various depredations in that vicinity."[39] Another paper exclaimed, "The Indians, inflamed by the appeals of Apes, are now ready for a nullification of all the state laws."[40] One newspaper reported that the Mashpee were "lead on by one Apes, a well known half breed preacher of the itinerant order." He was described as having "considerable shrewdness and talent as a preacher . . . and, as is supposed, has had a material influence in organizing the disaffected Indians."

In these statements, and many others, the colonial ambivalence that attaches itself to the project of Native assimilation is laid bare. The Mashpee were of little concern to the presiding colonial power as long as they remained in abject poverty and lacked the tools to compete or exercise even a shred of agency in the economic straightjacket designed for their "improvement." But as soon as Natives were allowed to become educated or develop their own talents through the profession of Christianity, or by any other means, they became a viable threat to the community at large. The dominant culture had long maintained that Indians were inherently incapable of cultivating such "arts," but Apess's intervention at Mashpee quickly teased out the falsehood of such claims, making available instead the explicit intention to deprive Native peoples of such "mischief-making" abilities. The very talents that were supposed to "civilize" the Indian, on the contrary, rendered him "shrewd," "wily," and "unprincipled," making of him a treasonous "imposter" merely for exercising those talents to the advantage of himself and his community. No wonder, at the start of "Indian Nullification," that Apess, the preacher, could wryly announce himself still "the same unbelieving Indian that he ever was."[41]

But the hall of mirrors abuses persisted. Apess and two of his Mashpee cohorts, Jacob Pocknett and Charles de Grasse, were charged with using "force and arms" to "unlawfully" and "riotously . . . assemble and gather themselves," causing "great noise, riot, tumult, and disturbance . . . to the great terror of the people" of the Commonwealth of Massachusetts.[42] When Apess was sentenced to his month in jail in September of that year, white reporters remarked that "in our opinion, never was there a more just conviction, or a milder sentence." This despite the fact that potential jurors, voicing sympathy for the Natives, were released without explanation and a witness in the case, Judge Marston, openly "swore in court that he thought Indians were an inferior race of men, and, of course, were incapable of handling their own affairs."[43] The newspapers largely concurred, proclaiming that the Natives at Mashpee were "as helpless and incapable of taking care of themselves as little children or slaves."[44] Apess had little recourse but to reflect these pale inconsistencies, formed of the logics of oppression, back at his audience in hope that, somehow, they might give pause. He maintained that "since this affair took place, I have been kindly informed by a gentleman of Barnstable that my punishment was not half severe enough. I replied that, in my mind, it was no punishment at all; and I am yet to learn what punishment can dismay a man conscious of his own innocence."[45]

And it was in this spirit of enlightenment, within the rank and suffocating confines of the old Barnstable County Jail (the building still stands today, although it has been moved from its original location behind the courthouse),[46] that Apess took pen in hand and began to compose the opening lines of the Marshpee "Memorial," writing, "Where it is expected, by the inhabitants of this Commonwealth, that justice and equity will reign in the hearts of all— that national prejudices and peculiar feelings, attending religionists, will not be permitted to rule the hearts of any—but, that every enlightened and judicious Representative, as we trust they all are that compose this Body, will be willing to do as they would wish to be done by; we wish this Honorable Body to consider our oppression."[47] Such a calm and enlightened response, from an allegedly cunning and riot-mongering Indian, further rankled Apess's opponents. They unexpectedly found themselves cast in the role of frothing tyrants accusing noble Socrates of corrupting the youth of Athens. But perhaps most galling of all for Apess's detractors was the fact that, upon his release, he continued to travel freely about the country, preaching, lecturing, and "endeavoring to enlist public sympathy in his favor . . . stigmatizing and calumniating the Court and Jury who tried and convicted him, and flinging his sarcasms and sneers upon the Attorney and Jury who indicted him. And for all this, he is receiving the applause of an audience who must be ignorant of his character; and blinded by the pretenses of this imposter."[48]

As the above commentary implies, Apess, as soon as he was released from prison, began publicizing the abuses at Mashpee in a remarkable and tireless campaign, stretching from Rhode Island to Connecticut and then back up through Worcester, Springfield, as far north as Concord, New Hampshire, and then back down through Salem, Massachusetts, all in roughly two months' time. It is difficult to imagine anyone, no less a member of the oppressed

FIGURE 4. Old Barnstable County Jail in Barnstable, Massachusetts, where William Apess most likely spent a month in prison for "inciting a riot." Photograph by the author.

class, with the energy, will, and organizational skills to manage such a campaign with virtually no support, financial or otherwise. And the response was largely positive. The *Rhode Island Republican* reported that "the son of the forest told many historical truths which could not be very palatable to those who term themselves civilized. He spoke charitably, fearlessly, but unfavorably of the conduct of the white Missionaries among them."[49] And the *New Hampshire Observer* observed, "The object of the address was to awaken public sentiment to the expediency of a measure which will be proposed to the Legislature at its coming session" to extend the rights of the Indians.[50] Apess ended his whirlwind publicity tour in Boston, where, along with his "Marshpee Deputation," consisting of Daniel Amos and Deacon Coombs, he packed Boylston Hall and apparently brought the crowd to its feet with what the *Barnstable Patriot* sourly described as his "ribaldry, misrepresentation and nonsense."[51] One might imagine that Apess almost exhausted his rivals as he persisted in pressing the matter coming up before the Massachusetts Legislature.

In mid-January of 1834 the Mashpee delegation finally presented their "Memorial" to the House of Representatives in Boston. All three of the Mashpee leaders spoke, beginning with Deacon Coombs. *The Liberator*, which had taken a special interest in the case by this point, provided commentary, noting that Coombs was brief but "somewhat indefinite" in his remarks. Coombs was followed by the newly elected Mashpee president, Daniel Amos, who gave a short account of himself, his years spent traveling the globe on whaling boats, and his pride in never having been imprisoned for either crime or debt, apparently a rare achievement under the Mashpee regime as it existed. *The Liberator* wrote that Amos's words were few and his "language broken." These were not men who, whatever their strengths, were practiced at performing in the halls of power before all-white audiences. But when Apess rose to speak, we are told that he was "fearless, comprehensive and eloquent." He "illustrated the manner in which extortions were made from the poor Indians, and plainly declared that they wanted their rights as men and as freemen," and "endeavored to prove that, under such laws and such overseers, no people could rise from their degradation." Apess demanded to know by what right the Mashpee were held under such obligations and made what *The Liberator* referred to as some "dexterous and pointed thrusts at the whites for their treatment of the sons of the forest since the time of the pilgrims." Regardless of whether everyone was as inspired by Apess's speech as the correspondent for *The Liberator*, Apess probably prompted more than one legislator to shake off his ambivalence to the racially motivated laws by which Native people were governed. *The Liberator* concluded that "the cries of the Indians have reached their ears, and we trust affected their hearts."[52]

Apess's remarkable strategy of peaceful resistance in 1833 worked to nullify or negate, through public exposure in a provocatively heightened environment, the series of harmful practices and undemocratic abuses that had been codified into law over time to the detriment of Native peoples. Apess maintains that the plight of the Natives at Mashpee and elsewhere had nothing to do with racial destiny, but was a result of unjust laws "calculated to drive the tribes from their possessions and annihilate them as a people; and I presume they would work the same effect upon any other people; for human nature is the same under skins of all colors. Degradation is degradation, all the world over."[53] By conducting his lifelong study of racism and meticulously observing its operation within the dominant power grid, Apess was able to anticipate and, at least temporarily, short-circuit its mechanisms.

It should come as little surprise, however, that these same manifestations of power, which work to maintain dominant relations and discourses

MISCELLANEOUS.

MEMORIAL OF THE MARSHPEE INDIANS—January, 1834.

To the Honorable the Senate and House of Representatives, in General Court assembled:—

Where it is expected, by the inhabitants of this Commonwealth, that justice and equity will reign in the hearts of all—that national prejudices and peculiar feelings, attending religionists, will not be permitted to rule the hearts of any—but, that every enlightened and judicious Representative, as we trust they all are that compose this Body, will be willing to do as they would wish to be done by; and we wish this Honorable Body to consider our oppression. While ye are filled with the fat of our fathers' land, and enjoy your liberties without molestation, will not this Honorable Body be as benevolent to us, poor Marshpee Indians, who are sighing and weeping under bondage, as ye are to the poor Cherokees? and have we not groaned under the weight of degradation long enough? Are ye willing that we should go down to the grave with sorrow and disgrace, as our fathers have before us, when we are willing to try to take care of ourselves? And we fear that our petitions have been laid aside without much notice heretofore; and our complaints that come before common Courts, as well as this Honorable Body, have been looked at as being mere cyphers. But we hope that this indifferent spirit is dying away, and that the true spirit of the Christian philanthropist is beginning to reign in the hearts of the people, and those who compose their Legislative Bodies. If so, may we not expect to share a part, although we are looked upon to be but poor and insignificant creatures? And why are we so?—Because we have not had the opportunity; no particular pains have been taken to instruct us; we are wanting the same privilege that your Honors have, in order to make us what we ought to be, good and wholesome citizens; and we do say that we can never rise to a state of cultivation, under existing circumstances. We can assure your Honors that there is not one enlightened and respectable Indian upon the plantation, that wants Overseers or the present minister, Mr. Phineas Fish. We say that all of our rulers, and he who is said to be our preacher, were placed here amongst us without our consent; and it has been the policy of these interested men to work upon the feelings of some of our most ignorant and dissipated men and women, to keep us divided. We are sure that none but those who are in the habit of drinking, and such as do not attend meeting any where, would, or have signed his paper, to hear him preach; and many of them have said they did not know what it contained. Why we mention this, is, because we have discharged him, and passed Resolutions that we will not hear him preach; and we are of the same mind still. We do not believe he cares any thing for our souls, but the fleece we believe he loves well. If he did care for us, we believe that twenty years would have been long enough to have secured our confidence, and reared to himself a respectable church and society; but he has not a male member belonging to his church that has one drop of the royal, or real native blood in him. We therefore wish to have him removed peaceably from our borders, by this Honorable Body, who we believe will try to do us justice, especially when your Honors hear the Bill of Complaints, laid before

you by us, your humble petitioners, the Marshpee Indians.

Bill of Complaints.

Honored Gentlemen:

It is not possible for us to give you a full statement of wrongs that we have to suffer, in consequence of having Overseers to manage for us, who, we believe, felt more interested for themselves than for us; and we purpose only to give you a few statements of facts, such as generally can be sustained by us, whose fathers were the original proprietors of the soil where this stately edifice now stands, and whose laws have ground us to the dust.

First: We are certain that the Marshpee Government is unconstitutional, and far transcends the Constitution of the country, and of course is extremely defective and injurious to us as a people.

This law was imposed upon us by the consent of a few of our forefathers, aided by the designing white man, whose artful voice inspired in their breasts cheering hopes that their property should be secured to them, and they one day should be equalized and respected with the white man; for we have no idea that our fathers would have bound us, so as to take away all of our rights from us, for Indians have too much affection for each other, to use that kind of treachery towards their children. We believe they would as soon given up their own lives, but for the promise of bettering their condition, and that of their children. But since our fathers fell asleep, we have heard but little about law or liberty, or any thing else, but imposition upon the back of imposition, and in the following manner:

We have been obliged to submit to a hereditary government, as we believe, son succeeding father, and brothers brothers, to the Overseership: for this lineage of government has been kept up for nearly forty years, and we think it is time for a change. Neither do we think it right for us to abide by an unconstitutional law, made by our fathers forty years ago, and others, meaning the whites, who had their own interest in view, we believe, altogether—for our sufferings by that law have been immense.

For we as a people have not been permitted to worship God according to our own views and feelings, and as conscience dictated us; for the preacher that was placed among us was altogether by the power of the Overseers, without asking one of us whether we would like to have him or no, and of course ordained without the particular knowledge of us—to be supported out of our property for life, without being any service to us, or our consent to have it so. Is the like known any where amongst other towns in this State peopled by white men? This preacher has moved principally amongst white people, and taught them, whilst we have been compelled to support him, and sigh in bondage; and the presumption is, that the whites have had three times the benefit of the preacher and our funds, that we have ourselves.

This government also admits two ministerial farms upon our plantation, occupied by Phineas Fish and Gideon Holly. Mr. Holly succeeded his father, who was Preacher and Overseer—the latter now being Overseer—and these two gentlemen occupy about fifteen hundred acres of our best land, and do us no essential service whatever, but contrariwise, a bill of expense, and as destructive to us as a famine would be, in gradually wasting away the people before it.

We have been kept out of our own meet-

ing house and school houses till very recently;—have had no privileges to hold any kind of meetings in them, although we should have been glad to have done something to improve our minds, in the way of meetings, either for debating societies or the worship of God; and our meeting house has been vacated for nearly ten years by most all of our people. We have no idea it would average ten of a Sabbath, and our meeting house is almost worn out by white people. It is not actually fit for respectable people to meet in. When we wanted a meeting for the benefit of the town, the Overseers have appointed them in other towns, and incurred a large bill of expense in this way, while they have insulted and pushed us out of doors: our women and our widows neglected, and our orphan children crying for bread. The expense has been very great in this way of doing business, for they (the Overseers) generally had a fine dinner, and we believe the expense came altogether out of our funds. The General Court provides but three for us to pay, but they (the Overseers) provide three or four more for us to pay, and they all find such good picking, they are loth to leave us; but we should rather not maintain them any longer, for we do not see that they are any service to us in raising us in the world; but we find the same deep stain of degradation hanging upon our persons and property, all apparently devoted to the will of unholy and unprincipled men, that prowl around our borders.

This present government admits all the scum of the white population amongst us that cannot remain in those towns where your Honors dwell, and our young people are not slow to learn their vices; and it is impossible, under existing laws, to have it otherwise. It also admits those characters to more privileges upon our lands than ourselves, and if we say a word, we are then made out highway robbers, condemned, and hauled to the prison, and calumniated to the foulest extent by those very persons, who, we believe, have reaped the benefit of our property.

It furthermore withholds from us the necessaries of life that many of our people might enjoy; for it is a fact, that it gives power to the Overseers to take from us our grain if they choose, which they in fact have done. Whilst their husbands were absent at sea, our wives, and mothers, and sisters, would go to the Overseers for assistance. Sometimes they would hear, and at other times they would not; and when they did, they would give them a writing or order for the value of twenty-five or fifty cents, and then send them nine or ten miles to procure the value of it, and this as often as they go. We set too much by our women and children to have them served in this way any longer.

It also spoils our fishing, for white people think they have as good a right to our plantations and fishing privileges as ourselves, and of course throng us, and injure us all more or less.

This law also declares our whole plantation to be a public highway, and the inhabitants to be thieves and robbers, according to the plea made by Mr. Warren, the District Attorney, appointed by the Governor and Council; and this too, for merely inquiring into our rights, and shuts us up in prison. This law discourages our people, so that many of them have left their homes, and say they will not live under such oppressive laws, (the Overseers never encouraging industry,) and we believe it is the design of the Overseers so to oppress us as to drive all our people from the plantation. So that this law only adds disgrace to disgrace, and grinds us to the dust. The Overseers have also incurred many needless expenses by hiring other houses to have our meetings in, when we had them of our own, and appointed several men to do our business, and paid them out of our funds, when we might have done it ourselves; such as mending roads, carting wood, it being far from market, and by the time the poor got it there who had no team of their own, they had but little indeed left for themselves.

There are several tons of our most excellent ship timber that is cut and carried off yearly, and other valuable timber that we do not want cut; for we do not know but we shall want to build a ship ourselves, if we get able; and if not, we want the profit of it, for we have never learnt that any account has been rendered for any of it, to any one. Our cedar swamps share the same fate. Many of our most enlightened and virtuous men have been and cut and corded wood for themselves, and the Overseers have taken it from us, and sold it to whom they pleased; and even torn our fencing stuff from our fences, and carried it off, and sold it, and all the satisfaction we could get was, hold your peace, or you shall have nothing. This law admits just as much wood as the Overseers are a mind to cut and sell, and we believe it will average yearly, not less than twelve hundred cords per year of cord wood, besides other wood that is sold for fires around about us; and if we want any we have to pay one dollar per cord for pine wood, and one dollar fifty cents for oak, out of our commons, and then sell it to just such men as the Overseers say, and to no others; and we think that such a tax is enormous, to pay for our own wood.

It also admits the white people to take away from our meadows all the hay, if they choose, leaving only enough for one cow, if any of us happen to have one; and if we have any more stock, we have to go ten or twelve miles to cut hay upon shares, or buy it. This we are compelled to do, or our cattle must suffer and die; and from these men we have no encouragement to raise stock, or be enterprising in any way whatever. It also admits the white people to greater privileges in possessing our pastures, than ourselves; for our wood, and hay, and pastures, are all set up at auction, and the white people have the means to out-bid us, and take every thing from us; and the Overseers will not give us any chance for our lives, in these things. As to the poor, we are all poor together; for we, in general, take care of ourselves in farming, hunting, fishing, and some in going to sea. We have some poor that are not able to maintain themselves. The Overseers assist a little in helping us to take care of them, but if we did not help them they must suffer; and in the manner things are conducted, it makes it hard for all. If things were conducted differently, it would make it easy for all; but we cannot have it otherwise under present laws and task-masters, although we believe there has been enough to maintain our poor, and if we had what has been squandered, as we believe from circumstantial evidence, we all should be in a better condition than we are now.

How much the proceeds of our plantation would amount to, yearly, we are not able to give an accurate account, but from circumstances that we have had before us, we think we can come somewhere near it. We will say twelve hundred cords of wood, at nine shillings per cord, amount to eighteen hundred dollars; two hundred tons of hay, at four dollars per ton, amount to eight hundred dollars; there are twelve farms, at fourteen dollars per farm, amount to one hundred and sixty eight dollars; we have much pasture, we will say one hundred dollars for that, although we think we are within bounds; ship timber, we will put one hundred more; the whole amounting to twenty nine hundred and sixty eight dollars. We think the property ought to fetch that, certainly.

How much our expenses would be, when all told, we are not able to account accurately, but we believe we can come very near it. Our schools are kept in the following manner: in the winter we have two, the teachers receiving pay from twelve to fourteen dollars for three months each; in the summer we have two female teachers, they receiving one dollar per week for about sixteen weeks, making one hundred and ten dollars. There are seven poor, we believe, assisted by the Overseers; three are supported principally from the fund; for them is paid one dollar per week out of the funds, the others receive from two shillings to fifty cents, making about two hundred and fifty six dollars for their table expenses. As to clothing, they get but a little; they get a suit of coarse factory cloth, amounts to four or five dollars per suit, we will say thirty dollars; the Overseers let us have a few boards and shingles, to stop a few holes in our old houses, we would say it would be one hundred and fifty per year. We have a doctor that comes amongst us; we should presume he received about seventy five per year. The Overseers pay out of our funds about twenty five dollars per year, for mending roads; the whole of the expenses amounting to six hundred and forty six dollars per year.

We think there is a great contrast between our expenses and the income of our plantation. But how much the Overseers charge for their services we know not, (we presume they take care of themselves) but they take the remainder—the funds are generally all away.

And now, Honored Gentlemen, we think we have been in slavery long enough. As to the Overseers, we have no confidence in them whatever—we do not believe they have dealt honestly by us, and we believe if they have a mind to swindle, none has a better chance than themselves, for they keep debt and credit, and how easy it is for them to conspire together to do us wrong, if they choose! At any rate, after suffering so much, we are jealous of them, and do assure your Honors we want them no longer. The Overseers say there is a general satisfaction amongst us, and that the excitement is of recent date. But we say, for more than five years there has been a very great dissatisfaction amongst us, and if we should add five more to it, it would be nothing out of the way: and it appears from the movements of the Overseers, that their influence in past times respecting our petitions, has been against us—that we have been represented as being a set of indolent, drunken Indians; but we say it is not the case—for many, very many of our people, are temperate, and sober, and industrious, and are willing to do, if they (the Overseers) would not prevent us. And now, if we wish to take care of ourselves, we cannot see why we may not have that privilege.

We presume the above charges and complaints are sufficient to warrant us a redress, and the abrogation of an unconstitutional law. If not, we have no doubt but the Overseers would strip us of all our living in five years more; and we have no doubt but it was the intention of the Overseers to strip us from our all; and we most solemnly believe we have been wronged out of thousands and tens of thousands of dollars in the course of this Overseership—every man seeking his own wealth instead of another man's.

Honor to whom honor is due, custom to whom custom, fear to whom fear; and we would render therefore unto Cæsar the things that belong to Cæsar, and unto God the things that are God's.

Therefore we can say there is one item in the law that is good—that is this: that no one should be permitted to sell his land without a mutual consent, and we wish that item still to be retained for a few years, till our people become more enlightened, for many of them are ignorant in making trades, although we are happy to state to this Honorable Body, that we have many who are capable of doing business any where, and any kind of common and merchantable or seafaring business—to navigate a ship to any part of the globe.

And now we want a chance to instruct those who are ignorant, before that item is removed, for there are many that would not hesitate to strip us, who are ignorant, of our last morsel—and we shall consider it a favor indeed to have that item remain, and give us a chance for our lives in acting for ourselves.

And we do not want Overseers—as for them, we want them discharged, and never want their names mentioned amongst us again. And we would say of the preacher, Mr. Fish, we think no more of him than we do of the Overseers, believing they are all linked in together; and we want him discharged, for we want our house to meet in ourselves.

Yours Most Obediently,
THE MARSHPEE INDIANS.

We, the Marshpee Tribe,

Also pray for a grant of the liberties of the Constitution, to form a Municipal Code of Laws amongst ourselves, that we may have a government that will be useful to us as a people; for we are sure we have never had any since our original Sachem fathers fell asleep.

Also, we desire that this Honorable Body would grant us the privilege of choosing an Attorney, to advise with us in our municipal regulations, and to instruct us still further in the laws; and this gentleman to be chosen yearly, or as long as we may deem it proper for the safety of the Town, and to be supported out of our funds (his expenses).

We wish that some provision could be made for the appointment of one or two Magistrates amongst us.

We also pray, that our Town may be incorporated and called Marshpee.

We have made these requests, believing the white men are knowing to our oppression in the general; and that if such laws are still enforced upon us, it is still murdering us by inches. And we do not know why the people of this Commonwealth want to cruelize us any longer, for we are sure that our fathers *fought, bled, and died for the liberties* of their now weeping and suffering children, the same as did your fathers for their children, whom ye are, who are now sitting to make laws to suit your own convenience, and secure your liberties. *Oh, white man! white man!* the blood of our fathers, spilt in the Revolutionary War, cries from the ground of our native soil, to break the chains of oppression, and let our children *go free.*

Yours we are, most respectfully,
THE MARSHPEE INDIANS.

FIGURE 5. "Memorial of the Marshpee Indians" as it appears in February 1, 1834, edition of *The Liberator*. Courtesy of the American Antiquarian Society.

of white privilege, can be seen very much in operation today—when we see unarmed people of color gunned down by police officers; when protesters in urban centers like New Orleans, Ferguson, or Baltimore are tarred as looters, thugs, and rioters when they attempt to lobby against entrenched civil injustices; when Native peoples are regarded as disturbers of the peace or in opposition to modernity because they resist the continued exploitation of resources on their land, the pipelines, and oil-extraction processes that endanger the ecological well-being and continued livelihood of the inhabitants for the short-term interests of a few energy companies. The narrative is always set to tilt toward the operation and flow of power, the tools of media always ready to reaffirm the age-old racial stereotypes that seamlessly shift blame to the oppressed. But for a moment in time William Apess was able to cannily reverse the flow, through the application of "negative work," attaining the moral high ground even as the colonial powers thrust him in the Barnstable County Jail, charging him with inciting a riot that never actually took place. From this epicenter of injustice Apess began to pen the words that would lead to the reclaiming of basic rights of self-governance for the Mashpee. As he exhorts in the "Memorial of the Marshpee Indians," drafted during his month of jail time, "We think we have been in slavery too long."

DREW LOPENZINA is an assistant professor of early American and Native American literature at Old Dominion University. He is the author of *Through an Indian's Looking Glass: A Cultural Biography of William Apess, Pequot.*

Notes

All William Apess quotations (unless otherwise indicated) are taken from either "Indian Nullification," "A Son of the Forest," or "Eulogy on King Philip," from William Apess, *On Our Own Ground: The Complete Writings of William Apess, a Pequot*, ed. Barry O'Connell (Amherst: University of Massachusetts Press, 1992).

1. "Indian Nullification," 206; and "The Marshpee Indians," *The Liberator* (Boston), January 25, 1834, p. 15.

2. "Memorial of the Mashpee Indians," *The Liberator* (Boston), February 1, 1834, p. 20.

3. American Antiquarian Society, Ira Moore Barton Papers, Box 1, Folder 1, "Committee on Affairs of Mashpee Indians, Feb. 5, 1834."

4. Michel Foucault, *The Archeology of Knowledge and the Discourse on Language*, trans. A. M. Sheridan Smith (New York: Pantheon Books, 1972), 21.

5. "Eulogy on King Philip," 280.

6. I refer in particular to important chapters in Apess, *On Our Own Ground*, ed. O'Connell, xiii—lxxvii; Robert Warrior, *The People and the Word: Reading Native Nonfiction* (Minneapolis: University of Minnesota Press, 2005), 1—47; Lisa Brooks, *The Common Pot: The Recovery of Native Space in the Northeast*

(Minneapolis: University of Minnesota Press, 2005), 163–97; Jean O'Brien, *Firsting and Lasting: Writing Indians Out of Existence in New England* (Minneapolis: University of Minnesota Press, 2010), 145–99; and Maureen Konkle, *Writing Indian Nations: Native Intellectuals and the Politics of Historiography, 1827–1863* (Chapel Hill: North Carolina Press, 2004), 97–159.

7. "Indian Nullification," 169.

8. Ibid., 170.

9. Such language was often employed by the first New England settlers in their desultory efforts to convert the local Natives. This particular quote comes from a tract known as "New England's First Fruits," in *The Eliot Tracts*, ed. Michael P. Clark (Westport, Conn.: Praeger, 2003), 58.

10. "Indian Nullification," 170–71.

11. See Konkle, *Writing Indian Nations*, 99–100.

12. See Anne Marie Dannenberg "'Where Then Shall We Place the Hero of the Wilderness?': William Apess's Eulogy on King Philip and Doctrines of Racial Destiny," in *Early Native American Writing: New Critical Essays*, ed. Helen Jaskoski (New York: Cambridge University Press, 1996), 66–82.

13. From June through August of 1832, Apess had a running appointment at Franklin Hall, on 16 Franklin Street in Boston, where he preached every Sunday, often twice a day. Among the topics for his sermons, as advertised in *The Liberator*, was "an Address on the subject of Slavery." Running concurrently with Apess's Sunday sermons was a series of meetings called by the New England Anti-slavery Society to debate the subject of the colonization of slaves to Africa. Franklin Hall seems to have been the designated podium of the abolitionist movement in Boston, and among its noted speakers was Maria Stewart, who delivered her most famous address, "Why Sit Ye Hear and Die?" in this space in September of that same year. *The Liberator* (Boston), July 7, 1832, p. 107; "A Solemn Appeal," *The Liberator* (Boston), June 9, 1832, p. 90; *The Liberator* (Boston), September 15, 1832, p. 147.

14. The experiences noted here are further elaborated on in my forthcoming work *Through an Indian's Looking Glass: A Cultural Biography of William Apess, Pequot*, with the University of Massachusetts Press.

15. "Indian Nullification," 168.

16. "A Son of the Forest," 6.

17. "Indian Nullification," 177.

18. "Memorial of the Mashpee Indians," 20.

19. Benjamin F. Hallett, *Rights of the Marshpee Indians* (Boston: J. Howe Printer, 1834), 13.

20. Ibid., 15.

21. "Indian Nullification," 173.

22. "Marshpee Indians," *The Liberator* (Boston), issue 25, June 22, 1833, p. 99.

23. See "Indian Nullification," 178–80. See also Earl Mills, Sr., and Alicja Mann, *Son of Mashpee: Reflections of Chief Flying Eagle, a Wampanoag* (North Falmouth, Mass.: Word Studio, 1996), 10.

24. "Trouble in the Wigwam," *Columbian Centinel* (Boston), July 7, 1833, p. 1. According to the *Barnstable Patriot*, the "Nullifying Ordinance" read as follows:

"Having been heretofore degraded and despised, and a much abused people, we have determined to make our own laws and govern ourselves. For this purpose we have seen the Governor, who has no objection to our governing our own affairs. This is to give notice we have resolved if any person is seen on our plantation after the first of July, carting or cutting wood, without our leave, or in any way trespassing upon our lands, they shall be bound hand and foot and thrown off. Signed Daniel Amos, President, Moses Amos, Secretary."

25. William Apess's home in Mashantucket, Connecticut, was broken into in the spring of 1831 and Apess was severely beaten, presumably for his efforts at reform on the Pequot plantation. See Connecticut Archives RG003 New London County Court Files, Box 3, Folder 18.

26. "Indian Nullification," 181.

27. Ibid., 182.

28. Theresa Strouth Gaul, "Dialogue and Public Discourse in William Apess's 'Indian Nullification,'" *American Transcendental Quarterly* 15, no. 4 (2001): 281.

29. "Indian Nullification," 182.

30. Ibid., 180–81.

31. Ibid., 183.

32. Ibid., 184.

33. Ibid., 195.

34. Ibid., 187.

35. Ibid., 189.

36. Ibid., 187.

37. "Massachusetts Indians," *The Globe* (Washington, D.C.), July 18, 1833, issue 30, column B (originally reported in the *Boston Advocate*).

38. "Hostilities Commenced in Marshpee," *Baltimore Gazette and Daily Advertiser*, July 10, 1833, 80:13242, p. 2; "Indian War in Massachusetts!" *Hampshire Gazette* (North Hampton, N.H.), July 10, 1833, 47:2445, p. 3. "Trouble in the Wigwam," *Columbia Centinel* (Boston), July 13, 1833, p. 1.

39. "Indians in Massachusetts," *The Jerseyman* (Morristown, N.J.), July 24, 1833, p. 3.

40. "Marshpee," *Philadelphia Inquirer*, July 11, 1833, p. 2.

41. "Indian Nullification," 169.

42. Barnstable Court House Index of Defendants, A–K 1827–1886, Case 633, "Commonwealth vs. William Apess."

43. "Indian Nullification," 202, 227–29. Benjamin Hallett also notes that "every person on the jury, who said he thought the Indians ought to have their liberty, was set aside." Ibid., 167.

44. "The Marshpee Indians," *Trumpet and Universalist Magazine* (Boston), August 17, 1833, 6:8, p. 31.

45. "Indian Nullification," 203.

46. The Old Barnstable County Jail was replaced by a newer prison built sometime in the 1830s. While it is possible that its construction was finished by time Apess was sent to jail, Benjamin Hallett would write in the April 17, 1838, edition of the *Boston Press and Advocate*, "We understand that the elegant and costly building known by the name Barnstable Jail is now unoccupied. The first

one who applies will probably have the uncommon privilege of selecting his or her room" (1).

47. "Memorial of the Mashpee Indians," 20.

48. "Indian Nullification," 227–28.

49. "Monday; Indian; Preacher; Baptist; Gospel," *Rhode Island Republican* (Newport), October 30, 1833, p. 2. See also "Marshpee Indians," *National Aegis and Massachusetts Yeoman* (Worcester), December 11, 1833, p. 2; "Marshpee Indians," *Salem Gazette*, December 17, 1833, p. 3.

50. "Marshpee Indians," *New Hampshire Observer* (Concord), January 10, 1834, p. 3.

51. "Indian Nullification," 226.

52. "The Marshpee Indians," *The Liberator* (Boston), January 25, 1834, p. 15.

53. "Indian Nullification," 212.

ALYSSA MT. PLEASANT

*Laura Cornelius Kellogg: Our Democracy and the American Indian and
   Other Works*
edited by Kristina Ackley and Cristina Stanciu
Syracuse University Press, 2015

LAURA CORNELIUS KELLOGG: OUR DEMOCRACY AND THE AMERICAN INDIAN AND OTHER WORKS is a collection of the surviving writings of the Wisconsin Oneida public intellectual and advocate who was involved in organizations such as the Society of American Indians and other activist circles during the first half of the twentieth century. Editors Kristina Ackley and Cristina Stanciu have assembled short stories, poems, and essays written while Kellogg was enrolled in secondary school and at Stanford University and Barnard College, as well as publications, speeches, and testimony from later periods of her career. These texts are reproduced in their entirety, bringing back into circulation works, such as *Our Democracy and the American Indian* (1920), that have been out of print for nearly a century. In addition to these writings, Ackley and Stanciu have compiled a chronology of Kellogg's life and an appendix of selected newspaper articles published throughout her career. The editors' extended introduction complements this robust collection of writings and supplementary material.

In their introduction to the collection, Ackley and Stanciu position Laura Cornelius Kellogg as an intellectual and activist who, while controversial, was deeply grounded in the Wisconsin Oneida community, where she grew up and made enduring contributions to the tribal nation that have gone largely unacknowledged (8). As they contextualize Kellogg's life, the editors draw sharp distinctions between the present day, when Wisconsin Oneidas' discourse about tribal affairs exudes assurance of "continuance and persistence," and Kellogg's lifetime, when the nation faced tremendous social, political, economic, and legal challenges (1–2). They argue that Kellogg promoted an innovative vision of the reservation as a space of economic opportunity, and that her work on educational initiatives and innovative legal strategy relating to land claims presented important alternatives for Wisconsin Oneidas navigating the treacherous assimilation era. Additionally, they note Kellogg's attention to clan affiliation, stressing its long-term significance for some Wisconsin Oneidas who used this documentation for later initiatives surrounding the clan system (59). This nuanced discussion of Laura Cornelius Kellogg's work breaks with dominant interpretations of her life, especially those connected with the Iroquoianist school of scholarship that have long emphasized declension narratives in their interpretations of six nations experiences and have suggested that Kellogg's life was marked by tragedy. The editors instead develop an analysis of Kellogg's life that acknowledges the tremendous challenges Wisconsin Oneidas faced in the nineteenth and early twentieth centuries, the role that Kellogg sought to play at that time, and the enduring (if unacknowledged) significance of her work.

This collection makes an important contribution to a number of streams of scholarship in Native American and Indigenous studies. It adds to the growing body of publications that bring work by Native writers and orators back into circulation. Barry O'Connell's edited collection of William Apess's work, *On Our Own Ground*, which has circulated widely since its initial publication in 1992, is an early example of the recovery work that literary scholars have undertaken over the past generation. Collections of Samson Occom's writing and the oratory of Red Jacket are but two examples of more recent projects in this vein. This recovery work, which requires substantial, sustained engagement with archives in order to recover rare manuscripts and publications, complements and reinforces scholarship in American Indian intellectual and literary history. Additionally, as Ackley and Stanciu make clear in their introduction to *Laura Cornelius Kellogg*, and others have argued before them, collecting a body of writing by a particular author facilitates scholarly research and teaching about, and community understandings of, particular tribal nations' past and present realities. With this publication, Ackley and Stanciu enlarge our understanding of Wisconsin Oneida history and the work of Haudenosaunee women. They challenge readers to think more broadly about the Society of American Indians and early twentieth-century activism by Native people. And, importantly, they contribute to a growing stream of scholarship in Haudenosaunee studies by scholars such as Mishuana Goeman, Penelope Kelsey, Rick Monture, and Audra Simpson that emphasizes the critical work Haudenosaunee intellectuals and activists have undertaken over generations in service to their reservation communities and their nations.

ALYSSA MT. PLEASANT (Tuscarora) is an assistant professor of Native American studies at the University at Buffalo (SUNY).

JARED EBERLE

First Nations, Museums, Narrations: Stories of the 1929 Franklin Motor
    Expedition to the Canadian Prairies
by Alison K. Brown
University of British Columbia Press, 2014

IN 1929, Cambridge University's Museum of Archaeology and Anthropology sponsored an expedition to Western Canada to collect First Nations artifacts. As Alison K. Brown notes, at the time "First Nations were subject to extremely invasive policies aimed at assimilation, which, in turn, stimulated an extensive program of ethnographic salvage" (2). Brown's goal in looking at the trip is to "demonstrate how the analysis of historic collections can inform awareness of the legacy of colonialism as it relates to the revitalization of cultural heritage and to improving relations between indigenous people and museums" (2). Furthermore, Brown seeks to examine largely ignored questions of how Native people responded to both the expedition and the subsequent use of their cultural items that are now housed in the museum's Rymill Collection, the largest assemblage of prairie artifacts in a British museum. Finally, *First Nations, Museums, Narrations* offers a look at collection practices on the Canadian prairie, an understudied area in a field that had a copious amount of literature on the Northwest Coast.

The trip was informally called the Franklin Motor Expedition because it served as a promotional opportunity for the Franklin Motor Company, which provided the "air-cooled" car the group traveled in and published Donald A. Cadzow's resulting publication, *Air-Cooled Adventure among the Aborigines*, which mostly focused on promoting the vehicle but provided gendered and racial stereotypes of the journey. For one, Cadzow noted an encounter with the Saulteaux where he went to work "with the possibility of flight uppermost in my plans," showcasing both the "heroic ideal" of fieldwork and the alleged savage nature of the Indians (120−21). Additionally, the portrayal of the area as "untamed and beyond the limits of civilized society" gendered the expedition as a masculine and dangerous affair characteristic of narratives during the golden age of exploration (32). Finally, in emphasizing the car and technology, the expedition played on narratives of the progress of Anglo-European society and the decline of First Nations, which was a central justification of the salvage anthropology the men conducted (154). For Brown, the trip exemplified the blend between the "amateur" and "professional" periods of anthropology by including Cadzow, who had worked for the Museum of the

American Indian in New York with John and Robert Rymill, brothers who had little experience in professional anthropology.

Brown's real contributions come during the second half of the book, where she shifts from looking at non-Native ideas to how the First Nations experienced and responded to the expedition. Chapter 5 switches from discussing how non-Natives perceived the expedition to how First Nations "talked *around* the collection in cultural and spiritual revitalization processes in supporting community history" (35). Brown then provides a chapter on the exhibition's artifacts following her proposed biographic approach. To put it simply, Brown adopted the arguments of Igor Kopytoff and others who argued that "artifacts cannot be fully understood at just one point in their existence; processes of production, of circulation, and of consumption must all be taken into account" (25). Doing so not only provides the artifacts with a history but allows us to understand them as something more than "dead," decontextualized pieces. The discussion of the development of the Rymill Collection from the expedition naturally leads into Brown's concluding chapter on the relationship between Native collections and British museums and the necessary evolution of the how museums contextualize those items.

First Nations, Museums, Narrations is a helpful and thought-provoking book that encourages the reader to explore not only museum collections but also how we describe the artifacts housed within. Coming out of more than a decade of field research, Brown's book should be read by anyone involved in museums and Native collections.

JARED EBERLE is a PhD candidate in history at Oklahoma State University.

RICHARD MACE

Transformable Race: Surprising Metamorphoses in the Literature
of Early America
by Katy Chiles
Oxford University Press, 2014

KATY CHILES'S **_TRANSFORMABLE RACE_** endeavors to examine the concerns of Early Americans of the possibility of having one's racial identity changed. No less so than it is now, race was an important factor in self-identity and classifications by society. Chiles's text utilizes nativist studies and other texts to examine the presence of the mutable nature of race in Early American texts, arguing that "the notion of transformable race structured how Early American texts portrayed the formation of racial identity" (3). In undertaking this task, Chiles utilizes a broad spectrum of writers in interesting pairings to provide multiple examples of concerns and incidences where one is alleged to have transformed from one race to another. These pairing include Occom and Wheatley; Franklin and Aupaumut; Crevecoeur, Marrant, and Brown; and Equiano and Brackenridge.

As neither Occom nor Wheatley is white, they, to the eighteenth-century mind, represent the idea of becoming colored as part of God's design. Chiles examines the idea of transformable race through Occom's questioning of the different treatment he receives as compared to white missionaries, noting that he was paid the same amount by the Boston Commissioners for his twelve years of service as a white missionary for his one year. Occom concludes that he is as God made him and cannot help being any different than he is. Chiles notes that by juxtaposing "God has made me so" with "I did not make myself so" Occom's treatment at the hands of the Boston Commissioners has more so do to the fact of how they see him as compared to what service he has performed and what they view as an Indian body and the lesser value it holds. Like Occom, Wheatley's writings awakened questions of raced bodies. Chiles aptly highlights Wheatley's use of the phrases "sable race" and "die" in her poem "On Being Brought from Africa to America," with an understanding of the word "die" as something that alters a preexisting state and of the sable race as something "_becomes_ black through a dark dying" (56). Wheatley, whom Chiles notes reflects environmentalist accounts of the sun producing dark skin pigments, does so with a purposeful racialized undertaking, while also hinting that she herself is infused with that same kind of "die."

Chiles also utilizes Benjamin Franklin and Hendrick Aupaumut in her examination of how race is viewed. Chiles notes that neither Franklin nor

Aupaumut stridently hold forth on how the different races originated; the challenge in examining their writings is that neither implicitly argues whether social environment, modes of living, or separate creations cause the differences between each race. Regardless, Chiles contends that the importance of examining these writings lies in how the authors engage in race "as a category in relationship to evolving political identities" (65) as they argue that political bodies connect to the racialization of physical bodies, which connects to how Occom and Wheatley are viewed. Chiles highlights concerns that everything from the sun to diet to how you lived could transform your race. By using Franklin, who purposefully fails in keeping to Tryon's diet and wearing skins and furs to take up the habits of blacks and Indians and still remain white, Chiles shows that Franklin's contemporaries could see that diet and actions do not alter race or being.

Chiles most closely examines the idea of transformable race through the anomaly of a slave, Henry Moss, starting to turn white, or fictitious stories like Charles Brockden Brown's *Edgar Huntly*, in which a man who sleepwalked and lived in the wilderness returns to civilization and is no longer recognized by his family. She also notes other authors whose works contain elements of "passing" like Stowe, Chesnutt, Twain, and Larsen. Despite these occurrences, which are mostly in fictitious stories, *Transformable Race* does not truly examine how race is transformed or reconsidered. Instead, Chiles presents the fear that some European Americans had that their life in the wilderness of the New World would transform them into something other than the white Europeans they had been or would change how race came to be viewed. Chiles does bring in elements of passing or playing another race, yet these also are not truly transformable, but rather, in essence, elements of perception. Although the text at times does read like a dissertation, Chiles presents ample literary evidence of the concern about race and how these authors conceptualize how one becomes colored in colonial America.

RICHARD MACE is an associate adjunct professor of English at Pace University in New York.

MELANIE KENDALL TOTH

The Civil War and Reconstruction in Indian Territory
edited by Bradley R. Clampitt
University of Nebraska Press, 2015

THE EIGHT ENGAGING ESSAYS in this edited volume discuss the impact of the Civil War from relatively underexplored angles. The collection includes work from notable historians of the borderlands, plains, U.S. Civil War, Native American, and American social history whose work integrates recent scholarship on the Trans-Mississippian and western theater of the war to incorporate a broad range of experiences from the heart of Indian Territory. The chapters provide a general chronological framework that covers military, political, and social history of the Five Nations and other tribes from Removal to Reconstruction and the creation of historical memory. It was edited to appeal to student readers and would make a good addition to the reading list of an undergraduate history course.

Recent research in the field, especially *Between Two Fires* and *When the Wolf Came* have gone far in filling in the gaps since Annie Able, and these essays make good use of that material. Two essays concerning Reconstruction incorporate recent scholarship on the experiences of freedpeople. Several branch out into even lesser known areas beyond the Five Nations or focus on the experiences of civilians and women.

At the outbreak of the Civil War, Indian Territory was claimed by several nations that had arrived approximately a generation prior. The majority of the territory was home to the Five Nations: the Cherokee and Choctaws in the east, the Seminoles in the west-central region, the Creeks in the east-central lands, and the Chickasaws in the west. Brad Agnew's chapter challenges the common assertion that the period between Removal and the Civil War was a "golden age" for the Five Nations by highlighting ongoing internal and external tensions that would expand with the onset of war. Most scholarly work in this field focuses on the Five Nations, but recent work by the historian F. Todd Smith concentrates on the tribes settled at Wichita agency just two years before the war. This region is considered peripheral to the main conflict, but in his essay Smith shows how the Civil War's destruction was central to the inhabitants of these communities as they were forced to become refugees once again.

To set the context for this anthology, the Civil War historian Richard McCaslin describes the events of the battlefront in carefully researched detail. In parallel, Clarissa Confer crafts an analysis of the hardships faced by civilians throughout the Five Nations as waves of Union and Confederate armies, bushwhackers, and refugees disrupted every aspect of existence. Christopher Bean's essay investigates the Reconstruction of Indian Territory after the war. He argues that although Reconstruction was a "national process" of redress and reconciliation for the northern and southern states, in Indian Territory the government sought to undermine sovereignty and place the nations under "complete congressional control" (110). All tribes, regardless of alliances during the war, were forced to sign new treaties that included stipulations for freeing slaves and incorporating them as full citizens of their previous owner's tribe. Linda Reese's essay offers a concise overview of the various strategies each tribe negotiated to handle this contentious issue and the environment this created for former slaves. Reese claims that this process created a "second civil war" for freedpeople as acceptance on paper did not reflect reality and many were met with violence and discrimination as they sought to build new lives.

Two essays complete this anthology by developing the theme of public memory. Amanda Cobb-Greetham's original and beautifully wrought chapter incorporates oral history through interviews of Creek and Cherokee women conducted by the Works Progress Administration in the 1930s with recent scholarship on historical memory. Whit Edwards discusses the complexities of presenting the Civil War in Indian Territory to the public and the benefits of historical reenactments.

The whole of this anthology provides enough information for the average student to gain a solid comprehension of this complex subject. Its greatest feature, beyond readability, is the balance it strikes between politics/warfare and the human element. *The Civil War and Reconstruction in Indian Territory* was edited to appeal to scholars and historical enthusiasts alike. To ensure this, all historiographic material is provided in extensive endnotes following each essay that provide a wealth of material for further reading. The volume will appeal to students of the Civil War, Native American history, African American history, and women's history, as well as those interested in regional studies.

MELANIE KENDALL TOTH is a master's student in Native American history at the University of Oregon.

THEODORE (TED) JOJOLA

Thatched Roofs and Open Sides: The Architecture of Chickees and Their
  Changing Role in Seminole Society
by Carol Dilley
University Press of Florida, 2015

THERE IS ARCHITECTURE, AND THEN THERE IS *ARCHITECTURE*. This is the beginning premise postulated by non-Native, architectural historian Carrie Dilley. She draws her findings from a recent tribal survey she was hired to conduct on behalf of the Seminole Tribe by Florida's Office of Historic Preservation Office. The book presents in a straightforward manner the evolution and cultural representation of a vernacular building called the *chickee*.

Most readers would dismiss this building as a crude thatched hut, reminiscent of the Hawaiian Tiki house. As the discussion unfolds, however, one gains a wider and deeper respect of the role that this traditional building has served over time and place. Superbly adapted to the ecosystem of the Everglades, it reflects the social and economic norms of the Seminole culture.

This story is far more complex and interesting than it appears at first glance. After all, a hut is a hut, right? Yet the *chickee* is born from necessity, survival, and resilience. As the Seminole people hid among the swamps, they endured not only military campaigns intended to eradicate them but also turn-of-the-century engineering designed to gentrify their traditional landscape.

Faced with their survival, the Seminole adapted a semipermanent, hide-and-seek habitation. So-called camps evolved in the most impassable areas of the Everglades. The camps were organized along matrilocal patterns. Their layout comprised a variety of *chickees*, each of which was specialized. The most important of these and the central focus of its lifeways was a detached unit used for cooking. The *cook chickee* with its star fire was not only the hub of camp life, it was the symbolic center of their world.

Of course, what makes this discussion most compelling are the push-and-pull factors of modernization. Whereas the camps were once camouflaged from prying eyes, families eventually succumbed to the forces of land development and the economies entrained by it. These events changed the demeanor of the camps' people from isolationists to entrepreneurs.

The transformation occurred along the Tamiami Trail. Completed in 1928, the road is 275 miles long and links Tampa to Miami. This roadway created a corridor for exotic display and economic opportunity through the Big Cypress National Preserve and its Seminole environs. Dilley outlines the impact of this change in the *chickees'* form and function. The discussion is also informed by tribal voices that lived through the transformation, some of whom positioned themselves to make a living off the new trade.

Interestingly, not only did Native entrepreneurs morph their village encampments into sightseeing venues for swamp tours and alligator wrestling, a few became invested contractors who built customized *chickees* for both their people and non-tribal clients. Of course, all of this was evolving during a time when do-gooders, the BIA, HUD, and the surrounding county attempted to undermine Seminole culture by forcing them on Indian reservations, replete with substandard Western housing and a suburban existence.

Finally, there are plenty of technical minutiae drawn from historical materials and newer building surveys. A great number of its chapters are dedicated to the engineering and structural design of a *chickee*. That aspect of the discussion will not disappoint. Interspersed within these discussions, though, are the more nuanced elements of assimilation and how the Seminole feel about this.

These aspects, however, go largely unstated. The Seminole are necessarily a private people, and the author acknowledges that the book is tempered by respecting their predisposition against revealing the spiritual and sacred values associated with the *chickee*.

The book finishes on a rather disquieting note as to whether the persistence of the *chickee* is enough to preserve their cultural identity (in all fairness, the author resolutely says yes, while the reader may still have doubts). As with many other tribes who have imbibed the casino Kool-Aid, they are faced with language loss, materialism, and a growing generation gap. Elders lament that young people no longer embrace the *chickee*, much less want to live in one.

In conclusion, the author's treatise lays the groundwork for a solid discourse on function. Yet it is not as well rounded as it could have been had it balanced function with a more expansive discussion on form and meaning. Despite this, it adds an important chapter to a rather sparse, albeit growing, literature on Indigenous design and architecture. In the words of the author, it gives the structure "architectural significance." The book rebukes the view that tribes in the Americas only had teepees and igloos. That, in my Native scholarly opinion, is long overdue.

THEODORE (TED) JOJOLA, PhD (Pueblo of Isleta), is a distinguished professor and regents' professor in the Community and Regional Planning Program, University of New Mexico. He is the director of the Indigenous Design and Planning Institute.

HAYLEY G. BRAZIER

*Cattle Colonialism: An Environmental History of the Conquest
of California and Hawai'i*
by John Ryan Fischer
University of North Carolina Press, 2015

JOHN RYAN FISCHER'S *CATTLE COLONIALISM* is a comparative history of Californian and Hawaiian colonial conquests. At the root of this colonization, Fischer argues, were cattle. Spanish missionaries and British explorers first deposited cattle in California in 1769 and then Hawai'i in 1793 as "tokens in the game of imperial rivalry" (4). The book traces the development of Native Americans and Native Hawaiians within the cattle industry from the mid-eighteenth century to the mid-nineteenth century. The cattle industry was central enough to Pacific Ocean trade that it caused what Fischer identifies as a transition into a capitalistic market. The book's six concise chapters are divided into roughly two sections each: one dedicated to California and the other to Hawai'i. Fischer relies primarily on introductory and concluding paragraphs to compare and contrast the two, a smart approach to avoid regional confusion.

Over the course of a century, Indian neophytes developed a unique cowboy or vaquero identity, whose labor was central to the Spanish mission system. The secularization of the missions after 1833 subordinated Indian vaqueros whose livelihoods were lost to the increasingly powerful rancheros. Initially left to roam free on the islands, Native Hawaiians successfully captured, processed, and sold cattle's hide and tallow for the booming Pacific Ocean trade. Native Hawaiians developed a distinctive paniolo identity, Hawaiian for cowboy, which imported some vaquero practices. By the mid-nineteenth century, land reforms in both California and Hawai'i resulted in the dramatic capitalization of lands. For hundreds of years, the royal family and their ruling elite had allotted land and cattle to the paniolo, but during the privatization and Americanization of Hawaiian lands the paniolo were largely excluded.

Cattle Colonialism sits within a rich field of scholarship that has emphasized the significance of domesticated animals as tools of imperialism. These works include V. D. Anderson's *Creatures of Empire: How Domestic Animals Transformed Early America* and Elinor Melville's *A Plague of Sheep: Environmental Consequences of the Conquest of Mexico*. Therefore, Fischer's argument that cattle were central to the expansion of the Spanish, British, and American empires is already an understood and accepted theory within the field. However, Fischer's comparative focus on Hawai'i and California is new to the historiography, which has paid less attention to the role of animals in the development of the Pacific world.

Fischer's understanding of empire stands on the foundation of books like Alfred Crosby's *The Columbian Exchange*. Fischer does, however, critique Crosby's declensionist outlook of Indigenous populations post-European contact. Instead, Fischer emphasizes a story that highlights Indigenous adaptability, a central theme throughout the book. Fischer concludes that the "mere introduction of bovine species did not make that conquest a fait accompli" (201). Fischer argues that cattle provided Indigenous peoples a source of opportunity in labor, trade, and movement. It was human-created racism and imperialism, not cattle, that subordinated the Indigenous people of Hawai'i and California by the late nineteenth century.

A better title for this book may have been *Livestock Colonialism*, however lacking in clever alliteration. The European introduction of domesticated animals alongside cattle, such as the horse, also played a central role in the colonization of Hawai'i and California. Fischer does not fully convince his reader that cows, above all other animal and agricultural products, were "at the heart of these transformations" (220). Notably, horses appear on the pages of this book almost as often as cattle, although one could argue it was the cattle industry that employed many of these horses. Fischer emphasizes sources referring to cattle while downplaying the centrality of other agricultural and livestock products in the development of Pacific Ocean trade.

Of interest to *Journal of the Native American and Indigenous Studies Association* readers is Fischer's close attention to the development of Indian vaquero and Hawaiian paniolo identities. Despite his heavy reliance on European travel and missionary diaries, Fischer still paints a detailed picture of Indigenous styles of dress, freedom of movement, and the way in which land privatization affected Indigenous lives. Indeed, this is a book more interested in Native stories than European ones. Readers of environmental history may notice the minor role Fischer dedicates to the nature of the cattle themselves. The book downplays the cattle's capacity to transfer and alter environments as they moved between regions. Overall, however, *Cattle Colonialism* is an ideal read for those wanting a thorough introduction to Hawaiian and Californian colonial histories, with a strong focus on the two regions' respective environments.

HAYLEY G. BRAZIER is a PhD student in environmental history at the University of Oregon.

JESSICA LESLIE ARNETT

Attu Boy: A Young Alaskan's WWII Memoir
by Nick Golodoff
University of Alaska Press, 2015

ON JUNE 7, 1942, the Japanese invaded the Aleutian Island of Attu. They murdered the Bureau of Indian Affairs schoolteacher and her husband, and took the Alaska Native residents to Japan as prisoners of war. *Attu Boy: A Young Alaskan's WWII Memoir* is the firsthand account of Nick Golodoff, a six-year-old Unangan boy who survived the invasion and three years as a Japanese prisoner of war in Otaru on Hokkaido Island. Many of the village members died from starvation, malnutrition, and disease. At the war's end, the U.S. military resettled the remaining Attuans on the Aleutian Island of Atka. Nick Golodoff never saw his village on Attu again.

Golodoff's granddaughter, Brenda Maly, compiled this powerful memoir from tapes that Golodoff began recording in 2004. With the help of editor and friend Rachel Mason, *Attu Boy* was first published for the National Park Service in 2012. Maly and Mason supplemented and intertwined Golodoff's story with additional firsthand accounts from other Attuans taken by the Japanese. This rich and moving account of the Attuan experience brings long-overdue attention to a heretofore-obscure history of Alaska Natives and World War II. Scholars have recently begun to examine the Japanese invasions of Alaska, Alaska Native military service, and the removal and internment of Aleut citizens by the United States. Golodoff's memoir constitutes an integral component of, and fundamental resource for, the scholarship emerging from these studies and for the literatures that examine Indigenous people in WWII generally.

Organized into three sections, the first part of the book comprises Golodoff's personal memories. His story begins with his recollections of life in the village of Attu and the prewar fears and clues foreshadowing the Japanese invasion. He recounts the anxiety of village members returning from trapping and hunting with stories of the *Tuginagus*, or boogiemen. At the time, Elders talked about seeing mysterious people or ghosts, finding strange tracks, and hearing boat engines. He describes his fear when the Japanese invaded his village, and confusion as to why the Japanese did not simply leave the Attuans behind when they departed in mid-September. He remembers the arduous boat trip to Japan, the illness suffered by many of his village members, and the death of his father. After the war ended, he remembers waiting for the Americans to find them and that it took several months for the U.S. military to bring the Attuans back to Alaska. Of the forty-two Attuans taken to Japan, only twenty-five survived to return. Importantly, readers are reminded that these are the recollections of a young child. Golodoff remembers daydreaming about pies and cakes while hospitalized in Japan, and collecting golf balls for fifty cents a day, which he used to rent a bicycle during the monthlong stay in Seattle on the journey to Alaska.

Part 2 of the book consists of Golodoff's reflections after resettlement at Atka, working life, hunting and fishing, learning from the Elders, and memories of his family and community. The third part of the book combines additional firsthand accounts of the invasion and life as a prisoner of war. The memories of Innokenty Golodoff (Nick's father's brother), Olean Golodoff Prokopeuff (Nick's mother), Mike Lokanin, and Alex Prossoff are compiled and interwoven with information on the historical background of Attu and commentary provided by the editor. The book closes with a brief description of Nick Golodoff's return to Japan in 1995 as part of a conference on wartime compensation. Accompanying him on this trip were Sylvia Kobayashi and her husband, both of whom had been in a Japanese internment camp in the United States during the war.

Attu Boy draws our attention to the lived experiences of a small community of Alaska Natives, swept up into an international military conflict. It is at once a local Unangan story and a global story, and as such draws together complex and entangled histories of Indigenous people, state violence, and national and international geopolitics. For this reason, *Attu Boy* is a fundamental text for any scholar of Alaska, Alaska Natives, WWII in the Pacific, and the field of Indigenous studies.

JESSICA LESLIE ARNETT is a PhD candidate in history at the University of Minnesota.

KRISTOFER RAY

Cherokee Medicine, Colonial Germs: An Indigenous Nation's Fight against Smallpox, 1518–1824
by Paul Kelton
University of Oklahoma Press, 2015

IN 1972 ALFRED CROSBY shed light on the biological consequences of the European invasion of America. The invaders, he explained, brought with them a number of devastating pathogens. Perhaps most deadly was *Variola major*—better known as smallpox—which carried a mortality rate as high as 40 percent. Curiously, Europeans seemed not to die from the disease as frequently as did their Indigenous counterparts. For Crosby (and many scholars since him) the explanation was simple: centuries of exposure to the disease meant they had developed a level of immunity. Lacking that advantage, Indigenous peoples could only watch as *Variola* rampaged across the "virgin soil" of the American continents.

Paul Kelton reminds readers that there are significant problems with this virgin soil thesis. Most obviously, immunity to smallpox is impossible regardless of one's ethnic background. Europeans were not as affected in the Americas because many of them contracted the disease as children and were "inoculated" from further outbreaks. More substantively, says Kelton, the virgin soil thesis turns Indigenous people into passive (and impotent) recipients of disease, thereby dismissing their attempts to respond and adapt to biological realities. Perhaps most problematic, however, is that the thesis provides Europeans with absolution for the pathogen's spread. After all, it was beyond their power to handle. They did not willfully disseminate it, and thus they were not culpable for its devastation.

A rebuttal is needed for these assertions, and *Cherokee Medicine, Colonial Germs* provides it. Kelton's story evolves over five chapters. The first tracks the violent establishment of disease vectors in the Indigenous world generally and, after 1670, Cherokee country specifically. Chapter 2 explores the eighteenth-century emergence of the Cherokee rituals and ceremonies used to confront smallpox. Chapters 3 and 4 focus on the disease's impact on the Anglo-Cherokee War (1759–1761) and subsequently on the American Revolution. In the former, smallpox hit Cherokee country when towns were economically strapped, and diplomatically and militarily undermined by British duplicity and violence. It was a lethal combination, which notably depleted the population. During the Revolution the endemic violence of colonialism was more directly responsible for Cherokee desolation, although smallpox lurked in the shadows because the population had not recovered from the epidemic a decade earlier. Kelton's concluding chapter focuses on how the nineteenth-century American republic used inoculation as another form of civilization policy. Cherokees continued to adapt, however. Protestant missionaries may have brought vaccinations to the Nation in 1824, but conjurors incorporated Euro-American medical advances into their beliefs and rites.

Kelton's nuanced analysis of the meaning and evolving application of Cherokee medicinal practices makes this book a valuable contribution to the literature. He sheds light on the creation and employment of purification ceremonies as well as the ritual separation of infected community members. Meant to keep Cherokee medicine strong and maintain good reciprocal relations with the spirit world, separation in effect served as a de facto quarantine. So, far from helplessly lamenting their decline, in other words, Cherokee conjurors actively developed forms of treatment. Their efforts were no worse—and arguably much better—than those employed by Europeans in the era.

Cherokee medicinal practices can also provide a means by which to rethink the Cherokee experience broadly. For example, it is notable that ritual separation emerged in a period when Cherokee political/diplomatic identity revolved around towns, or at best regions. Quarantines protected against epidemic outbreak, but they also would have inhibited the development of "national" bonds. It is a point that pushes scholars to consider biological impacts on the process of nation building, although Kelton himself does not take that step. Instead, his narrative rests on older stereotypes of an extant, monolithic Cherokee polity that only meaningfully engaged with the British Empire. Dismissing other diplomatic/economic options—both European and indigenous—leads to an acceptance at face value of the symbolic language employed by headmen to chastise the British (Cherokees are "naked and starving," for example), as well as a devaluing of the copious indications that Cherokee geopolitical realities were more complex than prevailing historiography would admit.

Of course, Kelton's primary aim is not to rewrite the history of Cherokee political identity. He is remarkably successful in challenging the virgin soil thesis, revealing how one indigenous group dealt with an epidemiological catastrophe of the highest magnitude and forcing the descendants of settler-colonialism to think about culpability. *Cherokee Medicine, Colonial Germs* is an important book, and scholars will wrestle with it for years to come.

KRISTOFER RAY is a visiting associate professor of Native American studies and history at Dartmouth College.

SHAUN A. STEVENSON

The Land We Are: Artists and Writers Unsettle the Politics
of Reconciliation
edited by Gabrielle L'Hirondelle Hill and Sophie McCall
Arbeiter Ring Publishing, 2015

GABRIELLE L'HIRONDELLE HILL AND SOPHIE MCCALL'S edited collection *The Land We Are: Artists and Writers Unsettle the Politics of Reconciliation* begins not with official, state-sanctioned statements of reconciliation, but with a photograph of a work created by the artist Rebecca Belmore in the aftermath of the standoff between the Mohawks of Kanehsatà:ke and the Canadian armed forces, commonly known as the Oka crisis. Belmore's work, a giant wooden megaphone, was taken from blockade to blockade in 1992, inviting Indigenous peoples to speak to the land they wished to protect. *The Land We Are* takes up this invitation more than two decades later, as artists and writers work in collaboration to center land and art as a means to position reconciliation as a contested discourse.

In the Canadian context, the editors situate the emergence of the politics of reconciliation not with the 2008 Harper apology, but as part of the official government response to the Oka crisis, suggesting that this form of reconciliation consistently "diverts attention from the underlying question of land and also aims to produce a cooperative Indigenous subject" (9). Insisting that Indigenous land rights must be central in any discussion of reconciliation, *The Land We Are* looks to the role of art, its powers of subversion as well as its potential for cooptation, in order to probe the limits of the politics of reconciliation.

This temporal situation of reconciliatory discourse does not, however, preclude some contributors from critically responding to Harper's residential school apology (Garneau and Yeh), or Obama's signing of the Congressional Resolution (Long Soldier). Part 2 of the collection, "'Please check against delivery': The Apology Unlocked," includes the poetry of Jordon Abel, a collaboration with none other than Stephen Harper himself, as Abel reorganizes and problematizes the Harper apology.

Along with land and art, the integral role of collaboration is at the forefront of *The Land We Are*. Each of the contributions in the collection's four sections is an act of collaboration. Whether between differently identified Indigenous peoples, first-generation settlers of colour, or multigenerational settler-Canadians, each chapter emphasizes collaboration as necessary for a critical engagement with discourses of reconciliation. Key to this endeavour is critical self-reflection on the collaborative process.

This collaboration and critical reflection is best highlighted in the final section of the collection, "Insurgent Pedagogies, Affective Performances, Unbounded Creations." In particular, the chapter "Touch Me" brings the reader into the personal correspondence between artists Skeena Reece and Sandra Semchuk regarding a video shoot for an upcoming exhibition on reconciliation in which an Indigenous woman (Reece) bathes a "white matriarch" figure with the utmost care (Semchuk). The intimacy of this encounter is interrupted by the women's decision to include the collection editors' revisions to their letters in the margins. This piece, perhaps most complexly, illustrates the ongoing negotiations that attempts toward reconciliation must entail—not just between committed individuals, but between form, content, institutional guidelines and pressures, and a whole system of actors with different aims and motivations.

Section 1, "Public Memory and the Neoliberal City," contains one of the collection's strongest and most critical essays on the function of art in relation to reconciliation. Dylan Robinson and Karen Zaiontz challenge how we constitute and engage with Indigenous lands, interrogating Vancouver's integrationist reconciliatory framework that threatens the assertion of sovereign Indigenous rights, calling instead for a "civic infrastructure of redress" (22).

Parts 3 and 4 of the collection focus heavily on Indigenous/non-Indigenous collaboration and how to reconfigure settler relationships to the land and Nation state through encounters with iconic symbols of Canadiana (see contributions by Dector, Isaac, and Goto), and the ways in which violence to Indigenous bodies persists through uncontested Canadian nationalism (see contributions by Dewar, Goto, and Morin). Allison Hargreaves and David Jefferies conclude the collection by reminding readers that reconciliation should be understood not as a place of closure but as "a place from which to begin the hard work of rethinking relationships and renegotiating responsibilities" (200).

Throughout *The Land We Are* reconciliation is imbued with the urgency of resurgence, as the collection brings land, art, and collaboration to the fore of reconciliatory engagement. The collection is for anyone interested in art as resistive practice, and scholars of redress and Indigenous studies will find its critical engagement with reconciliation through art extremely useful. *The Land We Are* is a highly successful interrogation of reconciliatory politics that unsettles preconceived notions of Indigenous and non-Indigenous relations, while ensuring that readers understand engagements with reconciliation not as something to be resolved, but rather as something in the process of "always beginning" (208).

SHAUN A. STEVENSON is a PhD candidate at Carleton University.

KYLE T. MAYS

MTV Rebel Music: Native America
MTV, 2014

I, ALONG WITH MANY INDIGENOUS PEOPLE, waited with enthusiasm for the November 2014 premiere of the *MTV Rebel Music: Native America*. In a renewed moment of Indigenous activism in North America, seeing the nationally televised documentary, especially the combination of hip-hop and Indigenous activism, was truly a historical event.

The entire advisory board to the production team for *Rebel Music* consisted of Indigenous people, ranging from Cherokee to Esselen/Ohlone, from both Canada and the United States. In a time where Indigenous people are challenging colonialism in a variety of ways, including through social media and film, the documentary helped contribute to that struggle by showcasing contemporary artists who are not bound by settler imaginaries. There are many hip-hop-themed documentaries of the culture itself and individual artists, but this is the first to focus on Indigenous acts.

The documentary features the artists Frank Waln (Sicangu Lakota), Inez Jasper (Kole First Nation), Nataanii Means (Dakota, Dine, Oglala Lakota), and Mike "Witko" Cliff (Oglala Lakota). They cover issues of youth suicide, activism against the construction of the Keystone Pipeline through Indian Country, the missing and murdered Indigenous women, the #NativeLivesMatter movement, and how those issues influence their art. Frank Waln argues, "I definitely think there's a connection between traditional storytelling and hip-hop. My people have been storytelling for thousands of years, and this is just a new way to tell our stories." This is a powerful point. Indigenous artists' engagement with hip-hop culture illustrates that they are informed by history but not confined to it.

The documentary, though, is not all about hip-hop. Its presentation of the struggles of Native people on reservations and its connection to hip-hop is commendable. Those challenges include the many missing and murdered Indigenous women in Canada, youth suicide, and police brutality. As Inez Jasper suggests, "It's the system that's to blame, and the system needs to take responsibility."

Although the production was great and the music excellent, there are at least three lingering questions for the documentary. First, what is the history of Indigenous hip-hop in North America? There are more than a few hip-hop history texts, but we still know very little about the origins of hip-hop in Indigenous North America. While we want to show that Native people are products of the present—perhaps we might call this modernity—we cannot overlook that history.

My second question is this: how does urban space influence these artists? We know that, today, in both the United States and Canada, the majority of Native people live in cities. Yet there was no discussion of the importance of urban space, and how that contributed to the development of these artists. Yes, they come from reservation communities, but they are also influenced by other spaces. If hip-hop is anything, it is tied to the urban, and there are several urban scenes in the documentary. In fact, the artists attended a climate change march *and* recorded some dope songs together in New York City, the birthplace of hip-hop culture.

Finally, what is the link between blackness and Indigeneity? It is difficult to understand any form of hip-hop without a clear discussion of blackness. Indigenous hip-hop presents for us an opportunity to examine the intersections of blackness and Indigeneity that remain narrowly confined to certain academic subjects. For instance, while Cliff is speaking to youth on his rez, one cannot help but notice that he is wearing a T-shirt that has on its front the cover of the late Notorious B.I.G.'s album *Ready to Die* (1994). What is it about Christopher Wallace with which Cliff might be able to identify? Perhaps it is the ubiquitous presence of death that is always a part of black and Indigenous men.

This brilliant documentary is timely and necessary, and a welcome contribution to Indigenous popular cultural studies, Indigenous studies, hip-hop studies, and the public. Yet we need more. Hopefully *MTV Rebel Music: Native America* is the beginning of a host of works that explore the importance and usefulness of hip-hop as a modern expression of sovereignty. These artists also inspire; as Mike Cliff states, "My ancestors fought and died for me to even be alive. I have a responsibility. If we don't pick up that fight, who will?" Indigenous hip-hop artists might be the warriors of the twenty-first century.

KYLE T. MAYS (Black/Saginaw Chippewa) is a postdoctoral fellow in the Department of History at the University of North Carolina at Chapel Hill.

MICHELLE D. STOKELY

The Darkest Period: The Kanza Indians and Their Last Homeland,
1846–1873
by Ronald D. Parks
University of Oklahoma Press, 2014

IN THE SUMMER OF 1873, 533 Kanza left their diminished reservation in Kansas and relocated to Indian Territory. Historian Ronald D. Parks identifies the social, political, and economic forces that led to the loss of Kanza land and population in *The Darkest Period: The Kanza Indians and Their Last Homeland, 1846–1873.* Parks adequately uses source materials written by government officials, missionaries, and journalists to describe the historical events and attitudes of local farmers and merchants toward their Native neighbors. Largely missing from the story, however, are the Kanza's own understandings and interpretations.

The book situates the tribe within the Central Plains, identifying important aspects of topography and natural resources, including water, timber, and food sources that were essential for Kanza survival. These resources became increasingly necessary, and ever more valuable, as settler populations increased during the 1850s and 1860s, forcing the tribe to surrender large portions of its territory. Tragically, the Reservation's proximity to the Santa Fe Trail also placed Native peoples in the direct path of disease and commerce. Land is at the heart of this book; the Neosho Reservation became a refuge for the Kanza.

The author carefully describes the powerful social, economic, and political forces that undermined the Kanza's ability to retain their land and culture. Christian missionaries hoped for transformative success; several congregations built small missions and schools, but each effort failed. Settlers squatted on Kanza lands, arguing that the survey boundaries were inaccurate. Tribal efforts to retrieve stolen horses were used as demonstrations of hostility, prompting calls for military action. Newspapers fanned settler fears. Ineffective government agents came and went. Frontier violence became especially problematic as the Civil War produced "bleeding Kansas." Rail lines cut across the Plains and the bison herds declined. Other Native groups, such as the Cheyenne and Arapaho, also hunted the remaining bison. Drought, disease, alcohol, greed, and racism all played a powerful role in shaping the Kanza's predicament.

The strengths of this book lie in the author's ability to illuminate the above complexity and to use newspaper articles, diaries, missionary records, and government reports in his presentation. Parks readily accepts that his work is based on Euro-American writings, but he also states that "historical records yield, in my estimation, sufficient material to construct a narrative featuring the Kanza nation's most prominent events, personalities, customs, and subsistence strategies from 1846 to 1873" (5). Through these materials, Parks is able to identify the Kanza's principal leaders, locations of camps, topics of treaty discussion, and economic activities, but the reader is left wanting information on changes to tribal social structure in the face of significant population decline; the roles and contributions of Kanza women as agriculture replaced hunting; internal political dissention, particularly in regards to land retention and removal; the struggles to remain spiritually balanced; and much more. Parks recognizes the limitations of his source materials, noting, "Since all the chroniclers available to us are white, readers are held hostage to how deeply the writers cared to look into the humanity of the Kanza with whom they associated—that is, how willing and able they were to relate to the Indians as subjects" (167). Parks then provides a few anecdotes to balance the presentation. But is this really all there is to the story? Are there no recorded Kanza recollections available in the archives? And what of memories, passed on within Kanza families, describing undocumented events or providing alternative explanations? Scarcity of source material is a concern for all researchers, but reliance on only written documents limits Parks's ability to find that humanity which appears to have eluded settlers, missionaries, government agents, and newspapermen.

Despite its limitations, *The Darkest Period* provides a valuable framework in which to better understand Kanza relations with Euro-Americans at a critical moment in tribal history. Clearly, Americans placed significant pressures on tribal leaders and members to accommodate or acculturate. How the tribe responded can be only partially explained using diaries, newspaper articles, and mission reports. Readers should begin with this text and follow up with others that use an anthropological approach; incorporating an Indigenous perspective would provide a more balanced view of the tribe's history and culture.

MICHELLE D. STOKELY is an independent scholar.

CHARLOTTE COTÉ

*The Sea Is My Country: The Maritime World of the Makahs, an Indigenous
    Borderlands People*
by Joshua Reid
Yale University Press, 2015

IN *THE SEA IS MY COUNTRY: THE MARITIME WORLD OF THE MAKAHS, AN INDIGENOUS BORDERLANDS PEOPLE*
Joshua Reid brings readers on an aquatic voyage as he navigates through
and reconstructs the maritime history of the qʷidičča?a·txˇ (kwi-dihch-chuh-
aht), the People of the Cape, who came to be known as the Makah. Covering over 250 years of history, Reid shows how the Makah people, who live
on the northwestern point of the contiguous United States, were intimately
tied to their marine habitat, which informed and shaped their culture and
identity. Whereas most historical records focus on oceans as dividing lands
and territories, Reid's narrative creates this marine milieu as a substantive
space where the Makah and other coastal Indigenous peoples were deeply
immersed in networks of kinship and trade.

Reid offers an in-depth and stimulating analysis of the history of the
Makah through the lens of the borderlands. The borderland in Reid's study
stretches nearly five hundred miles, an area he calls ča·di· (cha-dee), the
Makah's name for Tatoosh Island, which was one of their important terres-
trial spaces. Covering a time span starting in the late eighteenth century up
to the early twentieth century, Reid examines the tensions, triumphs, and
challenges these seafaring people faced as they strived to maintain control
over the political, social, and economic exchanges within their marine borderland before and after the arrival of the babałid (non-Indigenous people)
(Reid refers to the Nuu-chah-nulth word for non-Indigenous as mama'ni,
which is incorrect. The proper spelling is mamałn'i [mamalhn'i]).

Reid challenges the dominant notions of borderlands and frontiers.
Whereas scholars have defined these through the lens of European imperialism, Reid conceptualizes the Makah marine space as a borderland where
interactions, challenges, and contestations are positioned within Indigenous
history and experience, and centers his narrative on great Indigenous leaders
such as Makah titleholder Tatoosh and Nuu-chah-nulth titleholders Wicka-
ninnish and Maquinna, who commanded the interactions taking place within
aquatic zones they created and controlled. While these leaders adapted indigenous protocols to serve interactions with babałid, the ča·di·, Reid asserts,
"remained a region where strong chiefs continued to control space on their

own terms and to meet their own priorities and agendas" well into the late nineteenth century (52).

Colonialism had a profound and pervasive effect on Indigenous peoples and cultures, who experienced disease pandemics, massacres, assimilation policies, forced removal and relocation, prohibition of spiritual and cultural practices, and boarding schools that threatened their cultures, languages, and identities, which was further intensified by socioeconomic and political marginalization along with racial prejudice. The Makah and Nuu-chah-nulth people witnessed and experienced severe challenges to their social, political, spiritual, and economic systems; especially hit hard was their whaling tradition, with both Nations ultimately making the difficult decision to terminate their whale hunts because the unregulated commercial whaling industry decimated the whale populations that sustained and nourished their communities.

When examining the impact of colonization on Indigenous peoples there is no one Indigenous experience; some individuals actively resisted, some individuals acculturated, and some successfully adapted to the changes being forced on them and their societies. Providing a more nuanced understanding of how Indigenous peoples engaged with settler-colonialism, Reid's study acknowledges Indigenous agency in these colonial encounters to show how some Makah members found ways to adapt by utilizing new technologies and opportunities that Euro-American society presented to them. Reid maintains, "When examined from a Makah perspective, these actions reveal dynamic, indigenous actors who exploited new opportunities within their own cultural framework . . . the People of the Cape combined customary practices with new opportunities to attain high standards of living. Their participation in the expanding settler-colonial world supported their ability to continue forging a unique Makah identity and to resist the cultural assault of federal assimilation policies" (165–67).

As a member of the Nuu-chah-nulth nation I congratulate Reid on his thorough and innovative study that positions the Makah and Nuu-chah-nulth voices at the center of his historical narrative, making this a significant contribution to the history of Indigenous peoples of the Northwest Coast.

CHARLOTTE COTÉ (Nuu-chah-nulth) is an associate professor in the Department of American Indian Studies at the University of Washington in Seattle.

CURTIS FOXLEY

*The Settlers' Empire: Colonialism and State Formation
    in America's Old Northwest*
by Bethel Saler
University of Pennsylvania Press, 2015

IN HER IMPORTANT BOOK *THE SETTLERS' EMPIRE*, Bethel Saler examines state formation in the Northwest Territory from American Independence through the ratification of Wisconsin's constitution in 1848. Unlike other historians who study state formation, Saler frames the early American republic as a "both a postcolonial republic and a contiguous empire" (1). By seeing young America in this light, Saler demonstrates that state formation came from the hands of settlers. Put another way, "settler societies possess an ambivalent double history as both colonized and colonizers" (2). This take on state formation importantly highlights how state formation was contingent on the actions of both the federal government and settlers who, more often than not, improvised their way through the process.

Although she could test her claim on a number of American states, Saler anchors her work in the last territory in the Old Northwest to gain statehood—Wisconsin. Before the agents of the American empire arrived in the region, the land that would become Wisconsin had a long history of housing Native American towns and European traders. As demonstrated by the historians Gary Clayton Anderson, Richard White, and Jacqueline Peterson, among others, Europeans and Native Americans throughout the Great Lakes region used the bonds of kinship and the region's flexibility as a "middle ground" to mutually accommodate one another. Saler's story essentially begins where White's ends. With the Treaty of Paris in 1783, the United States gained claim to the region and became "at once a settler republic and a continental empire, a postcolonial and aspiring colonialist nation" (15). The trick of early Americans, then, was simultaneously to forge their state and national identity while dispossessing and acculturating the residents of their newly acquired empire.

Saler inspects six cultural and political aspects that overlapped with one another in the colonial project of state formation in Wisconsin. First, Saler peels apart how Federalists and Republicans diverged from one another in managing the public domain. This section does the best out of all the chapters in demonstrating how U.S. Americans in the early republic were still negotiating and debating whom the public domain, and the nation itself, was principally for. These top-down developments show how the early state forged a gendered and racial hierarchy in the Old Northwest at the expense of the Native Americans, African Americans, and women in the region. Next, Saler analyzes how the treaty system "provoked ongoing formal and informal, written and face-to-face negotiations between Indian groups and a spectrum of local and national government officers" (86). This chapter is particularly fascinating, as Saler recounts how Christian Indian settlers from the East Coast, including the Stockbridges and the Brothertowns, relocated to the region and created a treaty polity in Wisconsin. The other chapters in *Settlers' Empire* analyze how fur trade gift economies transformed into markets based on capitalist ventures and commodity values, how missionaries provoked Native Americans to reform their "Indianness," how the state regulated marriage formation, and how settlers reworked their history to imagine a collective past. These chapters are less impressive than the others, and are not distinctive from the multitude of other works on the fur trade, missionaries in Native America, mixed families, and the interplay between history and nationalism. Still, at the heart of each of these stories is the important reminder that both the settlers and the government imposed cultural uniformity on the diverse population living in the public domain in order to create a state.

Saler's study is a great contribution to the historiography of state formation, reminiscent of Walter Hixon's *American Settler Colonialism*. Like Hixon's text, Saler's work is brilliant yet frustrating. Both monographs importantly show that state formation came from the hands of postcolonial settlers. While some sections of this text retread old ground, Saler's emphasis on gender brings something new and valuable to a field that often solely focuses on race. Her organization is also particularly wonderful. Her chapters on the treaty system, the fur trade, missionaries, and marriage can each stand on their own, making them structurally ideal as weekly reading assignments for college undergraduates. Yet this reader is cautious about presenting this text to bachelor students. Like Hixon's work, Saler's writing style muddles her argument. Still, historians interested in state formation, settler colonialism, and the Great Lakes region will find *Settlers' Empire* useful and thought provoking.

CURTIS FOXLEY is a master's student in history at the University of Oklahoma.

CHRISTOPHER J. ANDERSON

Capture These Indians for the Lord: Indians, Methodists,
   and Oklahomans, 1844–1939
by Tash Smith
University of Arizona Press, 2014

TASH SMITH'S BOOK *Capture These Indians for the Lord: Indians, Methodists, and Oklahomans, 1844–1939* offers readers an overview of the nineteenth- and twentieth-century mission work and shared experiences of white and Native American missionaries, ministers, and members of the Methodist Episcopal Church, South (MECS). The volume examines the interplay of encounter, assimilation, and religious tension in the Oklahoma region of the United States. While white American Protestants positioned themselves to enlarge their religious presence in the region, Native American clergy and laypersons protected the best interests of their spiritual past and unique religious and cultural traditions.

Smith points readers to recent scholarship that emphasizes perspectives on encounter, including research confirming that some missionaries were bent on genocidal removal of Native American religious and cultural traditions. He also provides a balanced perspective, noting that some white missionaries were more altruistic, interested in assisting the plight of Native American people who wanted to protect their heritage while at the same time embrace the Methodist movement. The volume is a tightly focused regional study of the missionary efforts of American Methodists during the nineteenth century. Smith describes and analyzes their intent to Christianize the peoples of several Nations throughout the Indian Territory, which later received statehood as Oklahoma. The Indian Nations examined in this study include Apache, Arapaho, Cherokee, Cheyenne, Chickasaw, Choctaw, Comanche, Creek, Delaware, Kickapoo, Kiowa, Potawatomi, Seminole, and Shawnee.

Smith provides a glimpse into the administrative organization of the Indian Mission Conference, a grouping of regional churches under the auspices of the Methodist Episcopal Church, South. The MECS was a denomination within the American Methodist movement that separated from the Methodist Episcopal Church in 1844. The Methodist Episcopal Church, founded in 1784, had conducted missionary efforts with Native Americans in Ohio, Georgia, and Mississippi. When the MECS separated from the MEC in 1844, Southern Methodists established the Indian Mission Conference, placing its missionary efforts under a national church administrative umbrella while at the same time elevating those congregations to the same level as their white counterparts.

Smith identifies the complicated interplay of white Christian missionaries and Native American peoples, noting, "The story of Southern Methodist Indian communities from the pre–Civil War decades and into the twentieth century is a story of how Indians developed autonomy and exploited the resources of a larger church structure" (12). Earlier in the book he writes, "What many [white] missionaries did not anticipate was the degree to which Indians accepted Christianity on their own terms and for their own needs" (5). Native Americans found ways to claim Christianity, specifically Southern Methodism, for their own purposes by taking advantage of national church structures and intertwining these directives to benefit the various Nations. Smith confirms, "The fact that Indian congregations created their own space within a larger Christian community was typically related to how they used denominational organization to their own benefit" (10).

This appropriation of white-dominated administrative offices and funding of the MECS meant the Native American Methodist converts, those who became ministers, translators, and laypersons in churches throughout the Conference, took on more influence and more power. Ultimately, Smith's volume demonstrates how "the experience of Oklahoma Indians in the Southern Methodist Church from the 1840s to the 1940s reveals the ways in which Native communities created their own religious space, even as ethnocentric pressures of assimilation marginalized Indians in American society" (192).

The volume's strengths include a focused study of one Protestant tradition engaging with Native American religions in a specific region of the United States. The volume also spotlights understudied missionaries and ministers such as J. J. Methvin, who spent fifty years in the Oklahoma area yet is not known to students of American history, even within the Methodist tradition. Finally, Smith's work employs understudied and underutilized primary sources of American religious history that make the book a valuable historical contribution. His examination of the annual reports of missionary societies, newspapers such as the *Christian Advocate*, and periodicals such as *Our Brother in Red* provides readers with firsthand accounts of missionary efforts in the central United States. The volume will be useful for researchers and students interested in American history, American religious history, Native American and Indigenous studies, and regional studies of Oklahoma. The volume will be of particular interest to faculty teaching courses that examine American missionary efforts to Native American peoples.

CHRISTOPHER J. ANDERSON is associate dean of libraries at Drew University.

NEW FROM MINNESOTA

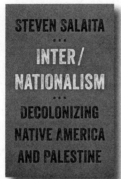

Inter/Nationalism
Decolonizing Native America and Palestine
Steven Salaita

"A powerful and moving analysis of what it means to decolonize settler societies through an unflinchingly ethical and incisively original notion of inter/nationalism, this book offers a searing, comparative analysis of what liberation means in North America and Palestine–Israel. Steven Salaita is, as always, bold, brilliant, and visionary."
—**Sunaina Maira**, University of California, Davis

$22.95 paper | $80.50 cloth | 232 pages | Indigenous Americas Series

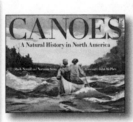
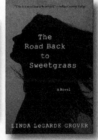

California Mission Landscapes
Race, Memory, and the Politics of Heritage
Elizabeth Kryder-Reid

How iconic American places cultivate and conceal contested pasts

$35.00 paper | $122.50 cloth | 368 pages
Architecture, Landscape, and American Culture Series
Available December 2016

Canoes
A Natural History in North America
Mark Neuzil and Norman Sims
Foreword by John McPhee

A natural history of one of North America's most enduring cultural artifacts, with over 300 photos and images

$39.95 hardcover | 416 pages

The Road Back to Sweetgrass
A Novel
Linda LeGarde Grover

A powerful debut novel of love, hardship, and family bonds on an American Indian reservation—from the author of the award-winning short story collection *The Dance Boots*

$14.95 paper | 208 pages

The World and All the Things upon It
Native Hawaiian Geographies of Exploration
David A. Chang

Centering indigenous perspectives on the age of exploration

$27.00 paper | $94.50 cloth | 344 pages

University of Minnesota Press | www.upress.umn.edu | 800-621-2736

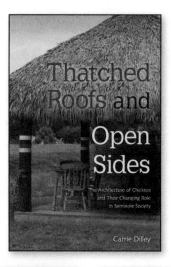
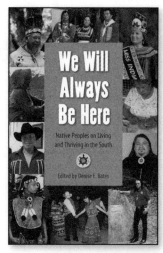

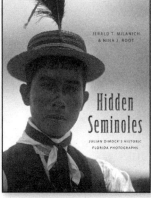